D0274374

JASON LEONARD
THE AUTOBIOGRAPHY

JASON LEONARD
THE AUTOBIOGRAPHY

With Alison Kervin

CollinsWillow

An Imprint of HarperCollins*Publishers*

First published in Great Britain in 2001 by
CollinsWillow
an imprint of HarperCollins*Publishers*
London

This edition published in 2004
Copyright © Jason Leonard and Alison Kervin 2001, 2004

1 3 5 7 9 8 6 4 2

All rights reserved. No part of this publication may be
reproduced, stored in a retrieval system, or transmitted,
in any form or by any means, electronic, mechanical,
photocopying or otherwise, without the
prior written permission of the publishers

The author asserts the moral right to be
identified as the author of this work

A CIP catalogue record for this book is
available from the British Library

The HarperCollins website address is:
www.harpercollins.co.uk

ISBN 0 00 719392 0

Typeset by Rowland Phototypesetting Ltd,
Bury St Edmunds, Suffolk

Printed and bound in Great Britain by
Clays Ltd, St Ives plc

Picture acknowledgements
All photographs provided courtesy of the following:
Authors private collection all on p1, p2 and p3 top right/
Allsport p3 top left; p3 middle; p3 bottom; p4 top; p5 top; p7 top;
p7 bottom; p8 top; p8 bottom left; p9; p11 middle right; p12 top right;
p12 middle; p13 top; p14 top; p14 middle right; p14 middle left;
p14 bottom; p15 middle; p15 bottom/ **Colorsport** p11 top/
Empics Ltd p4 middle; p4 bottom; p5 bottom; p6 top; p6 bottom;
p7 middle; p8 bottom right; p10 top; p10 bottom; p11 middle left;
p11 bottom; p12 top left; p12 bottom; p13 middle; p13 bottom;
p15 top; p16 top right; **Getty Images** p16 middle right;
Mimmo Frassineti/**Rex Features** p16 middle left.

Statistics by Stuart Farmer Media Services Ltd

To Sandra, Francesca, Harry and Jack, with love.

Contents

Acknowledgements

Thanks to: Peter and Cristine from Beech Road Research Ltd, Colin Herridge, Dave Whitney, Maria and Frank Leonard, Paul Rendall, Dean Cutting, Sandra Rodham, George Huw, Susan and Mark Walker, Gareth Lawman, Daniel Evans, the Rugby Football Union, Mark Evans and all at Harlequins, Harry Keogh at Drummonds, Philippa Brockway at Pearson Television, all at This Is Your Life, Jonathan Johnson, Clive Woodward and the England team and to my partner, Sandra Rodham, and our three children – Harry, Jack and Francesca.

What a Year!

I'll never forget standing on the Sydney pitch in the pouring rain. We'd played our hearts out in the World Cup final for 80 minutes. Now we faced extra time. Johnno got us into a huddle and said, 'don't panic'. He told everyone to be calm and collected and just carry on doing what we were doing and we would win. He had such confidence. We all had confidence in each other and in our ability to do it.

Clive ran down the steps to talk to us. He darted onto the field and Johnno stopped him. 'We're OK,' he said. 'Everything is OK. You can go back.' Clive looked shocked but he just backed off and let us get on with it. We'd been through a lot together as a group – we knew each other inside out. We'd been through defeats and victories, criticism and praise. We knew we were the fittest team and we knew we could rely on each other. We knew we could win.

The moment when Jonny kicked the ball that would win

us the World Cup, all I remember was the sound of leather on leather. I knew it was going over. He belted it with his wrong foot, under all that pressure, yet I was certain that it was good. I looked up and saw it sail over. The crowd roared. We'd done it. We were the 2003 world champions.

It had been a long time in coming. By the time they hung that medal round my neck I was the most capped player in the history of the game and had competed in four World Cups and three Lions tours. I'd won four grand slams and had three kids! Winning the World Cup was the highlight of a career that has been an absolute joy. I started in 1990 and ended in 2004. Who would have guessed, when I stood on the field in Argentina for my first international cap, that it would develop the way it has. I still remember that first cap so clearly.

Even now I can picture the smoke, billowing out from the far stand as applause rippled around the stadium. I stood in the middle of the pitch and tried to stare ahead without focusing on the hatred written on the faces of those who jeered and shouted in the crowd. The strength of their emotions was palpable – as real as the smoke that drifted on the warm afternoon air. Every one of those people standing out there seemed to hate the England team with a depth that I could barely comprehend. It seemed that the players on the pitch wanted to take us apart, and those watching in the crowd, from behind huge barbed-wire fences, wanted to pick over the bones.

The year was 1990 and the place was Argentina. I was about to play in my first game for England and I had never been more scared on a rugby field. The pressures of playing in my first international game paled into insignificance beside the physical threat which appeared to be confronting me. I had never felt such intensity before, had never known such an exhibition of raw human emotion – nor have I since.

As I stood, as tall as I could, all those years ago, heaving my shoulders back and facing the angry mob, I belted out the national anthem at the top of my voice. I thought about the shirt that I was playing in, the country I was playing for and the players I was standing alongside. This was it. A most glorious moment. My first England cap. Their anger and bitterness would not prevent me from cherishing this moment.

All the time, the smoke continued to snake through the air, getting thicker as it billowed across the pitch. I turned towards it and, just as I thought the atmosphere couldn't get any more hostile, a group of young Argentinians revealed the source of the fire as they held a burning flag in the air. I could hardly believe it – they had set fire to the Union Jack during the national anthem. This was now, officially, a baptism of fire.

It was a terrifying start to my career. The burning of the Union Jack signalled the commencement of the toughest, most vicious game that I have ever played in. The England rugby team was the first sports side from this country to travel to Argentina after the Falklands War and, with the shadow of that costly encounter colouring all Argentine opinion, we were considered the enemy. Their feelings towards us ran deeper than those one would expect to experience as a sportsman. We were seen as the enemy, in every sense. We were the living embodiment of the political and military clashes that had taken place between Argentina and Britain, and the Argentinians were looking for sweet revenge.

I knew, in that game, that if I got through and emerged with credit despite the bitterness of the hostile crowd, then

I would earn the respect of my fellow players. I knew that if I could succeed despite the adverse conditions, then my peers would know that I deserved my place alongside them – and that is what happened. Buoyed by the fact that I was flanked by some of the toughest, bravest and most talented men ever to grace a rugby pitch, I threw myself into the match and threw myself into the tour. I acted like a sponge – soaking up information and learning from the best in the game.

I passed the physical test in Argentina and returned from the tour very much 'one of the boys'. From then on, I was a key member of the England squad and would stay in and around the team for over a decade, taking in four World Cups and three Lions tours.

But even now, after all the games I have played, I still think that the first game I played, in those extraordinary conditions, taught me a valuable lesson – that you have to protect your teammates and you have to trust them to be there for you. If any one of us had faltered in that match, someone would have been seriously hurt. The fact that all the players stuck together and refused to bow to the intimidation, allowed us to succeed.

Over a decade later, I am playing a sport that few people would recognize from those heady days in Argentina. In Argentina, in 1990, we never imagined that players would one day be on lucrative playing contracts, that millionaires would sweep into the sport and embellish it with cheer-leaders, loud music and big promotions. Nor did we imagine that TV contracts would be massive news stories, nor that Twickenham would become such a sleek, professionally-run organization. The magnitude and speed of the changes have been quite staggering. There have been changes too for players at the top level. When I first started playing for England it was practically obligatory to drink as much as you could the night before a game, especially for a forward – I can't imagine how I'd have been treated if I'd sipped isotonic drinks and headed for the gym like we all do now. Back then, nutrition meant eating the biggest steak and the hottest curry you could find, and dehydration was caused by a queue at the bar, not intensive training.

Paul Rendall (known as 'The Judge') and Mickey Skinner ('The Munch') were my two guiding lights when I first started. Under Judge's expert tutelage, I honed my drinking skills to a fine art, and I really was amongst the very best in the team. As you will read, Judge is one of the first people to make my all-time drinking XV. I hope he is flattered by this great honour – he should be very proud of himself. Under Mickey The Munch I learnt much about knocking over Frenchmen and putting in hard-hitting tackles, but I also remember him fondly as an expert at getting out of training runs.

In my time as a player, I think I've seen rugby union change more than it did in the previous hundred years, or will in the next hundred. But some things remain the same. Camaraderie, team spirit and thrill still exist in the sport at all levels. Nowadays we are paid to play, and this influences much about our preparation off the field; but on the pitch the game is the same as the one I started playing as a boisterous Barking schoolboy. The fundamentals of the game remain intact, the people remain as they always were and the joy and pain that it can cause remain as acute as ever.

There have been low times, of course. I had an operation in 1992 which could have taken me out of the game forever. A surgeon had to cut a chunk of bone from my hip and insert it into my spine by going through the front of my neck. For that surgeon's skills, I am eternally grateful. I had recovered by the time England next played and I ran out in white without missing a game.

There have been fun times, too – always. For all my achievements in the sport, I know that even now one daft comment and the team will take the piss out of me as readily as they did when I was a fresh-faced youngster, eager to impress. Martin Bayfield has a lovely Jason Leonard joke which is one of my favourites. It goes: why does Jason Leonard have a see-through lunch box? Answer: so he knows whether he's going to work, or coming home. He also insists that line-outs would be a lot more efficient if I didn't stand there looking at all the girls in the crowd! I couldn't possibly comment on this, of course.

There have been frustrations along the way, too, like losing three Grand Slams in a row in the final games in 1999, 2000 and 2001, and the ultimate frustration – losing the World Cup final to Australia in 1991. But I've had my share of great triumphs too, such as the back-to-back Grand Slams in 1991 and 1992, the tremendous Lions tour of 1997 and of course the 2003 World Cup. When Jerry Guscott kicked that dropped goal I thought every prayer had been answered. He makes the drinking team, too. But even if he was tee-total I think I'd take him – just to thank him for that wonderful kick!

All the times – good and bad – have provided me with fantastic memories, and I do not regret a single second of my time as a rugby player.

I have also managed to combine having a family with international rugby, something which has been a great joy to me. Harry, Jack and Francesca, are a fantastic antidote to the pressures of rugby. When things are going well on the pitch, it's always amusing to return to the boys who happily ignore every demand I make, kick me out of the way and generally disrespect me. It's probably very healthy and it's certainly great fun. Sandra, my partner, has sacrificed a great deal to enable me to keep the caps mounting up. She has played a significant part in my career and I'm grateful to her – luckily she understands what it means to me to play this game. She's aware of the value I place on the friendships I've made and the happiness I derive from this tough, confrontational sport that absorbs us all so much.

In the last 10 minutes of an international match, when your lungs are bursting, your legs are aching and you think you're not going to make it through the game, you tap into a part of yourself that you're never sure you have! You challenge yourself and force yourself to perform – for the team. People say that I have given the sport a lot, but I don't believe I've given half as much as it has given me. It's taken me round the world, introduced me to some fabulous people and created a lifestyle for me that I could never have enjoyed without it – not bad for a barrel-shaped Barking boy who only wanted to play rugby to make friends, meet girls and drink beer, is it? I hope you enjoy the book.

CHAPTER ONE

Barking Beckons

When I first appeared, screaming and kicking into the August sunshine on a bright and warm morning in 1968, the midwives at Upney Hospital remarked on what a quiet, sweet placid child I was. I smiled gently and cooed at the passing nurses, giving no indication whatsoever that just a few months later I would be tearing the family home apart, emptying the contents of the fridge onto the floor and smashing eggs around the kitchen.

I was the perfect baby for the first few weeks. The only sign of the size I was destined to become lay in the amount of food I was eating. Mum says that I was only 7lb 8oz when I was born, but I very quickly put on weight because there was no food that I wouldn't try. I was always hungry, always wanting to eat and never fussy about what it was. Some things haven't changed!

I was the first of three boys for Mum and Dad, and I don't

think either of them had any idea how much work it was going to be, or how noisy family life would become with us all tearing around, wrecking their nice neat home. Suddenly, handles were being yanked off drawers, food was being pulled out of cupboards and tipped onto the floor, and everything moveable was either broken or eaten. Wanton destruction was my favourite game and, in the name of it, I used to smash everything I owned to pieces. In fact, there is just one toy in existence that I didn't totally wreck – a Tonka truck with one side totally caved in and the other side full of dents and scrapes. It's in an awful mess and Mum has this embarrassing habit of producing it from time to time as proof of how bad I was. In recent years I have come to dread journalists talking to Mum, in case she shows them the Tonka toy!

Mum and Dad were living in Hornchurch at the time of my birth, but we moved to Chadwell Heath soon afterwards and lived in a small, cosy, terraced house in a big family community, with my Gran and Grandad and my uncles Roy and Darren living in the house next door. Mum produced two brothers for me to pick on relentlessly – Scott who is three years younger than me and my baby brother, Russell. Having so many family members living nearby meant there were lots of big get-togethers, usually over food and drinks – we were all big eaters in the Leonard family, unsurprisingly. I think Mum must have spent most of my childhood either cooking and baking, or shopping; meanwhile Dad seems to have spent all his time apologizing. On one occasion, when I was three or four, I'd been playing around with the oven in the kitchen twiddling all the knobs around. Without realizing it, I had turned the gas on. The next thing I knew was that my grandma went into the kitchen to make my tea.

When she approached the oven with a match the whole thing exploded into flames and singed her eyebrows off. She says that one of them still hasn't properly grown back to this day! My other favourite trick was kicking the heads off crocuses. Grandad had a row of prized flowers in his garden and I went up to them one day, lined my foot up and kicked the top off every one of them.

My partner in crime in those early days was my Uncle Darren who, despite being an uncle, was born in the same week as me. The two of us would play together and refuse to involve my younger brothers who seemed incredibly young and childish compared to us. Three or four years doesn't seem much now, but then it seemed a lifetime.

I had a very happy childhood – idyllic in many ways. I was forever laughing and giggling, tearing about and causing mayhem. Home was a manic place and I was always in trouble over something or other – either because I was doing something wrong or one of my brothers was, although it was usually me! On one occasion, Darren and I disappeared up to my bedroom with an airgun and fired it at some guy who was working on his car in the street outside. It must have given him the fright of his life. Darren and I belted down the stairs and ran out of the house because we knew the guy would come looking for us. Sure enough, Dad says that a man came to the door soon after we'd gone, complaining that he'd been shot in the bottom and he was sure the culprit had been in this house. Dad had to assure the man that he would sort us out when he got hold of us.

On another occasion, I decided that it would be a really good idea to put a small firework in the keyhole of the woodwork door at school. Don't ask me why! I suppose I had this firework, saw the keyhole and thought it seemed like a good idea. Unfortunately the woodwork teacher didn't agree! In fact he thought it was a particularly bad idea and called my mum to the school to tell her so. Mum says she got more of a telling-off than I did!

Luckily I discovered sport before I could cause too much further damage and in it I saw a release for all my pent-up energy. The first sports that appealed to me were those that my dad was interested in – boxing and darts. Rugby came later when I got to senior school. I also had a passing interest in the Cub Scouts and karate but Mum says that as soon as she bought me the Cub uniform, I gave it up.

Dad was working as a sheet-metal worker when I was born and trained as a carpenter shortly afterwards. He thinks he's the real sportsman in the family because he plays darts and can hit the bull's eye after 20 pints. I suppose I'd have to agree with him really. I might have played for England and the Lions, but can't get anywhere near the bull's eye – with or without alcohol.

Mum competed as a swimmer when she was younger and taught my brothers and I how to swim. I went a lot at school and completed the bronze, silver and gold awards, but swimming never appealed to me as there was nowhere near enough violence in it. What I loved was boxing – going to fights with Dad in the East End, when he would surprise me by talking through every punch and explaining all the moves in detail. No one believes that their parents know anything when they're young and I was no exception, so Dad's boxing talk used to amaze me no end.

It was my interest in boxing that saw me involved in a bizarre activity which forms my earliest memory of school. I was in the hall, holding a challenge match to see if anyone could punch me in the stomach and hurt me. I know it sounds ridiculous, but I'm sure it must have seemed like a good idea at the time. There were boys at the school queuing up to hit me and see if they could inflict any pain. No one ever did, although a few hurt themselves trying. I think money was changing hands somewhere along the line and some smart kid was probably making a fortune out of it, but I just remember standing there, clenching my stomach muscles and watching the looks on their faces as they hit me and held their hands in agony.

I went to Warren Comprehensive from the age of 11 onwards – a good, decent school, but by no means out of the ordinary. It was a real football school in the East End tradition, with links to West Ham football club based just up the road. There was little interest in rugby there, because it was seen as a sport for posh kids and those with a public school education. Things have changed a lot since then and professionalism means that it's hard work and talent that are rewarded now, not whether you wear the right school tie; but back then we felt that it was 'them and us' as far as rugby was concerned, and our school tie was definitely not the right colour (even if you bothered to wear one).

I played some football as a youngster, but not football as most people would know it. I was actually recruited to perform a role which is not strictly in the rules or the spirit of the game – I was there just to chop people down. Put simply, I played rugby in a football team. There would be ten footballers and me, but I liked to think that I was the crucial player. I was given a job in defence which involved kicking anyone who got past the other players into the air and it worked a treat – there are probably still some guys wandering around today with scars to prove it.

However, I was always destined to find myself in a rugby

team, and because of my bulky physique, I started playing for the school side at prop. I don't have any particular
memories of playing rugby for the first time, but Mickey
Eyres, a teacher at Chadwell Heath who also played prop at
Barking Rugby Club, remembers seeing me and realizing
that I was a naturally talented player who would just go to
waste in the school system.

I played some local matches for the school side and was
invited to go to area trials, which resulted in me playing
Barking and Essex representative matches, but Mickey was
right – I didn't go far in the school system because I wasn't
at a rugby school. There were a couple of good rugby
schools in the area, such as Campion, and they supplied the
majority of players for the representative sides. I don't think
a kid – coming from Warren Comprehensive, at that time,
stood much of a chance. But being overlooked never entered
my mind – I played rugby for fun and had no real desire to
make it to the top. I don't think I even thought about it at
that time.

Mickey Eyres invited me to go down to Barking Rugby
Club one Sunday morning. He said that it would be a chance
for me to play at a higher level, alongside players with more
experience, and I decided to take his advice because it
sounded like fun. It's clear now that everyone around me
thought that I might have a real talent for the game, whereas
I liked rugby because of the friends you could make and
because it was a rough sport. I also loved the fact that everyone socialized afterwards and there were usually a few girls
hanging around.

I can clearly remember when I first went down to Barking
Rugby Club and how I was made to feel welcome straight
away. I walked into that old clubhouse for the first time,

aged just 14, and thought it was fantastic – an excellent place full of down-to-earth people. The sport itself allowed you to throw your weight around, plough into other players and fling them around the park. I almost believed that I'd died and gone to heaven.

When Barking had a look at me, they said I should be in the U16 side even though I was only 14. From that moment on, I would go on playing a long way above my age group. By the time I was 15, I was in the U19 side, and by the time I was 16, I was the U19s' captain. I started to concentrate all my time and enthusiasm into Barking Rugby Club and although I played a few representative games for the school, I focused on club rugby, so it was there that I really developed my game.

Once I was at Barking Rugby Club, I started to take rugby seriously, realized that this was a sport I was good at and loved. Everything else paled into insignificance besides rugby, the one activity to which I was totally devoted. I became determined to be fitter and stronger than everyone else, so I started weight training, and used to run to Barking from Chadwell Heath for every session. It was about 4 miles to the rugby club and once I could do the run easily, I bought myself a weightlifting belt and planned to fill it with weights to give me more of a challenge. Mum spotted what I was up to and stopped me before I injured myself. Dad says he remembers coming up to my room after I got back from Barking one night to find me totally out of breath.

'Are you OK, son?' he asked anxiously.

'I'm just a bit tired from the run back,' I said, not letting him past me into my room.

The next day he found a bus stop sign with a solid concrete base tucked away in the corner of my bedroom. I had decided that I needed more of a challenge that night so had decided to run back clutching a big lump of concrete. Dad put it outside and I think we confused bus drivers in the area for weeks!

As I was spending so much time at Barking, education, school work and exams that had never meant much to me anyway, mattered less and less. I had never worked very hard or concentrated particularly when I was at school so I never troubled the masters in the top group. This meant the school lost interest in me academically and I was encouraged more in my sport than with my books, to the extent that I abandoned all interest in school work and devoted all my time to the sports field. Not that I was alone in this, for I can remember when they gave us the option of playing sport on Wednesday afternoon, which meant you had time off lessons. You've never seen such a rush for the door – there were all these kids who'd never touched a ball before suddenly rushing out of classes like they'd been selected to play for England.

As I was working through the age groups at Barking, I was continuing to be less than impressive at school. My rugby got better while my school work got worse and I left just before my sixteenth birthday, which was as early as I could. My parents tried to persuade me to stay at school and get qualifications that would help me later on, but at 15 I didn't worry too much about 'later on' – I was only interested in the 'here and now'. What really turned me on was rugby. By that stage I had decided that I wanted to play for England and never tired of telling people that one day I would.

My parents eventually gave up trying to persuade me to stay at school and I began training as a carpenter alongside my dad for the first six months of my working life. I remember on my first day in the job, the guy running the site said, 'Look, son. I'll give you fifty pence for each sheet of plasterboard you can carry up the stairs,' because they needed materials to be taken to the top floor. They thought they were being very clever and that it would take me all day to shift them, so they'd only owe me a few quid at the end of it. Unfortunately for them, I was stronger than they'd given me credit for. I lifted a couple of the boards onto my shoulder and ran up the stairs, stuck at it all day and was quids in. In addition, I'd spent the whole day weight training, so I was happy.

I used to turn every occasion into a training session so that even walking the dog became serious exercise. On one occasion I took Sadie, our Staffordshire bull terrier out, with me. She loved going for walks but I don't think she was quite prepared to be put through a training session. By the time I'd been jogging and sprinting round the track for hours, she was absolutely exhausted. I turned round to stretch off and she ran home as fast as she could. Dad says he was working in the garage when the dog came running in, whimpering, and hid under the work bench, cowering and hoping that I wouldn't see her. She wouldn't go out with me again!

I remember the kids that I'd been at school with saying, 'Aren't you worried about having no exam qualifications?' and I'd say: 'Why would I be? I'm working now – what do I need exams for?' With hindsight, I realize that I should have worked harder at school, done the exams and kept my options open. However, I got a trade, so that was good, but I would rather have had the chance to go to college or university. Of course, if I'd done that I might not have broken into the England set-up quite so quickly because I just know that the appeal of the social system would have been too great for me, and they'd have probably taken me out of the students' union in a body bag!

My first year in the U19s was fantastic because we won the Essex Cup for the first time ever. It was amazing – you'd have thought we'd won the World Cup from the reaction we got locally. We were playing Harlow, a strong side that had won for the previous five years – the equivalent of Manchester United maybe playing Charlton. We beat them against all the odds and the clubhouse was turned into a party venue for the night – I don't think I made it home for the best part of a week.

The clubhouse at Barking Rugby Club was a fairly basic place in those days. It was a real old shack, with men's and women's toilets – but no one distinguished between them, and men would walk out of both. The walls inside were painted light green, so it didn't matter a bit if anyone was sick or threw beer all over them. There was no carpet – just plastic lino on the floor – so that every morning they would simply sweep out through the front door everything that had been deposited the night before. I always pitied the poor guy who had that job.

In addition to the main bar, there was also a little snug which was tiny and was members only – I don't think anyone under the age of 80 ever went in there, but those guys were some of the funniest I've ever met. There were two old fellows down there who reminded me of Statler & Waldorf – the grumpy puppets on *The Muppets* who start the programme off every week on a balcony. I always laugh when I go in there now, and even though Barking has acquired a new clubhouse, they're still sitting there in the snug. I'm not sure that they ever move. They look about 80, but then they looked about 80 when I was a kid. I always go in and say, 'Ain't you dead yet? I'm sure I sent flowers to your funeral. Are you sure you're not dead? They're not digging you up and propping you up against the bar, are they?'

Just after I'd played in the Colts' memorable and much-celebrated victory over Harlow, I got my break in the senior team because they were a prop short and they thought I might want to play. I was warned that I was under age and uninsured, but that the captain and coaches all believed that I could handle the step up in intensity. I jumped at the chance and when they warned me about how tough adult props could be, I told them not to worry, I'd be OK.

We played Braintree in that match – my first adult game – and coaches from Barking stood at the touchline, worried to death about what might happen to me. They knew that they'd be shot if I got into trouble or if the RFU found out that I was being played under age. When the first scrum went down they must have been hoping and praying that I'd come out in one piece. They were all staring, waiting to see how I'd cope when the front rows first came into contact, but five seconds later all their fears were allayed as the prop opposite me shot up into the air – I'd lifted him right off the ground. They all relaxed then and enjoyed the rest of the game and a few pints. I loved playing at that level and went back to play senior rugby as soon as I could, but first I had to finish the season with the Colts because I was their captain.

We had a new boy in the Colts side, a lad called Glyn Llewellyn whom our coach, Lawrence Consiglio, had spotted. Glyn had been watching us play East London because he was at East London Poly at the time and fancied watching a match. When Lawrence saw this 6'6" bloke with a Welsh accent standing there he rushed over and asked him if he fancied playing. Glyn said that he did and we began the process of signing him up to the club. The problem was that before you could play for Barking in those days, you had to go for a formal interview with members of the committee, so Glyn went along and sat before a few committee men who asked him about his rugby. 'I've played for Neath and Welsh Schools,' he said. One of the committee men couldn't believe it and kept nudging the one next to him and saying, 'Sign him up, sign him up.' But the others continued with their routine. 'And do you have any social references?' Social references? Can you believe it – social references? This was Barking Rugby Club, for God's sake. Give him a shirt before he gets away.

Glyn eventually managed to provide them with the references they required and took his place in the team. He was a No.8 at the time and was absolutely brilliant. He took the place apart and used to scare the life out of the opposition because Welsh rugby was a lot tougher than anything played in England at the time. We didn't have any touch judges in Colts games so you couldn't get sent off unless you were seen by the referee. Glyn would make maximum use of this and, knowing the referee couldn't see everything, would blatantly punch his opposite number in the first line-out and say, 'That's how we play in Wales.' Glyn and I have stayed good mates over the years and his first cap for Wales coincided with my first Five Nations game in 1991.

Both Glyn and I were recognized by selectors in the regional and area set-up, and began moving slowly through the system that would result in me running out for England and Glyn for Wales. The first stage was Essex trials, which didn't seem particularly difficult to me since I'd been playing a tough level of rugby since I was 17. After that it was to Eastern Counties, where I started to feel challenged and realized that I was now at a higher level. But I still felt as though I had the upper hand in the scrums and knew my way around the park. I was fit, streetwise and willing to try anything.

Those characteristics eventually came to the attention of the England U19 selectors and I was called up for the U19 game against Italy at New Brighton in 1986. I played with guys like Paddy Dunston, Paul Manley, Howard Lamb, Rupert Moon and Paul Hull. It was a great honour and we were a good side. The only match we lost that season was against France and even that game was close. When we played Wales, the young tight head was John Davies – a few years later he told me that he remembered me from that match as he only weighed about 14 stone in those days, so wasn't too hard to toss around.

The England Colts experience taught me discipline, but I relied on the Barking first team for my lessons in 'street rugby' and how to stay strong. After finishing my year in the Colts, I slipped back into the first team at Barking and immediately took up my position in the front row. Along with playing in the first team came various rituals, including the tradition of throwing new boys out of the bus on the way back when they made their first away trip – you then had to walk back to the clubhouse naked. I was thrown off the bus with this other guy who was also making his debut. We were a mile from the clubhouse, completely naked and in about four inches of snow. The two of us tumbled out of the bus and ran to hide behind a tree. I shouted to the guys on the bus to at least let me have my shoes – I wasn't bothered about the fact that I was stark naked, but was just worried about having to run through the snow barefoot. Our teammates on the bus were naturally having none of it and they turned and drove off, waving to us as we cowered behind the tree, covering ourselves with our hands.

I asked the guy who was with me what he was going to do. He said that he only lived a mile to the south of the point where we'd been dropped off, so he would run back home, get changed and meet me at the club. I lived miles away and decided I'd better head for the clubhouse which was about a mile to the north of us, so off we both went in opposite directions. I was running between parked cars, hiding behind them until it was clear, then running to the next car, hoping that no one would see me. I thought I was doing quite well until a police car pulled up alongside me, an officer got out, covered me with his jacket and told me to get into the back of the car. Once I was inside, he told me that a little old lady had rung 999 when she saw a naked man running past her window. The copper then radioed back to the station and told them that I'd been picked up, whereupon he looked at me and said, 'You're fit, aren't you?'

'Yes,' I said. 'I'm quite fit. I play a lot of rugby.'

'What position?' asked the copper.

'Prop,' I replied.

'Blimey, you're fit for a prop. Bloody fit,' he added, looking impressed. Then he looked at his watch. 'You were spotted in Barking Park Road five minutes ago. That's a mile away. You've just run a five-minute mile with no clothes on, no shoes and in four inches of snow.'

It was at this point that I realized that the little old lady had seen the other guy who'd gone running in the opposite direction. It was a shame to have to tell the copper as he was so impressed with my fitness, but I did tell him in the end.

He laughed, swung the car round and we went off to the police station. By the time we got back there, they'd picked up the other guy and took us both back to the club. They marched us into the club and said, 'Does anyone know where these boys' clothes are?' All the guys in the clubhouse just looked up at the ceiling. The police prodded the ceiling with their truncheons, one of the tiles shifted and down fell all our clothes, so we got dressed and bought the coppers a beer.

The fun side of rugby still appeals to me and although the sport has become more professional while I've been involved, I still think that the social side of the game is important – rugby won't be rugby the day that opponents don't go out for a drink with one another after playing. The sport will have changed for the worse when guys who battle like hell on the pitch can't socialize off it. It's different when you're playing for the Lions or England so it's important to keep in touch with the club game. At least it is for me. And I know I'd be a poorer person without the guys at Barking.

CHAPTER TWO

A Step Up

Barking was a great club for me to start my rugby career in.
It gave me everything I wanted, and more. But in the end, by
the time I was 19 years old and had experienced two hard
years in the first team, both I, and all my mates at Barking,
knew that it was time for me to move on.

The guys at Barking were very good about helping me
to find the best move after it became clear that it was time
for me to leave, just as they had protected me the year
previously and had urged me not to leave too soon.

I think that many people at the club were concerned about
me leaving too soon and being put in the U21s, where I'd be
likely to learn less about the real world of adult propping
than I would at Barking where at least I was gaining invalu-
able experience against old, wizened, wily, gnarled props.
Playing in the first team at Barking gave me a streetwise edge
which would help me to cope later, when I came up against
experienced internationals.

So I was 19 before I decided that it was time to move on. I'd already played a couple of U21 games for Saracens on an invitation basis, and I liked the club. They were in the second rather than the first, but I still liked the atmosphere and the people down there. The only other club that I had thought about joining was Wasps, but the England props Jeff Probyn and Paul Rendall were well established there, so I wouldn't have a chance of getting into the first team until they retired.

I liked Saracens because there was a good chance of me making it into the first team quickly and, although it was more serious than Barking, there was still an element of fun about the club which appealed to me. It was then a small club with lots of people who'd been around for years, so there was a great community spirit and a friendliness about the place which reminded me of Barking. I loved it and everything it stood for. It was a good, honest club full of hard-working people. There was nothing glamorous about it but there was a lovely atmosphere down there, and a feeling of everyone pulling in the same direction and working towards the same goals. Bramley Road was a great little stadium – even though the locals used to walk their dogs across the pitch during the day, so you'd be knee deep in dog shit during training sessions.

Saracens first approached me when they saw me playing county rugby and they invited me along. After the introductory couple of matches for the U21s, I took them up on the offer of a place and headed down to Bramley Road. The timing of my arrival was extremely lucky for me, but not for the regular prop, a guy called Richie Andrews, who went off to get married to Di – and I stepped in to fill in for him in his absence.

While he was saying 'I do', I sneaked in and stole his place; while he was on honeymoon, I perfected the role; and by the time he got back, I was a permanent fixture in the team. Luckily, we're the best of mates now, but he can't have been too pleased at the time.

In my first game for Sarries firsts, against Bridgend, Tony Robinson, known as Robbo, was playing tight head and was completely mauled by his opposite number. I remember afterwards, Tony Russ, the coach, said to him, 'You useless lump, you were beaten by a complete nobody.' Robbo was really embarrassed at the time, but was relieved later to discover that the 'nobody' turned out to be Mike Griffiths who was selected to tour with the Lions at the end of the season. Robbo took great pride in reminding Tony of his words when the Lions squad was announced.

When Richie Andrews came back from his honeymoon, he played tight head and I kept the loose-head spot. It had been a quick progression from playing casually at Barking to running out for Saracens, and I knew I was extremely young to be a Division Two prop, but I was ready – I had always been big, had always played a few years above my age and I'd had a couple of years of playing full-on adult rugby so I knew what to expect and what I would have to cope with.

While I was at Saracens, I carried on working on building sites – helping out, doing the lifting, slowly learning a trade and earning enough money to allow me to train whenever I could. I know that a lot of people thought we were getting paid by clubs at the time, but we weren't – we got our beer and kit paid for and there was transport to training, but that was it.

When I wasn't on site, I would be either fitness training in the gym or on the track, or rugby training. It all meant that I was extremely fit and quite lightweight for a prop (16 stone), so I tore around the pitch, causing as much trouble for the opposition as I could. That season we won all the games in the Second Division and were promoted to the First Division. Our results must have caught the eye of the selectors, because in 1988/89 I made it onto the bench for England U21 v Romania U21.

I had a great time at Saracens. I remember once when we were on the bus driving back from a match and Tony Russ fell asleep. We always had a rule that there was no sleeping allowed on an away trip so we decided to punish him. He had these enormous, bushy Denis Healey eyebrows so it seemed obvious that the best punishment was to shave one of them off. Unfortunately, it was decided that I was the best person to perform this task, so I crept up on Tony slowly, clutching a razor. I had got to within an inch of his face when he opened the eye I was about to shave above and said, 'I wouldn't, Leonard. I really wouldn't. Not if you ever want to play for Saracens again.' Needless to say, I didn't.

Getting into the First Division at a London club also meant I was a contender for a place in the London divisional squad. I played in only one London game, when we took on the South West at Imber Court. I ended up in the team because Judge was unwell. As soon as I heard about his illness and the fact that they needed a replacement, I raced across town to make it for the start of the game. It was well known that England were looking for a successor to Paul Rendall at the time and that they had tried to find a successor in 1989 without any luck.

Paul was the best prop around and England knew that they would need a good replacement for him, or risk the huge advantage they had in the forwards – with the likes of Paul Ackford, Wade Dooley, Mike Teague, Peter Winterbottom and Dean Richards. They knew that they couldn't afford to let the front row weaken or they'd weaken the whole scrum and the line-out – the platform of the English game. They had to find a good replacement.

I watched Judge carefully, trying to set myself up as a possible replacement for him. He was a great scrummager and the best line-out supporter (these were the days where you didn't lift, you 'supported'). The difference between supporting and lifting was very subtle – it was basically all in the shape of the hands. The easiest way to lift was to grab handfuls of your second row's shorts and hoist him into the air. Therefore, to prevent this, referees insisted that you had an open hand at all times. If a ref caught you with your fists clenched you'd be pulled for lifting.

Judge realized this early on and had developed the very impressive skill of lifting with an open hand. It was very effective and Judge was the best at it in the world. The crafty old sod wouldn't teach me what to do, so I had to watch him carefully. Because we were in direct competition for places, he didn't want to give me too much information about the task. I'd ask him 'Am I doing this right?' and he'd say 'Yes' although I knew I wasn't. As soon as I was established in the side, and when I was in the World Cup squad, he started helping me a lot more, explaining that you could get away with lifting by catching the jumper under his last rib and his chest side on, and just support him under the rib cage, so you could do it open-handed and therefore not be officially lifting.

It used to be funny during games. The second row would be in mid-air, and the referee would know that there was lifting going on. He'd think 'I can see that bugger's lifting, but his hand's open so there's nothing I can do.'

This was the sort of stuff you had to pick up along the way from the experienced guys. After London and the brief flirt with England U21 came England B. I was selected to play for them against Fiji, at Headingley. Geoff Cooke, the England manager, was keen to try out younger props, so Mark Linnett and Andy Mullins played for the first team, while Jeff Probyn and I propped against Fiji B. The match went well and it was good to play alongside Jeff. When Cooke called me up and said that I was down for the next representative game – England B v France B, away – I knew that I was in the reckoning and that one day they might take a chance on me in the first team.

CHAPTER THREE

Brothels, Bath Taps and Bottles

I always imagined that hearing I'd been selected to play for England for the first time would be special. I thought I'd answer the phone one day and the manager would grandly announce that I'd been chosen to represent my country, how proud I should be of myself and that he'd congratulate me. I even thought I might shed a tear. I never imagined that it would be Lawrence Consiglio, telling me that he'd read in the paper that I'd been selected. 'Hello mate,' he said. 'It says in the paper you're playing for England. You never told me.'

'That's 'cos I didn't know. Thanks for telling me,' I replied, and suddenly I was an international player.

After that call, there were loads more, as people saw the papers and talked to other people. I had relatives, friends and rugby mates on the phone, all congratulating me and telling me how pleased they were. I don't remember feeling anything at the time except surprise. I was amazed that I'd had no letter telling me about my selection, and I thought it was odd that all these people knew before me. I had wanted to be the one to tell Mum and Dad, not the other way round. In the end, I thought I'd better go and check for myself, so I headed off down to the paper shop. Sure enough, the squad for the 1990 tour to Argentina was listed, and in the four props there was a J. Leonard from Saracens Rugby Club. It had to be me.

The day was full of phone calls and questions as everyone I'd ever known called up to say 'well done'. I spent the whole day hoping for something from the RFU confirming it was true. I couldn't believe that they weren't going to tell me themselves. Was I going to find out all the arrangements for the trip and the Test team from the papers as well?

People think I'm exaggerating when I talk about what it was like back then, but it really was that bad. It was as if the selectors thought that their job was finished once they picked the side. I understand that if you've been selected, you'll find out soon enough, but when it's your first cap, it would be nice if they could mark it in some way by telling you before everyone else. Still, I suppose they knew the players would find out somehow, so they didn't worry too much about telling us.

At least I didn't get a '2p or a 10p call' – that's the way they used to tell players whether they were in the team or not in the early 1980s. The selectors used to sit round a payphone at the Lensbury Club (remember, these were the days before mobiles). In front of them, they would have a list of the players they had selected, and those players who had not been selected. If you were selected, they would call you using a ten pence piece, and explain to you why you had been picked and what the arrangements were. If you hadn't been picked, it was slightly different – they would use a two pence piece and before you could ask why you'd been dropped, the pips would go, the phone would cut off and the selectors would go back to the list and ring the next person.

I eventually got a letter from the RFU which outlined the plans for the summer tour. We were going to Argentina, and would be the first England sports team to tour there since the Falklands War in 1982. No wonder the selectors didn't want to tell me!

The tour was to be headed up by Geoff Cooke, the England manager, and would be seven matches long, with two Tests. They were taking four props and were going to rest Paul Rendall, who was about 107 years old by this time. The selectors were desperate to find a replacement for him, so all the young props on the tour knew that this was their golden chance. Rendall was a big character in the England team at the time – he was known as 'Judge' because he performed that role in the kangaroo courts on tour. These courts were a regular feature of tours back in the amateur days and would be held whenever the tour judge saw fit, to put any players who 'misbehaved' on trial. Misbehaviour counted as anything from talking to a female to not talking to a female, to wearing inappropriate clothes. Players who were called out late to tours would often be tried for arriving late. It was just a bit of fun, a nonsense occasion when we would all take the mickey out of one another.

Because Judge was left behind for the Argentina tour, I knew that I was in with a good shout for the England loose-head spot if I played the best I could. Jeff Probyn was chosen as the guaranteed tight head and Mark Linnett and Victor Ubogu were the other two. Vic, Mark and I were specialist loose vheads, so we knew we were up against each other for the honour of filling Judge's boots, and there is no doubt that Mark was in pole position as we left Heathrow, bound for Buenos Aires.

Argentina was a difficult place to tour – it was hard work, and there was enormous tension and a feeling of imminent danger all the time. We couldn't go out very much, and when we did leave the hotel, it had to be in numbers – always twos and threes rather than alone in case we came across some group in a bar or someone who took exception to us being English. We couldn't relax because we were forever looking over our shoulders.

Because there was nothing to do in the hotel and the players had started to feel a bit cooped up, Chris Oti and Victor Ubogu decided to go out one evening, coming back to the hotel afterwards, raving about this great bar they'd been to. 'There were loads of women in there,' said Victor. 'No men in sight, just full of women. It was a great place.'

As you can imagine, the England players thought this sounded like heaven on earth, so, the next night, half the England rugby squad went along with Victor and Chris, to find this magnificent bar. We arrived there and all seemed well until we had to pass a 6'5" doorman to get in. I thought that seemed a bit heavy-handed for a bar full of women, but we carried on inside and wandered up to the barman, who was also about 6'5" but with the added attraction of having a huge scar down the side of his face.

By this stage, I knew that this was no normal bar. We went to buy drinks, and they were 50p each. Every other place we'd drunk in, in Buenos Aires, it was about 15p a pint – even in the hotels. It was still a really cheap beer for us, but it was three times the price of the other bars, so I knew something wasn't right. Why would there be such a huge mark-up? When I looked around there were indeed just girls in there – all sitting round the edge of the bar. The man with the scar on his face told us that the girls weren't allowed to talk to us unless we spoke to them, so we had to make the first move. I couldn't believe it – it was obviously a knocking shop.

I told Victor and said we'd better go, but he didn't believe me. 'No, no, Jase, the girls aren't like that, they're nice girls,' he said. 'Are you nuts?' I replied. 'Just look at them.'

Victor looked around the room, and I could see that he was slowly realizing exactly what sort of place he'd brought us to. We all made a quick exit, with Victor running behind, still insisting that the girls had all seemed very nice and very friendly, and not at all like prostitutes. Yes Victor, of course. We believe you.

The tour began with a game against Banco Nación. It was expected to be an easy, warm-up match because Banco were just a club side, but it turned out that they were not just any old club side – they were Hugo Porta's side, and Porta was the greatest player in Argentine rugby. He was a real hero and the club were the current champions. Still, you'd expect an international side to beat them. On that day, Mark and Victor were selected, with Jeff Probyn on the bench and me in the stand. Mark was in at tight head because he had been on the bench covering loose head and tight head the previous season. England were beaten 21–29 in that game and everyone really laid into the team afterwards. Loads of questions were asked and selection plans changed. Mark had got himself into trouble by saying that he could play on both sides, because it was obvious to the selectors that he was a much more natural loose head.

The next game was against Tucumán, a team with a

reputation for turning over tour sides. I didn't know too much about the team or the place before the tour, but in the build-up to the game, and certainly during it, I learnt a great deal about the area. Tucumán is, apparently, the place that took the greatest number of casualties in the Falklands War, so to say that feelings were running high would be an under-statement. You didn't dare walk around the streets. It was extremely daunting. We decided that we should stay in as much as possible, which I found difficult because even stay-ing in the hotel was dull – there were no televisions in the rooms, nothing to distract you from the situation. It's odd how much it mattered, not having any televisions, con-sidering we wouldn't have understood a word of what was going on anyway, but it's still nice and somehow reassuring to have a TV on, and to flick through the channels and recognize the programmes – like the news, sports updates and game shows.

In the end, I decided to ask why there were no televisions. The hotel receptionist said that it was because the New Zealand team had been there a few weeks before us, and after losing a midweek game, they'd all gone nuts, got drunk and thrown the televisions out of the windows. They clearly thought that all rugby players would be of a similar tempera-ment, so had decided that we couldn't have them at all. It's one of the very few times that I've been treated like a rock star on tour.

When I heard that I had been selected for the game against Tucumán, I knew it was my big chance. Geoff Cooke decided to completely change the front row, and I would be playing with John Olver and Jeff Probyn whom I'd played with in London divisional games. We'd worked well together, so I was optimistic. By this stage, I knew of the problems that we would encounter at Tucumán. I knew that at the best of times they were viewed as being the bad boys of Argentine rugby, and that the match against the All Blacks (the one that had led to all televisions being thrown out of the hotel) had been a fight from start to finish, with the game almost being stopped halfway through. So, I could only imagine what sort of treatment we would be in for, with the memories of the Falklands crisis to aggravate them even further.

Tucumán play in an orange kit and are known as the Clockwork Oranges. Indeed, oranges are a bit of a theme at the club – there are orange trees on the way to the ground, and the fanatical supporters pluck them off on the way to the game. To eat? What do you think? No. To throw at us! During the national anthem, we were standing there, singing our hearts out in order to be heard over the booing Argentinians, and oranges were flying past our noses. Just when we were starting to think we were onto a bit of a lost cause, we saw something of a commotion on the far side of the ground. When we looked more closely, we could see smoke and hear people chanting and shouting, then we could see what was really going on – they were burning the Union Flag. They stopped the anthem halfway through before things got really out of hand.

Once the game started, the oranges kept flying. I remember being hit by them in the line-out, in the scrums and all over the field. The crowd was very close to the pitch – about 10 yards away – so we were covered with oranges all the time. And it was not just fruit missiles that we had to contend with. At one point during the game, Dewi Morris complained to the referee that he'd found a pair of scissors, an empty whisky bottle and a bath tap on the pitch. Who brings a bath tap to a rugby game?

The stadium itself was like a football ground, with barbed wire around the top of the fence to stop fans climbing over and onto the pitch – it was an intimidating place. When I first saw the barbed wire, I thought it looked awful, but by the end of the game, I was quite glad it was there to keep the supporters from us.

We played well in that game and we beat Tucumán 19–14, but to be honest, it had been little more than a brawl in places, and was like nothing I had ever experienced before. There was sheer bloody-minded violence going on – just nasty, vindictive incidents which were designed to seriously hurt our players. In the first ten minutes Wade Dooley was muscled up the wrong way (he really is the wrong person to punch and barge into) so he turned round and smacked someone, and that was it – the whole pack was in there. Suddenly, minutes into my first international game, I was about to get involved in my first international fight.

I don't mind playing a hard game, and I believe there's a place for that in rugby, but what we experienced in Argentina on that tour was completely out of order. What it did show me was how good it is having people who'll stick up for you – I had Wade Dooley on one side of me, Peter Winterbottom on the other and Jeff Probyn a few feet away, so I never felt like I was going to be short of back-up. The opinion that the older players had of me after that was great – they thought I'd coped well, especially because I was only 20, hadn't stepped back from anything and had given as good as I got. I had proved my worth and hadn't backed down, which made me feel pleased that I could cope at this level and under all that pressure; and it also showed the selectors that I was tough and not afraid of confrontation. In games like that you can't hold back and as I was a youngster with much to prove, I wasn't going to be pushed about, so I was in the thick of it as much as the experienced boys.

Brian Moore later commented that seeing my contribution in that game was one of the highlights of the tour. He wrote: 'The match at Tucumán, surely the most hostile place to play in the world, was a real test for the young players. It was patently obvious in that match that Jason Leonard, new to the squad at loose head, was going to be an outstanding player. He stood his ground. If the tour produced little of merit for English rugby, then at least it produced Jason.'

It's great when teammates say things like that about you, but the truth is that it was the support of people like Brian, throughout that tour, that enabled me to perform so well. The pieces of advice I was given will stay with me for ever – I just ran around like a sponge for the whole trip, soaking up everything I could.

I remember, before that match, a lot of the players had told me to just concentrate on my own game. If you make a mistake, don't harp on about it, forget it and carry on, that's all you can do. I find myself saying that now to young players, because if you make a mistake in front of 70,000 people, you feel stupid. All of a sudden it can make you go into your shell and put you right off your game. I managed to follow that advice, and still do.

Because that first game had gone well for me personally and we had won it, I started to relax and enjoy the tour a little bit more. I'd got in one good game, whereas my two oppos had had a bad one. It meant that there was no reason to drop me, and I kept my place for the Test matches. In some ways it wasn't very fair on Vic and Mark because they didn't get back into the side then, and that was just because of one game on the tour. Anyone can have a bad game but they were quite harshly punished for theirs. I played in one more game after Tucumán, before the first Test – against a Buenos Aires team called Cuyo Select. We lost 21–22 but I felt I played pretty well, so I thought I might just make it into my first Test team.

The morning that Geoff Cooke was going to announce the Test team, I felt a little nervous. When I'd left for the tour, I never thought I would be in contention for a Test place, but now that things were looking so good, I was very keen to make it. I remember sitting there in the team room at the hotel while they read through the list, through the backs, and then the forwards – number one, Jason Leonard. Yes – I was in. The players congratulated me, as did Victor and Mark, and I sneaked out of the room to call Mum before we started training.

I was one of four new caps chosen for the first Test – Dean Ryan, David Pears and Nigel Heslop being the other new-comers. Together we participated in the dirtiest game imaginable. Punches and boots were flying and we took the brunt of it all in the front row. Jeff Probyn, playing at tight head, got a kick in the face. It was quite unbelievable. We won the match 25–12, and I crawled off the pitch, having had a real baptism of fire as a Test player.

The penultimate game of the tour, before the second Test, was against Cordoba and was captained by John Olver – a big schoolkid who is second only to Mickey Skinner in the practical jokes department. They spent the whole tour trying to hit each other in the face with cream cakes, or tipping buckets of water over the balcony at each other, like seven-year-old boys on a school outing. In the Cordoba game, like in most of the matches on tour, there were local referees who were very biased. At one point in the game, Olver felt the referee was offering our players no protection at all, and they were getting lumps kicked out of them, so he turned to the referee and said, 'I've had enough of this, if you don't sharpen up, I'm taking my players off the pitch,' and walked away.

I was on the bench for the match and was standing on the sidelines at the time. I remember thinking to myself that Olver's words might calm the situation down a bit, when all of a sudden Olver ran in and deliberately kicked one of the Argie players – the whole crowd went mad. We couldn't believe he'd done it, but I think he'd got so sick of the whole thing that he decided to take the law into his own hands. Even us players on the bench were shouting 'Get him off, get him off' along with the crowd, because we didn't want to look like tourists – we were scared for our lives. But somehow he managed to stay on the field and England won our third victory of the tour.

We lost the second Test 13–15, meaning we'd tied the series which was a massive disappointment. That second Test was the first time that Argentina had beaten England anywhere – so it was not great to be part of that particular record breaker.

Once the rugby was over, we all started to relax a little bit, and although we still couldn't go out and about on our own, we were able to see some of the countryside in the organized trips that the RFU had set up. Argentina has some wonderful countryside, and a traditional, rural lifestyle. Someone in the England team management decided that it would be good to see this lifestyle from the backs of horses.

We arrived at the foot of this enormous mountain at some ridiculously early hour and were given our horses. I took one look at mine and knew I'd have problems. It was clearly an unmanageable horse that objected to having 16½ stone on its back. The theory was that the horses would take us up to the top of the mountain where the views were beautiful, but my horse didn't want to go anywhere. So everyone jumped on their horses and click, click off they all went up the mountain. Except me. My horse refused to move no matter what I did – talk to it, coax it, kick it. I tried all the things you see in those old cowboy movies but nothing worked – not a thing.

By this stage, the rest of the guys were really motoring, and had got halfway up the hill. Because the horses do this all the time, they just follow the backside of the one in front, so they were all off in one long line. But not my horse. I ended up dragging it up the mountain, swearing to myself as I went. I eventually got to the top about an hour after everyone else, and they were all killing themselves laughing. I've got a video of the whole thing somewhere because Terry Crystal, the team doctor, and Kevin Murphy, the physio, videoed me walking up the mountain pulling this horse behind me. They were laughing so much that the video shakes when you watch it.

By the time I got to the top, I was soaking wet with sweat and exhausted, but the trouble was that the rest of the team had been standing there for an hour, so by the time I made it to the peak, they were ready to go back down. I like to think that they assumed my horse would be OK going down, or they wouldn't have left me. Unfortunately, my horse was far from OK going down and refused to budge, so I had to drag him back down the hill again. I've never seen a group of grown men laugh so much as when I got back down to the bottom, having pulled this horse all the way up, and all the way back down again. Everyone else had had such a pleasant afternoon, and had taken lovely pictures of the beautiful landscape – I was just completely exhausted.

The tour to Argentina was also where I was first introduced to the delights of the international players' courts – one after the first Test, and another after the second Test. At the first court, Mark Linnett was judge in Rendall's absence, and Carling was court artist for the trip. He was ordered to whiten the faces of Paul Hull, Chris Oti and Victor Ubogu and that's how they were made to spend the evening following the first Test. After the second Test it was decided that revenge should be taken on the court artist, Will Carling, and it was with a painted black face that he walked into the dinner that evening. Geoff Cooke was not impressed. Five minutes later Carling was in the toilets, scrubbing the ink from his face. Cooke felt that the captain should behave more responsibly. It was the first time that I came across expectations that people had of Carling, and how he was always expected to stand apart and be a leadership figure, yet in order to gain the respect of the guys, he had to get involved with us to a certain extent and not be seen as Cooke's man. I think he was in a very difficult position.

The tour to Argentina was a real breakthrough for me, but it was a dire trip in every other respect. We'd drawn the series, been mauled wherever we'd gone in the country, on the pitch, and felt threatened wherever we'd gone in the country, off the pitch.

When I look back, it was a fascinating time in which to begin my rugby career. I was young and surrounded by some of the toughest rugby players around. I learnt so much, so quickly. It was also interesting because we were all still true-blue amateurs – we had to beat the Argentinians before we could go back to our day jobs. I had to take time out from chippying and I was absolutely broke when I got home. There was much talk in the papers of the increasing pressures on players and how unfair it was on them to have to train harder and play harder, but there was no real talk of anything ever being done about it. I really thought the sport would stay amateur for ever – we seemed so far away from anything professional at the time, being given just meagre expenses and absolutely no payment. The RFU took it for granted that you would lose money to play for England.

At the time, and through the early part of the 1990s, I was seen as one of the new, young, professional breed of players who worked hard and trained hard. I was focused on fitness and was just desperate to be the best I could. Some of the older players like Paul Rendall and Jeff Probyn had grown up in an era where you only trained if it was forced upon you, whereas I never felt like that. I enjoyed training because I wanted to be a good rugby player.

Some of the players at Harlequins noticed how enthusiastic I was, and how much I wanted to improve my game, which I think appealed to them because Harlequins were a strong, ambitious team at the time. Players like Brian Moore and Peter Winterbottom started talking to me about the possibility of me leaving Saracens and going to Quins. Will Carling also asked me if I'd be interested in getting involved and said he thought it would be good for me because of the strength of the pack I'd be playing in – with Moore, Ackford, Winterbottom and Skinner. I knew Will was right and that my game could improve dramatically with those boys. But I told them I'd think about it and wait until I got home to England.

There was a rumour at the time that Will told me that if I didn't move to Quins, I'd never play international rugby again. Like most of the rumours about him, it wasn't true. He told me he'd love me to go to Quins, as did some of the other players, but I was never threatened and Will never suggested that I would or wouldn't play for England based on which club I played for. The talks I had with the players in Argentina were interesting, but I still wasn't sure as I headed back to England to think through my options and to start pre-season training with Sarries.

CHAPTER FOUR

Moving West and Meeting Best

Argentina 1990 was a disappointment. The England team did not play well and many people believed that the tour should not have gone ahead in the first place. The guys had gone to Argentina off the back of a packed season, and there was the World Cup the following year. There was a feeling that the players would have been better off staying at home and getting some much needed rest instead of getting beaten up in South America! But for me, it was a personal triumph. The papers had been complimentary about me, I'd got on well with the other internationals, earning their respect, and I had an offer to join one of the country's biggest clubs – not bad for a few weeks' work.

When I got back to England, I had everyone ringing me up to find out how I was, how I'd enjoyed myself and what I thought of the other England players. All the Barking lads tried to get me out for a few beers and I have to confess I took them up on a few offers, but I knew that I had some important decisions to make – so I couldn't go out partying and reliving the tour every night.

The most pressing decision concerned the Harlequins offer. The chance to join the club was very exciting, but I was determined not to get caught up in the flattery of the offer, and to make exactly the right choice for my rugby career. It wasn't as easy a decision to make as it might appear for I felt great loyalty to Saracens and was safe and comfortable there – why change and cause myself more aggro?

I felt I needed to spend time thinking about what to do, but I knew I couldn't hang around for too long because the Harlequins offer wouldn't last forever – someone else would be brought in to the front row if I didn't grab the chance. They needed a prop, and they would get someone else if I wasn't interested. I sat down and thought about the pros and cons.

The pros were: it made perfect sense to leave Saracens and join the West London club because there were so many experienced players based there. I only had two caps, but I was already the most-capped forward at Saracens at the time and I knew that it would be harder to learn and progress if I wasn't surrounded by players who were at the top of the game. If I went there, I would be playing at loose head, Brian Moore would be my hooker, Andy Mullins my tight head; Paul Ackford would be the second row behind me and Troy Coker the other side of the second row. Then there was Mick Skinner at blind side, Winterbottom on the open side and Chris Butcher at No.8. Where on earth would you find a better line-up than that? The choice between Saracens and Harlequins came down to the choice between playing for a pack where I was a big fish in a small pond, or a pack in which I was a small fish in a big pond.

But there were downsides to leaving – there was the fact that I really liked it at Sarries and after just a couple of seasons, I thought of myself as a Sarries boy at heart. I wasn't sure how I'd get on playing for a different club on the other side of London – I didn't know if Harlequins was really 'me.' It was still an amateur game, so it was important to take into account the way you felt about your club, as well as what it might doing for your career. The other negative factor in joining Quins was all the travelling. I had been used to going to Saracens which was just down the road in Enfield. I could jump in the car from Barking and make it in around 30 minutes but it would take three times as long to get to Quins, and that was after a day's hard graft lugging tools around and doing manual work. Then I'd have to be on the train back again and I'd get home at around midnight with a full day's work to look forward to the next day. They were difficult times. I know many people look back on amateurism through rose-tinted spectacles and talk about how glorious it was. Well, not for the players it wasn't. We all had to combine training, playing and working, and sometimes it was extremely difficult.

The other thing I had to consider was an offer that Saracens had made me when I returned from Argentina. They were aware that I was being 'courted' by other teams, and the Harlequins offer was well known, so the club officials had to think of something to do, to try and keep me. In the amateur days, it was difficult for a club like Saracens to keep a player from a major side because they couldn't just make a counter-offer to a player and give him more money to stay – none of us were being paid in the first place. In the amateur days, clubs had to think of other ways to entice and keep players. Saracens' way of keeping me was to offer me the vice-captaincy of the club. It was a flattering offer, but it simply wasn't what I wanted to do. I was 20 years old and just wanted to be the best rugby player I could. What was the point of diverting my attentions and efforts to captaincy at that stage? The issue of captaincy has never bothered me in the slightest, anyway. I'm a player through and through. When, later in my career, I ended up being linked with the England captaincy, I found that other people became far more excited about the whole thing than I ever was. I know it's an honour to be captain of a side, but for me, it's a greater honour to be the best player in that side. Having said that, I was flattered by Saracens' offer, and the fact that they thought so highly of me was an enticement to stay at Bramley Road.

I was in this frame of mind – totally confused about what to do – when I went to Saracens for the first training session of the season, the first since I had returned form the tour.

In the end it was the events that occurred at that session which forced a decision out of me. I went along knowing that I'd be the fittest there by a long way because I'd just come back from a hard tour of Argentina. Most of the others hadn't played since the previous rugby season so they'd be winding themselves back up, whereas I had spent the last few months being wound up to the maximum. The session was odd from the start, mainly because none of the Saracens first team coaching staff were at it – they had gone on holiday. All the players turned up at Bramley Road, where Saracens were playing at the time, and prepared for the session.

Saracens was a lovely little club back then – very friendly and full of familiar faces. But Bramley Road, the ground, was not so lovely. Whenever it had been raining, the pitch would be three feet of mud with loads of dog shit from the local dogs all over it. We would often find other little gifts on the ground from the neighbours too (most of whom hated the players because they said we made too much noise at nights and at the weekends). There were things like broken glass, nails and ring pulls. It meant that when you went down on a loose ball in training, you could come back up with a cut on your leg, arm, face or whatever part of your anatomy touched the ground. There were people at Saracens whose limbs went septic overnight after playing on the pitch and they had to be rushed to hospital to be pumped full of antibiotics.

Then, when there hadn't been much rain, the pitches would have the opposite problem and they would be rock hard. It was like training on concrete, and if you went down on a loose ball you'd worry about breaking your shoulder.

It was the hard pitch scenario for the first session of the season and our coach for the evening was a guy called Ivor Jones who, as far as I knew, had never coached anything higher than Hertfordshire first division. He had certainly never coached a national standard first team before, and it seemed to me that he had something of a chip on his shoulder about the standard of players he was working with. Being an old-style prop, he obviously felt most at home when talking about set-piece play, so he decided that we were going out to practise scrummaging.

I said that I thought this was a bad idea because of the state of the pitch, which was like concrete, and the guys would be better off doing some fitness work and ball handling on the hard grounds. It was the first session of the season – we really didn't need to practise our scrums with any urgency, especially since there was no way we could even get a stud into the ground, it was so hard.

'Look, we can't scrummage on this pitch, mate. We can't get our studs in,' I explained, carefully and politely.

'That's OK. Wear trainers,' he barked back. I was feeling slightly less polite by this stage.

'What? How can we get any purchase on the ground in trainers?'

Ivor didn't answer. He just led the way to where he wanted us to work and we followed him in our trainers, muttering about how ridiculous it all was.

The results were painfully predictable – every scrum hit the ground, every time. We just couldn't get any grip on the turf at all. Bang – both packs hit the deck, face down in the dirt. Up we got and bang – back on our faces again. I can remember my nose smacking against the hard ground and wondering whether I'd break it by the end of the session. We were also putting real strain on our unprotected ankles and knees. It was all crazy.

In the end I said, 'I've had enough of this. You're a fucking idiot. We can't scrummage like this'.

'No, no. It's because you're not doing it properly, that's why it's not working,' he insisted.

'Not doing what properly?' I asked.

So he then started to go through my technique and tried to tell me exactly where I was going wrong. He said that, for starters, I was binding wrongly. I didn't say anything, but I was thinking to myself, 'Well, no one in the England team seems to think my binding is wrong.' I just gave him a look which implied that I didn't agree with him and for the next four or five minutes it was like something out of the old Harry Enfield sketch with the old git in the father-in-law sketch: 'You don't want to do it like that, you want to do it like this. Not like that, like this.'

In the end, I just looked at him and said, 'You are so fuckin' wrong.'

'Don't talk to me like that. I know what I'm doing – I'm the coach. Listen to me,' he replied. As if the fact that he was calling himself 'coach' automatically meant he deserved respect. By then, I'd had enough. 'I've just spent the summer with the best hooker and tight head in the world and that's how they like me to fucking scrummage. If it's good enough for them, then it's fucking good enough for you.' I flounced off the training pitch like a prima donna – it was all high drama stuff! As I left, I could hear him asking, 'Who the fuck's that?'

When he realized who I was, I think he must have been mortified, but it had taught me a lesson – I needed better than this. I wanted to be somewhere where quality training was taken for granted. It might sound a bit over the top to say it, but the training session at Saracens was the straw that broke the camel's back. I could suddenly see, with crystal clarity, that I wanted to be with the best players and the best coaches in the country. The barrel-shaped boy from Barking was going to sign for the poshest club in the world.

My first move was to ring Will and Pete to check they were still interested. They were. 'Any chance of coming round, just to see what the club's like? Can I come to a training session or something?' I asked. They said that wouldn't be a problem, so along I went. Dick Best was the coach at the time – one of the best coaches in the world, and several notches up from what I'd experienced in my last session at Saracens. I enjoyed every second of it and from that point I knew that I would leave Saracens and join Quins.

So I had to go back and explain to the guys at Saracens that, despite their offer of the vice-captaincy, I was going to join Harlequins. They were so disappointed because they had hoped that the lure of captaincy would keep me at the club. At one point I had most of the Saracens hierarchy in my flat, desperately trying to convince me to stay. They had all returned from holiday by this stage and couldn't believe that I was off. I had everyone including the club president in my flat, trying to persuade me to stay. I can still picture them all piled into my tiny front room in their Saracens blazers, urging me to stay. But I had made up my mind by then. I knew what I wanted to do. By this stage, what had happened in the training session was behind me. The officials had heard about the pre-season training and they kept assuring me that nothing like that would happen again, but it wasn't about the session – it was the fact that I had enjoyed watching Dick Best training the boys at Quins and felt confident that I could build a better future for myself there. Slowly, I got the Saracens guys to realize that this was the right move for me – it wasn't an impetuous decision based on one dodgy training session, but a considered approach to my future. I ran through the players at Harlequins, and – to their credit – they all accepted that it was a good move for me and wished me luck. Saracens still retain a special place in my heart to this day. They are good people and no one was more pleased than I when Nigel Wray stepped in and sorted out all their finances for them.

The only problem I encountered after leaving the club was with a committee man who was particularly upset that I was leaving – I think he saw it as a personal betrayal. It practically broke his heart. He used to drive round to my flat and sit outside in his car, trying to get me to change my mind.

Eventually he realized that nothing was going to change and his car disappeared.

It was time to move on. I have to admit that I was worried about joining Harlequins. Despite the reassurances of the players on the England tour, I knew it had a reputation of being run by gin-swilling former public schoolboys and I had heard all the rumours about players being paid to play and being given good jobs in the City. I didn't really know what to expect.

Rugby was going through a difficult time back then. The sport was in a period of vast change. Many called it shama-teurism because the steadfast ways of the amateur players were being eroded. We were allowed to capitalize on our rugby skills a little by being paid to give talks or attend evenings, but we couldn't be paid specifically for playing on the pitch or for anything to do with the playing side of the game. This led us into all sorts of awkward corners because none of us was sure where playing started and stopped. We were only famous because we were players, so our fame was playing-related. If we capitalized on fame, were we capitaliz-ing on rugby? At one stage, the RFU responded by saying that it meant we could not appear in any promotional litera-ture in our England rugby kits but, for example, it would be OK to appear in England football kits. That's how ludicrous and unsophisticated the distinction had become. Even lawyers, like Brian Moore, had no idea what the compli-cated and fast-changing rules of amateurism meant any more. What chance did I have?

When I first walked into the Twickenham clubhouse, I was pleasantly surprised. It was nowhere near as stuffy as I thought it would be. Of course, there were a smattering of regimental types and most people associated with the club had been educated in all the 'right' places, but there was a warmth and a community spirit at Harlequins that, I admit, I had not expected. I felt welcome immediately, and all my fears about how I would cope drifted away.

I never felt out of place at Quins – not at any stage. Obviously I came from a more working-class background than the traditional Harlequin, but there were many other players like me. I was aware that, under normal circumstances, I'd never have come across some of the city slickers, but I thought it was good that rugby was bridging the gap and expanding both my, and their, world.

I remember when I first got there, some old guy shook my hand with great gusto and asked, 'What school did you go to?'

I told him and he looked at me blankly as he repeated, 'Warren School, Chadwell Heath, huh. Where's that, then?'

'It's in Chadwell Heath,' I replied, adding, 'It's a comprehensive.'

'Oh really,' he said.

That more or less killed the conversation, one that I must have had around a hundred times in my first few weeks. The people at Quins were accustomed to being able to converse with one another by exchanging school information. The question was asked of newcomers to the club as soon as they'd exchanged weather details. But after a few weeks, they realized that it wasn't a conversation that got us very far and so they stopped asking.

I'm reluctant to be very critical of those amateur officials that ran the sport back then, though. Although they could be frustrating at times, and many of them had a narrow outlook on life, they meant well, and they effectively ran the club. I had no problem with them.

Indeed, the only difficulty I had in those early days was the awful travelling – from one side of London to the other, three times a week. My work was still in east London, so I had to be over there during the day – I didn't want to move or sacrifice any part of my working life because I had no idea how long I would end up staying at Harlequins. I was worried that one injury or a drop in my standard and I'd be back at Barking. If I'd started working in Twickenham, I'd be in a mess. I was also enjoying working with Dad, and the bunch of lads that I'd got to know. So I made the long journey across London every Monday and Thursday for training, and on Saturdays to play. Even if we were playing away, the bus still went from Harlequins, so I still had to get over to the other side of London.

I did eventually move a little bit closer – not all the way because I was still concerned about my future with the club – as far as Battersea. This made life easier on several counts, mainly because Paul Ackford used to drop me off at home as he went past my place in Battersea on his way back to Clapham. After a few weeks, it became a ritual. I'd jump in the car with Ackers and he'd tell me some tales about life in the police. He was a police superintendent in those days and I remember him telling stories about disarming bank-robbers – they were all colourful stories and I often wondered whether he made some of them up. If he did, it was good practice – he's a leading journalist now.

As I mentioned earlier, I had been interested to see how 'amateurism' was interpreted at Harlequins, and many of my rugby mates at Sarries and Barking kept asking whether I used to come back into the changing room to find my boots stuffed full of money. There were so many rumours about Harlequins flouting the amateur regulations – but the answer was 'no.' Despite Quins' reputation for throwing money at players, they didn't break the rules of amateurism – the only thing they did was to offer big City jobs to players. These jobs allowed players the flexibility to get to training sessions but they always had to succeed on their own merits. They weren't handed a job on a plate – they had to be good enough to achieve the standards required. I appreciate that giving out jobs was not in the strict spirit of amateurism, but it was not contrary to the laws either.

The idea of a big City job never appealed to me – I'm not a desk job sort of guy. Besides, some of those guys used to work very hard, putting in 7 a.m. to 6 p.m. days, then rushing back down to The Stoop to train in the evening. I never felt it was the best preparation for the game – how can you ask your players to put in a good training session when they're working such long hours? I'm sure that there were lots of financial perks if you were involved with a big City job, but it never interested me in the slightest.

Instead, the club tried to help me by getting me work near the ground and through the membership. There was a note put up in the club, and handed out to some of the members, saying that if they wanted any building work done, they should contact me. I got one old woman who was a Harlequins member who wanted me to fix her gate. That was it. It makes me laugh now when people talk about the old shamateur days and how we were all raking in the money. My only experience of shamateur sport was fixing some old dear's gate, and I was too embarrassed to charge her!

Colin Herridge, a great friend of mine, was the secretary of Harlequins at the time, and he would try to find me jobs in the Twickenham area on Mondays and Thursdays, so that I wouldn't have to leave work ridiculously early to get to the club. Colin hated to see me running in to training, already late, and having come from a tough day's work on site followed by a trek across London. But he appreciated that I couldn't leave my job early because I was paid by the hour, so if I left early, I got paid less.

As I became better known as a player, Colin would get me to do personal appearances in local pubs and clubs to help earn me some money so I had enough petrol for the car to get around town. It was an odd time when I first began at Quins in 1990/91. I was just starting to make it in international rugby and my face was in the papers, people were beginning to recognize me and I was being asked to go on television shows – it must have looked as if I was earning a fortune when in fact I was just trying to make ends meet.

Luckily money and material possessions have never mattered much to me and they didn't matter at all in the early days when I was young and loving the way my rugby career was going. All I wanted to do was improve on the field and at Harlequins I was in exactly the right place to do that. The guys really looked after me in that first season and they all took a hand in improving my technique immeasurably. I developed more in the first season at Quins than I had at any other time in my career. It was great.

There would be Brian Moore on one side, advising me on my binding, Paul Ackford working with me on my technique in the line-out and Winterbottom talking to me about my movement around the park. And, above all that, there was Dick Best.

Best has become a bit of an enigma – there are a million and one stories about him and how hard he is on players, but no one really knows him very well. I feel I got to know him through my time at Quins, and my time with London

Division, and he is the most astute, forward-thinking coach around. Having said that, he has a temper that you wouldn't believe – he didn't get the nicknames Sulphuric and Beast for nothing. Having said that, I never got one of the tongue-lashings for which he was famous. I just got cold stares and sarcasm when I upset him – I'm not sure whether that's worse!

I first met Dick when I turned up to a London Division U21 training session. I was still at Saracens at the time and arrived with a few of the boys who'd been drinking with me till the early hours of the morning. I was in a terrible state and had slept all the way to the session, which meant that the guy who'd been driving us had got lost and delayed us even further – not exactly what you want to do when trying to impress a new, well-respected coach.

When we walked in the changing room, Paddy Dunston, one of the guys I was with, went straight up to Dick Best and apologized, whereas I went to get changed. It wasn't because I was being rude but I just wanted to get ready and get out on the park. Also, there were several guys who I hadn't seen for ages, so I wanted to catch up with them. By the time I got out onto the pitch, most of the players had had their meeting, warmed up and were about to start training – I was a good hour late. I walked past the training pitch, past Dick, and towards where the players were gathered.

'Last time I saw you, you were pissed in Newcastle,' I said to one guy, patting him on the back. 'Ah, and how are you? I hear you're not with the missus any more. Sorry about that,' I said to another. It was all just light banter. But the players I was talking to were looking nervously over my shoulder. I couldn't work out what was wrong. Then I turned round to see a face like thunder.

'Hello, I'm Dick Best,' said the guy.

'I'm Jason Leonard, nice to meet you, mate,' I replied and shook his hand, smiling, politely.

'Get one thing fucking straight – I ain't your fucking mate,' he said. 'Now go and train.'

Dick was a tough coach, and he made my life hard that day – but he was fair. I was late and stinking of booze, so what was he supposed to do – congratulate me?

But by the next year, when I broke into divisionals, he'd become more vicious. I remember turning up late to one of his training sessions then, with Jeff Probyn. We got changed at record speed and ran out onto the pitch.

'Hello, Dick. We're here,' I said.

'No good to me. Just run round the pitch till I call for you,' he replied, without even looking round.

'Which way do you want us to run?' I asked, determined to be as awkward as possible.

'I don't fucking care which way you run. Just run.'

We ran around that bloody pitch all evening. All evening. We were talking most of the time as we went round – telling bad jokes and gossiping about everyone. Then, at the very end of training, Bestie called us over to do this thing called the Tunnel Of Love that he does at the end of every session.

First, he put us into two lines, with each of us holding tackle bags. The remaining players had to run down the tunnel of bags to the other end. You had to try and do it without either being knocked down through the tunnel or knocked off your feet. There are around 15 bags each side in the tunnel, so it's a chance for everyone to knock seven bells out of everyone else. Guess who went through the tunnel first? Yep, me and Jeff, after we'd been running non-stop for about two hours.

I think Dick was quite miffed that we both managed to get through without being dumped, because he'd specifically instructed the boys to knock us over. But we made it through.

Dick has his moments and he can flare up, but it's usually when he feels his authority is being undermined in some way. As a coach, he is absolutely superb and his coaching skills have played an enormous part in my growth and development as a player.

He is extraordinary at retaining information about players. He once did a team talk, before one of our games at Northampton. I said to him, 'Do you want to say a couple of words?' and he said, 'No, not really.'

I managed to persuade him just to say a few words about the opposition and what we would be in for that afternoon until eventually he agreed, whereupon he gave a short talk which was the most incisive piece of analytical summary of the opposition I've ever sat in on. I think he realized that a lot of the boys were tense that day, so he put us at our ease. First he went through Northampton's star players, telling us where they were going wrong. He started with Ian Hunter and said, 'Great player, great runner, great defender, one of the original big English backs, apart from injury he would have had a lot more caps. He plays on the wing and full back, sixteen stone and fit as you like, a superb athlete. If you run at him, he'll cut you in half and knock you over, but he has his weaknesses – for example, he's weak going into the corners. If you kick the ball into the corner, away from him, because of his height, he finds it quite difficult to bend down and pick it up.

'That's when you've got to strike him. You can't wait for him to have picked the ball up because he's a very precise kicker. You have a very good chance of charging him down if you go for his feet while he's about to kick to touch, because he takes so long.

'Also – just a quick warning for you – if you see him tuck the ball under one arm, he's going to run. He's not going to pass, he's going to run.'

Despite playing in the England team with Ian Hunter and playing against him for Quins, it wasn't until Dick actually said all that that I realized how he played. When Dick had said it all, I realized how astute he was. I thought, 'Jesus, I play with this bloke all the time and I've never noticed before what he does.'

He added lots of comments about other players as well, some insights into the way they played and some funny stories about players to lighten the mood – most of them rude. We ended up going out and beating Northampton at Franklins Gardens. It was great.

But while Dick had a real talent for understanding rugby and remembering exactly what he'd seen in a game, his man management was never very good. He is an emotional sort of bloke, which he admits himself, and does tend to wear his heart on his sleeve. If he believes something's right, he will say it there and then rather than wait for a quiet moment. If he doesn't agree with something, he stands up and says he doesn't agree straight away, sometimes without thinking things through properly.

Sometimes he'd start having a real go at players – I'd urge him to calm down and not fly off the handle, but his response was always the same: 'Why should I?' Some players had a very difficult time with him and, ultimately, that is why in my view he left Harlequins. I'm sure he partly blames me for what happened, because I was a senior player, but there was nothing I could do to save him at that stage – the rest of the club had decided they couldn't work with him, and that was the end of it. I respected him enormously and know I'm a far better player for having worked with him. He'd give me new ways that I could train and play and he was always right. He made life easier and never wanted thanking or pats on the back – he just wanted to get on and do his job. Sometimes I'd go up to him after training and say, 'Cheers, Bestie. That worked really well.'

He'd just be standing there, taking a drag of his fag, nodding his head and rolling his eyes. I really enjoyed my time with Dick for Quins, England and the Lions. One thing was for sure – there was never a dull moment.

CHAPTER FIVE

All Aboard the Fun Bus

Nicknames are such an important part of rugby that it was only a matter of time before I got one. Mine was Fun Bus. Unsurprisingly, it came from Martin Bayfield – the team joker. It was back in the days when we were given three training shirts before every England match – one white, one blue and one red. I was proudly sporting the red shirt when Bayf stopped in his tracks, spun round and said, 'Look – it's a red London bus.' You have to remember that these were the amateur days, when we all liked a pint or 20 (me more than most). I didn't have the most slender of figures and the players loved to take the mickey out of my size.

Looking back, I suppose Fun Bus is an appropriate enough name for someone who's big and likes to party. If there's any more offensive meaning to it than that, then I'm afraid it's lost on me!

When I first started in the England squad, I was intrigued

by all the names that everyone had been given. Rob Andrew was Squeaky because of his squeaky clean image and because every woman wanted to mother him. Will Carling was Bum Chin for obvious reasons, Brian Moore was Pit Bull – again for obvious reasons. There was Peter Winterbottom, the Straw Man, while Jerry Guscott had two names – Jack because he would always look after himself (as in 'I'm all right Jack'), and Joan Armatrading after her song 'Me, myself, I'. Then there was Phil de Glanville, who was called Hollywood because of his film-star looks.

On one memorable occasion which no other player seems to be able to forget, I turned to Paul Rendall, who as explained earlier was known as Judge, and said, 'Judge, why don't you have a nickname?'

I don't know what possessed me to say it. I'd just got so used to calling him Judge that I never considered it a nickname. But the abuse that I got for the question was unbelievable. First, there was the silence – they all stopped, stared at me and looked from one to the other – then there was the hysterical laughter, pointing, nudging and general humiliation. Finally, the more serious issues. Judge took me to one side and said, 'Look, no one minds you making a complete prick of yourself every now and again, but for God's sake don't let the backs hear you say things like that. You're lucky on this occasion – they didn't hear, but you must be more careful. You're a forward and have a reputation to uphold. Stupid comments are for backs only.'

There was a light-hearted but fairly long-running rivalry between the backs and the forwards at the time and if the backs had heard a forward saying anything quite so stupid, they'd have had a lot of ammunition to fire at us.

I must admit, I gave them quite a few bullets in those early days, and I'll probably be best remembered for my famous washing machine story, which happened just before I played my first home game for England. A journalist came to interview me a few days before and said, 'You must be so proud to play for England, to be running out at Twickenham.'

'Yes,' I said. 'I am proud.'

'How proud?' he asked.

'Oh, well – really proud, you know. Really proud.'

The journalist was determined to get a nice colourful quote from me about just how much playing for England meant to me, but I had no idea how to explain to him in words that he could print, just what it meant. How can you describe something like pride? All you can do is compare it to proud moments that have gone before, and I was certainly prouder when I heard I'd be playing for England at Twickenham than I had ever been before. How do you put it into words? I had no idea, but this reporter just kept on asking and asking me and I just kept saying, ' Look, I was very proud. Very proud. That's all – just very proud.'

So the reporter changed his approach a little and started asking more specific questions.

'What's it like running out at Twickenham in front of an international crowd wearing a shirt bearing the England red rose?' he asked.

'It's great,' I replied again. I was starting to feel a bit guilty at not being much help, but I didn't know what to say. Eventually, I added, 'When you run out there, you feel pumped up, you feel ten foot tall, you're running on air.'

'Great,' said the reporter. 'Now, tell me more about that shirt and what it means to you.'

'Oh God, I don't know. It just makes me proud.'

'How proud?'

'Really proud.'

'Yeah, but how proud are you?'

'As proud as you can be.'

'How proud is that? Tell me again how proud you are of the shirt.'

By this stage I'd had enough and I just gave a flippant answer to shut him up, so he'd stop asking a question that is nigh on impossible to answer.

'I'm so proud that when I put my England kit in the washing machine, I watch it going round and round because I'm that proud of it.'

I said it in such a silly, sarcastic voice that the reporter knew that I was taking the piss, and actually laughed at it as he said 'OK', and moved on to talk about something else. But when the article came out the next day, he had included my comment and treated it as if I had been serious. It had this huge headline on it which said I was so proud that I watched my shirts go round and round. Because the England team were all in camp at the Petersham Hotel at the time, I knew that I would be in for some big stick from the boys. And I was!

When I walked into the breakfast room on the morning that the article appeared, they all just looked at me, moving their heads round and round as if they were watching a shirt in a washing machine. They wouldn't speak, they just kept moving their heads round and round. 'I was being sarcastic,' I said. 'I was just joking. The reporter knew that I was just joking. I——' but it was no good. They just stared at me without commenting, their heads rolling round and round as they did so.

As the years have gone by, so this little story has gone into folklore, and people tend to quote it as proof of my devotion to the England cause. I'm as dedicated as the next bloke, but I'm not stark, raving nuts, and the truth is that I don't even know how to operate a washing machine!

The one thing that I learned from the whole episode was never, ever to be sarcastic to a journalist because once something appears in print, you're stuck with it for life. The washing machine story has found its way into every national newspaper at one stage or another, it's been repeated in books, on television and by countless individuals. What made the whole thing so much worse was the fact that, at the time, the England team was full of jokers with biting wits, so one false move and you were suddenly the butt of everyone's jokes – as I was.

The banter in the group was so strong at the time that some players would not talk for days at a time for fear of opening their mouths and saying something that the other players might tear apart. I can still remember that awful feeling now. The feeling you'd get when you said something in all innocence and someone in the group would say, 'Hold on a second. What are you talking about?' and you'd know that a barrage of abuse was coming your way.

Obviously, being the new kid on the block, I got slaughtered and ripped to pieces whenever I gave them any opportunity, so I had to be particularly on my guard. It was experiences like that which taught me that I had to be extremely careful about what I said and how I behaved. I learned very quickly that it's not what 99.9 per cent of the population thinks that matters, it's what the guys in the squad overhear or hear about that counts.

I bore this in mind when, just before the 1999 World Cup, I was asked to star in an advertisement for the television programme *Zena – Warrior Princess*. They wanted me to run on dressed as Xena, to promote the new series. When they first approached me with the idea, I immediately turned it down because I just knew how much abuse I'd get. But they raised their offer. I turned it down again, and so the amount of money rose once more. It kept going up and up and up until they were offering me more for five minutes' work than I'd get in three months of rugby, but I knew that I couldn't possibly go near it. Can you imagine the abuse I would have got? I would have been called Xena for the rest of my rugby playing days, for starters! I can live with being called Fun Bus, but not Xena!

The 'grounding' I received at Barking rugby club prepared me pretty well for the hustle and bustle of life off the field as an international rugby player. They used to rib me mercilessly about everything at Barking – particularly my eating, and the fact that I am so accident-prone.

My propensity to get into minor skirmishes with motor vehicles is now legendary. It started when I was just ten years old sitting on the kerb, and I was reversed over by a Transit van from a carpet company. The driver was so sorry and so worried about the injury that he might have caused me that he gave Mum and Dad enough free carpet to cover the entire house.

On that occasion, I'm convinced that it was the driver's fault, so he was right to compensate Mum in that generous fashion. The same cannot be said of the time that I rode my bicycle straight at two nuns, with one friend on the handlebars and another behind me on the saddle. I did shout at the nuns to move, but I think they objected to the colourful language and chose to ignore me completely. When I realized that I was about to hit them, I panicked and promptly rode the bike straight into the road where I was hit by a car.

My love of food is equally legendary and the boys at Barking love telling the story of the time that a group of us went away on holiday to Corfu. When we went to a nightclub one evening my friends noticed that I kept disappearing all the time – I'd go, then 15–20 minutes later, I'd be back. They thought I must be up to no good, the way I kept sneaking off, so they followed me, only to realize that I was going to the chicken vendor just outside the club where I'd tear through a chicken or two, then come back inside the night club and carry on, hoping no one had noticed that I was missing!

My mate Dean Cutting says that he always thought his house was haunted when I was staying over, because at about 4 a.m. every day, he'd hear sounds downstairs. He'd peer round the banisters and see a light on, but be too worried to investigate any further. Then, a few days later, his wife would say to him, 'Where on earth has all the food gone? I bought loads and it's disappeared.' That's when he'd realize that the noises he'd heard were me, eating my way through the contents of his kitchen after a night on the beer. If I'm honest, there are quite a few old Barking mates that I owe a fridge full of food to.

On one memorable occasion, my love of eating and my inability to avoid danger collided (an appropriate verb to use, as you will see!). It happened when we were in a cab going to the local Indian, playing 'last one out the cab pays the fare'. I wanted to be first out of the cab, so I went darting across the road without looking where I was going. My mates were still in the taxi, but I had decided that I could sidestep my way through the traffic and get to the Indian first. I was wrong on the first count and right on the second. I didn't manage to sidestep with anything like the skill I thought I had and a car crashed into me, tossing me up into the air. I rolled around on the road, but quickly jumped up. The lads and the driver caught me to make sure I was OK and became concerned when they saw blood on my trousers. After their persistent nagging, I was encouraged to drop my trousers so they could inspect the wound (I had neglected to tell them that I had cut my hand at work earlier in the day and wiped it on my trousers). So now I was standing in the middle of the road, with my trousers around my ankles, the female driver trying to inspect the damage she had caused.

Once I had convinced all parties that I was OK, they let me pull up my trousers and run off to the Indian. I was happily sitting there, having ordered a beer and already eating poppadoms, when the rest of the boys came in ten minutes later after helping the shaken woman driver on her way.

The best thing about the accidents that I have had is that I never seem to get hurt. I'm always being knocked by cars, falling over things, down things or into things, and emerging completely unscathed at the end of it – although I can't speak for the cars, of course.

My mother's youngest brother, Darren, who's the same age as me, once fell under my influence and managed to get himself into trouble when we were both young. We were going to the shops to get some Bazooka bubble gum, our favourite, and were running down the street when we came across a dog tied up outside one of the shops. It looked at us appealingly and my cousin bent over to stroke it, but as soon as he'd got himself remotely close, the dog turned and bit him ferociously, tearing his face. He turned round and looked at me, with blood running everywhere, hoping to hear words of wisdom and gentle advice. 'Don't worry, you go home and get your face sorted out, and I'll get the bazookas. I won't be long,' I said, before dashing into the shop, leaving him standing alone on the pavement. I'm sure I meant well!

At one stage, after leaving school, but before becoming a professional player, I had a job as a postman. It seemed the perfect job for an aspiring player because work was over by lunchtime, so I had the rest of the day in which to train.

I arrived on my first day, was given my bike and bag of post and set off on the streets of Barking to make my deliveries. I had been going for around 20 minutes or so when I suddenly turned a corner and pulled the handlebars off the bike. I tried to mend the thing but just couldn't get it to fix back together properly, so I had to go through the entire postal round carrying the broken bike and the duff handlebars as well as my bag of post. I was exhausted by the time I got back to the depot, carrying the bike and its parts over my shoulder. The poor guy who fixed the bikes was used to people handing him bikes with punctures or faulty lights, but he looked a bit alarmed when I threw the bike back at him in bits!

The lads at Barking have become quite used to telling these stories about me, and they become more and more embellished over the years, but I can get a little bit of revenge now by relating a tale about my Barking friends. The occasion was my first cap for England – on tour to Argentina in 1990. Gary Usher, one of the boys at Barking, was getting married on the day that I was due to be running out in an England shirt for the first time, so the lads had hatched an elaborate plan to hear the match, which involved altering the time of the service, and driving a car with a loud stereo up to the front of the church hall, where the reception was being held, minutes before kick-off. The guys ran out to the car, just before the match started, and crowded round to hear the commentary. Meanwhile the dance was going on inside and all their partners were getting really fed up as they were hanging around a car stereo instead of being romantic. Then a loud cheer went up. It was unbelievable – Jason Leonard, their old mate from Barking, had scored. They started leaping around and hugging one another. The women came outside and started dancing round the car as well, singing and cheering. In fact, they were making so much noise that they didn't hear the commentator correct himself and admit that he'd made a mistake. It wasn't the guy in the number one shirt who'd dived over the line, but the man wearing No.11, which meant that Chris Oti was the try scorer, and not Jason Leonard. But the boys were so busy celebrating and making so much noise I don't think some of them realized for days that I hadn't scored!

When I'm not with the Barking lads, one of the England players who got me into the biggest trouble was – predictably enough – Mickey Skinner. If there was something mad, bad or dangerous going on, then you knew with all certainty that Skinner would be at the centre of it.

My favourite Skinner story comes from a trip to Australia. Thankfully I wasn't on it, or I'm sure I'd have been caught up in it. Skinner suggested to the lads on tour that it would be a great idea if they all went bungee jumping. So off they trooped – I think there were about eight of them. They headed for the jump site and Skins tucked himself away at the back of the queue.

'Before we go,' said Skins, 'everyone should stick their valuables in here and someone who's not jumping will look after them.'

He handed round a bag and everyone put their wallets, watches and other valuables into it. Skinner said that he would hold it while they all leapt off the cliff on the end of a piece of rope. The last guy jumped before it was time for Skins to get ready. As the guy running the jump turned round, Skins ran for his life. He had no more desire to bungee jump than fly to the moon. Instead, he went out on the razzle with all the money in the valuables bag. The guys at the jump couldn't believe it. They waited at the bottom for ages, expecting him to come leaping over the top, then suddenly realized, one by one, that not only was he not coming down, but that he had departed swiftly with all their valuables. They mounted a fairly feeble attempt to find him, but, given that they had no money and he had a significant head start, he got clean away!

The England management and the Rugby Football Union were far from impressed when they heard what had happened, but I think they were used to Skins messing around by then – just as they were getting used to my antics. They had already had to deal with me totally ripping off their car service – they gave me the number for the RFU taxi account when I injured my neck, but I was told, in no uncertain terms, that I could only use it for rugby business. I was very good about this to start with and made sure that I never abused it for personal use. This lasted about a week, then I was ordering taxis to go everywhere. After a few months, and just before the RFU found out and cancelled my access to the account, I was ringing up and ordering drivers to pick me up in the best cars they had. I'd head down to the pub and have my driver waiting outside.

It's impossible to finish a look at some of the daft stories from my life without taking a quick look at some of the boys with whom I've had the pleasure of playing, drinking and fooling around, and with that aim in mind, I have compiled my all-time drinking and touring XV. These are the players that I would take on tour if we were planning to beat the opposition in the bar. Hopefully, you'll agree that this is a side with World Cup-winning potential!

15. **Gavin Hastings** – a great, great team player and such a good ambassador for the sport. He is one of the lads, knows how to enjoy himself and is a wonderful player. He likes a drink and everyone likes him. A must for my touring team.

14. **Rory Underwood** – a vital inclusion in any drinking XV because Rory doesn't drink, and you need to have someone on tour who can remember where the hotel is and how to get back there. Rory would be able to double up as a bus driver and look after us all – making sure that we get back to our hotel OK and aren't found lying in the gutter the next morning.

13. **Rob Henderson** – is in my team because late nights, alcohol, gambling in casinos and junk food are his favourite pastimes. No early nights with this boy on tour. Needs to be in a room on his own because of his unsociable snoring habits.

12. **Jerry Guscott** – a great friend whether playing for England, the Barbarians or the Lions. He's seen as being a bit stand-offish, but he isn't at all. He's one of the lads – a great player and a good drinker, too, especially now that he has retired. There are no signs that his drinking

capacity will do anything but improve in his retirement years and I, for one, hope that he continues to excel in this area.

11. **Derek Stark** – a must for this trip because he can talk you into any pub, club or casino you wish to get into, especially in Edinburgh where he will walk you past customers who have been queueing for hours to be let in and ensure that all the drinks are on the house.

10. **Jonathan Davies** – the man had everything: step, swerve, pace and vision . . . and that was just in the bar. A natural selection for this team.

9. **Dewi Morris** – the man nicknamed Monkey is known for not being able to take his beer, so he is on the tour as the comedy turn – for us all to laugh at when he gets drunk and turns into a gibbering wreck before our eyes. He's also one of the nicest, most decent men around and a good team player – so he makes it into this special team.

1. **Paul Rendall** – Where on earth do you start? This man has taught me almost everything I know about propping and drinking. I've tried to follow every example he's set but I simply haven't got the stamina. The older he gets, the better he gets. The ultimate tourist.

2. **Keith Wood** – this soft-spoken Irishman, with the appearance of Uncle Fester out of the Addams Family, gets the nod for the hooking berth. Wood is an accomplished model, whose picture has been hung above the

fireplace in homes across the country to scare young children away from the fire.

3. **Jeff Probyn** – he's really not very far behind Judge in the drinking league, so another must-have member for this team. He is affectionately known as Fibbin from the days when a journalist spelt his name Fibbin instead of Probyn, bizarrely enough. Wherever Judge is, Fibbin's not far behind. You just have to be careful never to get into an argument with him, because he's convinced that he's always right. Just remember – if he says black is white, then it bloody well is. OK?

4. **Martin Bayfield** – now one of the most sought-after after-dinner speakers, but he is also an extremely accomplished drinker and comedian. A very funny bloke who's able to make people laugh all the time. He has to come on tour.

5. **Wade Dooley** – this man, quite rightly, has one of the best reputations for drinking. The man is a legend. Known as Boring Bob to all and sundry, he lives up to the name, but – boring or not – he wins his place on this tour through pure, natural drinking talent.

6. **Richard Webster** – rightly wins his spot in this back row after his magnificent performance on the 1993 Lions tour to New Zealand. Enjoyed the local hospitality so much that he finished the tour two stone heavier than when he started. At one point he was so slow we thought he had grown roots.

7. **Peter Winterbottom** – Wints is the quiet man of this select team, but he can more than match the pace set by the rest. His ever-increasing waistline is a constant topic for discussion and looking at it provides considerable amusement.

8. **Dean Richards** – no tour would be complete without Deano and Jerry having a few beers and fags and playing cards until the early hours. Deano might not strike you as the perfect image of the modern player, but the sight of him without his teeth in is what touring's all about. He wins his place on this tour largely because of the exceptional moment when he gave Ross Kemp (Grant Mitchell) a clout, saying 'Take that. Your brother's not with you now.' Ross just looked at him in amazement.

CHAPTER SIX

The Greatest Year

What a time to join the England team. My first full season of international rugby turned out to be the start of one of the most exciting periods in the history of the English game. We were one of the world's top teams and there was a sense of optimism and excitement around us – with the prospect of the World Cup hovering tantalizingly ahead. It was a year in which I would help Harlequins to victory in the Pilkington Cup and the year in which England would, at last, prove they were one of the best teams in the world.

But my first match at Twickenham was to be a different sort of game altogether – against the Barbarians. These matches are supposed to be fun, and are played with the aim of entertaining the crowd rather than an eye on the scoreboard. You're not supposed to take it all too seriously, but the match was very significant for me for several reasons – it gave me my first chance to play at Twickenham, it confirmed me as one of the top two props in the country, alongside Jeff Probyn, and it confirmed that the selectors fancied me as a loose head, which I was delighted about.

I think a lot of people, even those who have played rugby for a long time, are slightly unsure about the differences between loose head and tight head, and they certainly don't understand why we can't play on both sides of the scrum. From my point of view the positions are very different and demand opposite body angles and the use of different muscles.

You also need to change your mindset for the two positions because the job of a loose head is to assist the hooker who is aiming to hook the ball back, by keeping the opposition tight head up so your hooker can see what he's doing. The tight head's role is the opposite – he is trying to keep the loose head down so the hooker can't see the ball (that's why you see the tensions and battles in the scrums – you've got one guy to pull everything down, and another guy trying to keep it all up).

Obviously, the body angle for the loose head is different, as are the pressures on the body. All the tension for a loose head is on the left-hand side of his body because he's got his binding and his hooker on his right, and is using the strength of his left arm to keep the tight head's arm up. The tight head, on the contrary, has all the pressure on his right-hand side because he is trying to drag the loose head's arm in with his right arm to make him as unstable as possible.

All this means that moving between the two positions is very difficult, because you build up strength and skills on one side of your body, making it hard to cope with the pressure on the other side. I have moved between the two during my career and it's been OK, as long as I've played one position for a certain length of time – long enough to get used to it. If you flit between the two, as I have on occasions, then you find it hard when the pressure's on. In a big match, when you're tired, you immediately start reverting back to your favoured position, which means that you have to be aware and alert all the time, and keep telling yourself 'I'm on the other side, I'm on the other side' to stop yourself going into scrums in the loose-head position when you're playing tight.

Luckily, I had no such problems in late 1990 when I ran out as loose head for both the Barbarians match and England v Argentina. The first of these games was significant for good and bad reasons. The bad reason was Richard Loe, the New Zealand prop who had been selected for the Barbarians (though it's hard to think of anyone who incorporated the Barbarian spirit less than he did). My most dramatic meeting with him came when I was on the floor, trying to get up. He stamped down on my head and tore at my left ear. There was blood everywhere and I went off so the England team doctor, Ben Gilfeather, could tape it up. At the end of the game, Ben removed the tape, took one look at the injury and announced that he would have to stitch the back of my ear. It seemed a sad way to end my first Barbarians game and my first match at Twickenham, but I wasn't unduly bothered – at least England won and I had the excitement of my first international post-match function to look forward to.

I had heard much about these and how much the players had grown to resent the way in which they were completely taken over by committee men and blazer-wearing officials from the shires. Luckily, my first dinner wasn't like the post-Five Nations events, so I was broken in gently! It was held at the Petersham instead of the Hilton and there weren't the usual round of long speeches. It was there that Geoff Cooke presented me with my first cap (it wasn't given to me on the tour to Argentina). It was great to receive it but, to be honest, I wasn't sure what on earth to do with it afterwards. The players made me put it on, which was funny to start with, but then I thought 'What now?' The caps are maroon so they're not exactly the easiest items to conceal and they really stand out in the crowd. I ended up tucking it into my pocket.

The second of the pre-Christmas internationals was, suitably enough, against Argentina. We were all quite keen to prove to the Argentina players and fans that the summer tour was a blip and that we were really capable of playing much better. We felt it was important to send out a signal – a year before the World Cup – that we were alive and kicking and ready for action. And I'm pleased to say that we did, beating Argentina 51–0 in the only game that Hugo Porta never scored in. We notched up seven tries – it was amazing. But I think the match will always be remembered for the actions of Federico Mendez, the Argentina prop who was playing in his second Test at the age of just 18. He managed to completely floor Paul Ackford, the 6'6" policeman in our second row. Mendez punched Ackers in the jaw, really swinging at him. Ackers, who is not much of a fighter, didn't see it coming, and when it caught him, he was flat out. He stayed on the floor for several minutes before Ben and Kevin Murphy, the physio, came on and carried him away. When they lifted him to his feet, he was all over the place, staggering around, barely able to focus. The sight of these two little men trying to cart this enormous, punch-drunk guy off the pitch will stay with me forever. He was like a baby giraffe, his long legs giving way every few minutes, so the doctors had to use all their strength to keep him on his feet.

For us, of course, it was an opportunity to have a lot of fun at his expense. We never tired of telling him that he'd been knocked out by a schoolboy. It transpired afterwards that Mendez had lashed out because he was fed up with being pushed around by Jeff Probyn in the scrum. As a way of getting back, he reached up and grabbed Jeff's balls. Jeff was not at all impressed with this, so he lashed out with his boot at Mendez and the Argentinian, in turn, had punched whoever was nearest to him – poor Ackers. At least, that's what we thought straight after the game. A while later, Ackers admitted that he'd been grabbing Mendez's balls which is what started the whole thing off. Whatever actually happened, Ackers came off worse – on the pitch and off it.

The dinner afterwards was in the Rose Room at Twickenham and Ackers was the butt of everyone's jokes. He had to sit there with his great swollen lip while we threw napkins, chanting: 'My boy's had enough. My boy's had enough.' Which was where the nicknames Jelly-Jaw and Bambi On Ice came from.

The incident with Ackers took the shine off what was, otherwise, a great match. Even today, I'd say it was one of the best matches that England has ever played. To hold Argentina back and stop them scoring was great, to stop Hugo Porta scoring in his last match was a bloody miracle, but to have slowly amassed over 50 points while doing it gave us enormous confidence and buoyed up our spirits before the Five Nations. I knew that I was playing well in a good team, but I also knew that Paul Rendall was hovering behind me.

The first game in the 1991 Five Nations Championship was against Wales at Cardiff Arms Park. England hadn't won in Cardiff since 1963 – the year that John F. Kennedy was assassinated. A helpful journalist also told me that 1963 was the year in which Nick Drake-Lee was selected for England – the only prop younger than me ever to have pulled on an England shirt.

Geoff Cooke was worried that Wales would present a tough start to the Five Nations – for psychological reasons as much as anything else. The thought of playing at Cardiff Arms Park never bothered me too much because I'd never been there before, so I didn't feel the same fear about it as those who'd lost there a few times. The whole team was desperate to have a good Five Nations after the disappointment of the 1990 Championship in which we lost the final game against Scotland, thereby handing the Scots the Grand Slam, Triple Crown, Calcutta Cup and championship victory. For many in the squad there was a need to erase the memory of this fast – and victory in 1991 would do that nicely.

I was aware that playing against Wales was going to be difficult because of the unique atmosphere of Cardiff Arms Park. The more experienced guys in the team had told me that playing them always felt like you were playing the whole of Wales – the singing, the reception, the attitude and that national anthem saw to that.

Geoff must have sat down before the match and wondered what we could do to reduce the effects of all this. Most of us wished he hadn't because he came up with this bright plan to subject us to weeks of listening constantly to the Welsh national anthem. I think they call it aversion therapy – if you're subjected to something you dislike for long enough, you'll become immune to the effects of it. They do it with people who don't like spiders and people who are scared of heights – we did it with the national anthem of Wales.

At every single training session it belted out, every team meeting, every time we got on a coach. By the end of the week we were sick to the back teeth of it, shouting 'Get it off' whenever it came on. It was a relief when we got to Cardiff, where Geoff realized that he'd made his point and stopped playing it. The atmosphere in Wales was unbeliev-able – very intense. They knew that this England side was good and they were desperate to hang on to their record of being unbeaten at the Arms Park for 28 years. We went out to look at the pitch a couple of hours before kick-off. When we walked back in, I got a real insight into how much the English were disliked at that time, as every single player in the England team had spit down his back. What on earth did the fans think they were doing? If they thought it was a gesture of support for the Wales team, they were wrong, for it just annoyed us intensely and made us all the more determined to beat them. I have noticed that sort of attitude slip away from the game as it has become more professional and as more players cross over and play for different clubs. I think that is a very good thing. The extreme parochialism has gone as the sport has become more professional, which has helped the game.

By the time the Welsh national anthem struck up in that opening game of the Five Nations, I think most of the England team knew all the words. And as much as we had taken the mickey out of Geoff for playing it constantly, it worked. It was obviously more impressive when thousands of Welsh voices sang it than it had been on a tinny stereo, but the fact that it was so familiar definitely took the edge off it, although I don't think that anything would have put us off that day. We were so determined to win in Cardiff.

One of my opponents in that match was Glyn Llewellyn – the guy I'd played with at Barking. The boys at Barking were very excited about the fact that both of us were being capped on the same day so I mentioned to Bill McLaren, the commentator, in the week before the match, that two former Barking boys would meet on the international pitch for the first time in their debut championship games. Bill said, 'You're the tenth person from Barking to tell me that.'

When I'm on the pitch, I go into my own world and never acknowledge anyone; I just think about the game and how I am going to play. The Llewellyn brothers still moan now about what a miserable old sod I was in that match, because the pair of them were trying to catch my eye but I didn't even bother looking at them. I don't see people and things in the same way when I'm on the pitch – I'm just thinking about the job that needs to be done, and they were wearing a different coloured shirt to me, so all I was thinking was 'Right, I'm going to knock seven bells out of you.'

I wasn't the only one in the team who was focused in that way – everyone had a different way of psyching themselves up and preparing themselves for the match, but there was not one person in that team that day who wasn't fully motivated, fully prepared and desperate to win. The match turned out to be a battle of the kickers – Simon Hodgkinson against Paul Thorburn. Hodgy got his, Thorburn didn't and we walked away with a 25–6 win, with 21 of our points coming from Hodgy's penalties.

After the game, despite all the excitement of winning, the players decided not to talk to the press. This caused uproar, with Dudley Wood, the secretary of the RFU, running around trying to find us, and the journalists fuming because we didn't turn up to talk to them. At one point Dudley

Wood said, 'Right, if they won't talk to the press, get rid of them. We'll get another fifteen players to play instead.'

The reasons for our decision not to co-operate were quite complex – it wasn't that a specific journalist had upset us or that we didn't want to talk to the BBC. It was because we were completely fed up at the way we were being treated, and we knew that the way to get things done was to make a public fuss.

A lot was being asked of the England players at the time, and there was very little support coming back from the RFU. It was one thing to play an amateur sport and not be paid for what you did on the pitch, but quite another to have hours and hours of your time off the pitch spent doing interviews, talking to the press, sponsors and advertisers. This was all so that more and more money could be generated which we would see nothing of. At that time, the England team were professional in every respect except that they weren't being paid. Everyone else in the game was making good money from it, the game was growing and it felt as if lots of people were living off our backs. Resentment had started to creep in and it was showing itself in many ways. The cancellation of the post-match press conference was just one of them.

There was also the fact that the team just wanted to be together and savour the moment. It might sound a bit daft, but the guys had been through a lot together and the loss in Scotland the year before had hit them hard. They'd just broken the Cardiff taboo and rather than talk to the press, who had slaughtered them a year previously, they wanted to have a few beers and enjoy the moment.

To a certain degree, it all back-fired because the press went for us with both barrels, but that didn't matter as much

Here I am aged six months. It was clear early on that I was never going to play in the backs!

Three years old and getting used to life in front of the camera.

Playing rugby at Barking in the Essex U19 Cup final gave me my first taste of victory.

Those were the days! Life before professionalism, on a building site with my work colleagues. There's always time for a cup of tea.

Doting grandparents – my mum Maria and dad Frank with Harry, my son.

Happy families – Sandra, Harry and I spend some time together.

What a handsome trio – me with Mick 'The Munch' Skinner and a tiny fan.

Pit Bull – a rare picture of Brian Moore with his mouth shut!

A Harlequins sandwich – Peter Winterbottom and Chris Sheasby wrap up Jez Harris.

On the way up – a happy bunch of lads as Saracens earn promotion to the first division.

The three wise men –
Jeff Probyn, Brian Moore
and I prepare for battle in
the 1991 World Cup.

An Inspector calls –
Paul Ackford shows the
Italians who's boss in
the 1991 World Cup.

One of England's finest –
Dean Richards in typically
aggressive mood against
the Irish in the Five
Nations 1991.

Grand Slam victory – Brian Moore and Mick Skinner lead the way as
we celebrate beating France in 1991.

'I'll have that!' Wade Dooley leaps for the ball in the line-out,
as he attempts to take on Ireland single-handedly.

The worst moment of my rugby career – Tony Daly touches down to help Australia win the World Cup in 1991.

The Power and the Glory – Wade Dooley scores against Wales at Twickenham in 1992 as England head towards their second Grand Slam in a row.

Practising his old farts –
Will Carling in Sun City
during a break from the
1995 World Cup.

A true rugby great –
Lawrence Dallaglio
is a good player and
a good friend.

A tragic loss – Richard Langhorn,
the Harlequins player who died
unexpectedly during a
routine operation.

Leonard the Lion – working hard in training on the 1993 Lions tour to New Zealand.

86 caps and counting – I lead England out at Twickenham to play Argentina in 2000.

Playing for the 'Sequins' – I get stuck in during a game in 2000.

as the fact that we had all stuck together and worked as a team. There was a great deal of power in the players when they were united – we'd shown that on the pitch and now we'd shown it off the pitch. You could argue that English rugby took its first big step towards professionalism that day because the players showed that they had power, too. They had a voice which was actually quite loud and from that time onwards, the players' views were considered – not much, but it was a start, and the RFU sought to avoid any future episodes like our media boycott.

The relationship between the players and the RFU was always difficult because their role seemed to be to stop us doing anything which might give us any pleasure at all! At the beginning of the 1990s it was a particularly difficult relationship which would get even worse until 1995. We also had a poor relationship with the press, so I suppose our mini-boycott, which upset both press and RFU, was inevitable.

The relationship between journalists and any group of sportsmen is bound to be tricky, but I think it was very hard at the beginning of the 1990s because players and journalists had enjoyed such a good relationship in the past. They would all go on these boozy tours together and no one back home would be any the wiser. But the whole sport was changing. Players like Will Carling had made the whole England squad more high-profile, and the papers wanted to know about our personal lives as well as our rugby skills.

I think what bothered most of the players more than anything was the way in which the papers seemed to be particularly negative towards us all the time; it felt particularly annoying when the guys had just started winning. They lost one match in 1990, but you'd have thought the whole season was an utter disaster from the press coverage they received.

Most players are willing to accept what appears in the paper as long as it bears a resemblance to the truth. If you've played badly, you know you've played badly. If you've played well, you know too. But if you've played well and someone writes in the paper that you had a bad game, it's very annoying. I've been on the end of some daft reporting in my time – when I've wondered whether the person writing the piece was at the same game as me. There is one journalist, who will remain nameless, who became a running joke – even with the rest of the press guys, because he'd fail to turn up at games (and presumably watch them on television).

Our boycott at least alerted the rugby authorities to the fact that we weren't happy with the demands made upon us, and they started to think about employing proper press officers to deal with journalists.

That night, in Cardiff, I was given an insight into how much the Welsh love their rugby and how much they hate to lose! It was astonishing seeing all these people on the streets of Cardiff devastated that their record had finally come to an end; it was the first time I had seen people in tears after a game – there were grown men sitting in the gutter crying, which was a real eye opener. Rugby mattered to me and to the other members of the team, but how many Englishmen would you find in tears in the gutter after a Twickenham defeat? It was just a different level of intensity that was quite incredible to witness.

Once I'd stepped over crying Welshman, it was time to get dressed up in my black tie and enter the secret world of the post-match function. Most players take wives or girlfriends with them on match days, but I was young, free and single when I won my first cap, so I was alone. That evening there were two dinners at two different hotels in Cardiff – one women's dinner and one men's dinner. It meant that we all got into a coach from the hotel we were staying in and travelled to a hotel down the road. The men get out of the coach at their hotel, and the women carried on to their dinner. After the dinner, the women got a coach back to the men's dinner to join them for drinks. Isn't that ludicrous? So old-fashioned.

It has to be said that my memory of that first dinner is a little shaky – something to do with the pressure of competing in Cardiff . . . or perhaps it was the beer! In fact, my only recollection of the meal was Mickey Skinner pushing Kevin Phillips's face in the strawberry gateau while the speeches were going on!

We all used to drink a lot after matches then, the post-match functions being a chance to get hammered with the opposition players and have some fun. Then, we would only have been playing a club game the next Saturday, at the most – now, there's every chance you're straight into training the next day for an important midweek clash. The fact that we are professional also puts pressure on us to behave differently. What we did as amateurs was considered nothing more than high jinks or high spirits; it was considered to be boisterous stuff and quite harmless. As a professional, however, if you're caught behaving anything like that you're termed a drunken lout and thug. We don't completely abstain from alcohol now, but we've certainly completely calmed down.

Back at the end of the 1980s, just before I started playing serious rugby, the England players would happily go out and have 20 pints a night – it was all part of the lifestyle. When they played Ireland they would stay in the same hotel as the

Ireland team and stay up on the Friday night drinking with the players before the game on Saturday. They'd have eight or so pints before playing on Saturday, then another shed-load after the match. That just doesn't happen any more – we'd never be able to cope with the pace of the game today if we went into it in the same state that they used to, whereas it was part and parcel of the game back then.

That particular night in Cardiff, the players were celebrating with unusual vigour because the win was so special after almost 30 years without winning there. It was a great win for me, but for players like Brian Moore, Rob Andrew, Paul Rendall and Wade Dooley it was completely beyond their wildest dreams – they'd lost there before and winning was extremely special. Peter Winterbottom had been involved with England since 1982 and had hated every loss in Cardiff. For him, the victory was particularly sweet.

After our first match victory, match number two gave us the chance for revenge over Scotland. They had already lost their first game of the Five Nations 9–15 to France so we knew they'd be slightly demoralized, and we also had the Twickenham advantage. The team had learnt a lot in the past year and had grown as a team. I think, most importantly, everyone in the side understood what the strengths of the team were, and had stopped trying to play attractive rugby, knuckling down to play a winning style. The guys had gone from being romantics to realists and it worked. We beat Scotland 21–12 – once again most of the points came from Hodgkinson. It might have been boring, but it was effective. We had a great line out that won everything, a powerful scrum and a reliable kicker, we kept the ball in the forwards and kicked everything we got. Two matches played, two matches won. Lovely.

The next stop was Ireland – a long weekend in Dublin, with the Triple Crown ours if we beat them. Everyone loves Dublin – it's a great place to play rugby because of the tremendous atmosphere, the generosity of the fans and the Guinness! But for this Ireland game there was considerable pressure on us to stay as sober as possible, because if we won, we would take home the first Triple Crown for 11 years. The match was our closest. We didn't lead until Rory Underwood scored ten minutes from the end, giving us a 16–7 win, but our celebrations after the match were cut short a little by the news that France had beaten Wales by six tries. The French, it seemed, were on fire. At the press conference after our game, Ciaran Fitzgerald, the Ireland coach, told the journalists in great detail that he thought France were the better side, and that he thought they would beat us when we met in two weeks. For the second year in a row, the final game of the championships would be the grand slam decider.

The final match of the 1991 Five Nations was to be played at Twickenham on 16 March. We planned a match of forward domination and that is exactly what we did. We had huge territorial advantage, dominated the line-outs and charged upfield, throwing the French into complete dis-array. I suppose, looking back, it was a match between the styles of the two countries – French flair against English grit. France tried to play wonderful, flowing rugby and we stopped them – most of the time. They did score a couple of fantastic tries, but it was England who controlled the game from the start, forcing the French to make mistakes and staying strong enough to capitalize on every one.

When the final whistle blew on a 21–19 win it was an ecstatic feeling. It had been such a hard game, but the victory was worth every minute of it. Carling was chair-lifted off the field to collect the trophy and the rest of us trooped off, while hundreds of fans ran onto the pitch, patting our backs and cheering us off.

The level of emotion that the win generated was amazing. I don't think I really understood at the time what they were so incredibly delighted about. We'd won, which was great, but I'd always thought we would. I had never been on a losing side in a Five Nations match and I don't think that you truly appreciate how good victory is until you have. It wasn't until we lost a match in 1993 that I came to fully appreciate how great a grand slam is – to beat all four teams, one after the other, is very hard. To be undefeated – when all you need is a loss of form or some bad refereeing and it can turn a game against you – is difficult. Just the bounce of the ball can ruin a game, so to win against all four countries is a real sporting achievement.

The celebrations after the game went on long into the night. There was the big, formal dinner at the Hilton which is all the more painful when we are playing France because all the speeches have to be translated into English first. I don't think, in all my rugby career, that I ever stayed around for the whole dinner. I always sneaked away once I'd eaten my main meal – I wasn't going to hang around for dessert and the speeches, always preferring to go out and enjoy myself. It got me into trouble a few times. A few years later Will wanted to give out these special silver trophies to com-memorate 50 caps, replicas of an England cap and a great honour to receive one. Unfortunately, when he called me to the front, I was nowhere to be found. I think that was the first time that the RFU realized how many of us used to sneak off because when the spotlight fell on my table, there were only two guys there. Will decided to try and present the trophy on another occasion.

'Is Jason Leonard here this time?' he asked jovially, a few weeks later. I wasn't! Apparently, he tried four times to give me that thing, but eventually had to speak to me and tell me to stay at the dinner because he was fed up carting it round with him wherever he went.

CHAPTER SEVEN

The Immoveable Game Plan

After everything I have experienced in rugby union, losing to Australia in the 1991 World Cup final still haunts me. It certainly ranks as one of the worst moments in my rugby career. We were so close – so very close – to lifting the Webb Ellis trophy in front of a Twickenham crowd. We were so near to being crowned the best side in the world but, in the end, we threw it away. I think everyone who played in that side would agree with me that we let it slip through our fingers.

In telling the story of the 1991 World Cup and why we lost to Australia, it is important that I start right at the beginning, with the tour to Fiji and Australia which preceded it, because it was this tour, and what we learnt about the Australians on it, that went some way to colouring our attitude to the World Cup final and, paradoxically, may explain why we lost it! The tour to Fiji and Australia was seven games long and took place in July 1991. It was a seven-match tour which included two Tests – one in Fiji, in Suva, then a Test against Australia in Sydney, both of which I played in.

We were fairly average against Fiji, not on top form, so that three-quarters of the way through we were stuck at 12–12 and heading for an embarrassing draw. It was a difficult match for England because both Ackers and Dooley were injured – the two guys whom we had come to rely on in the second row. We missed them all over the park, but especially in the line outs and scrums. Eventually, thanks to tries from Rory Underwood and Rob Andrew (his first try for England) and a dropped goal from Rob, we won the game 28–12. Luckily for us, the final scoreline masks how close the game really was.

We went to Australia suitably chastised, realizing that we could not afford to give the Australians an inch or they would do to us what the Fijians had come so close to doing. On the Australian leg of the tour we lost to New South Wales (19–21) and Queensland (14–20) before facing the Test side. It was a stern reminder that while we might be the European champions, we were still a long way off the best in the world. In the end, the Australian first team proved too good for us and they beat us comprehensively, the reason for their victory being the simple fact that they managed to get as much ball in the forwards as us. It might sound arrogant, but we firmly expected our forwards to dominate in every game we played. More significantly still, they used their ball much better than us. Faced with a ball-winning team who could spin the ball through the backs, we came a poor second.

It was, however, a fantastic match (from the spectators' point of view) but frustrating beyond belief for us. As a forward it was a very difficult game to play. I knew that we were providing ball which the backs were just kicking away while the Australians were providing ball that was being used to score. Some of the backs, notably Jerry Guscott, had a good game – but they weren't able to compete with the Australians who racked up the points. Australia were in superb form – inventive, quick and deadly. It became clear that they were the masters of the fast, free-flowing game and that we were playing a game which couldn't compete. The war of attrition that had led us to victory in the Five Nations didn't work against a wide, southern-hemisphere style game. We lost 15–40 and Australia swiftly became favourites to lift the Webb Ellis trophy. We came back to England and started to prepare for the World Cup.

Although we had not done well on the summer tour, Geoff Cooke, the England manager, stayed true to the team that had lost to Australia, and incorporated us into his World Cup squad. He didn't count a bad tour against us like so many managers would. He looked at the bigger picture and realized that we were the best players around. With Geoff, you didn't feel that one bad game ruled you out. It's hard to play any sort of creative rugby when you feel like that. Geoff understood that, and we understood that as long as we built as a team and improved, we weren't going to be kicked out for a bad match.

Before Geoff came into the England set-up, that wasn't the case, and there were lots of tales about players really struggling with the management. There's an old story about a centre who said to a young fly-half, 'Don't give me the ball when you get it, kick it up in the air.'

At the end of the game, the fly-half said, 'Why didn't you want the ball?' The centre replied, 'Well, if you don't give me the ball, I can't drop it. If I don't make a mistake, they've got no reason to drop me.'

That's a bit what it was like in the days before I joined, apparently. Players were so worried about not getting things wrong that they couldn't relax and play properly. Geoff changed all that. From 1988 onwards, there was a stability in the England set up which bred confidence.

In the period immediately prior to the 1991 World Cup, we had warm-up games against Russia, Romania and an Emerging England side. It was not the best preparation you could ask for, but at least we had the chance to play some games before going into camp, at Tilney Hall, for a week before the tournament started. It was good to go into the hotel and meet up with the other players early, and have so much time with the team, but it did get incredibly monotonous towards the end. We stayed in the World Cup all the way through, playing the first game and the last game, so we spent five weeks cooped up in that hotel, staring at the same four walls. I have to admit that a couple of times, some of us sneaked out to have a couple of beers at The Sun in Richmond (my local!). We jumped into a cab and ran into the pub – absolutely parched – had a few bevies, much to the astonishment of the regulars, then hailed a cab back to the hotel. We needed to break the routine of *breakfast, train, lunch, train, meeting, dinner, bed* – the same every day. We needed to relax and have a couple of hours away from the rest of the players.

By the time the tournament started on 3 October 1991, with the match between England and the All Blacks at Twickenham, we were bursting to get out onto the field and to play some rugby. New Zealand were the defending champions, after winning the inaugural tournament in 1987, so we, as the hosts, had the honour of playing them first. What a way to begin the biggest sporting event in Britain for 25 years.

There was enormous pressure on England – the public fondly remembered 1966 and there was a feeling that 1991 might be the year in which a World Cup once again came to England. The newspapers had Will's bum-chin all over the front, back and inside. It was the top sports story on radio and television, and the ramifications of all the matches had been analyzed, discussed and predicted. We'd had to sit back and watch all this unfolding. Now, it was time to play some rugby.

England were in Pool One with New Zealand, Italy and United States. We could confidently predict that we would beat Italy and USA, but beating New Zealand was slightly trickier, although by doing so we would come top of the pool and earn ourselves a big psychological advantage. It also meant avoiding a quarter final clash with France in Paris, something that we were very keen to do.

Games against New Zealand always have quite a theatrical feel to them because of the incredible reputation which precedes the All Blacks and because of the haka. This match was no exception, indeed, there was more drama than usual because the opening ceremony took place before we came out onto the pitch.

Once the match began, our forwards played well and I had a good game, but we simply couldn't match New Zealand's strength. Despite going into the break with a 12–9 advantage, we lost 12–18. After half-time, the All Blacks turned up the power and started varying everything until they had thrown us off course and they could muscle over the only try of the game. The biggest challenge of the match, from my point of view, was keeping Richard Loe under some sort of control. He's a big, big bloke, is a demanding prop and can be trouble if he thinks he has the upper hand for a second. It took all my might to nullify his effect and keep the scrum strong.

It was a disappointing start to the tournament, but we were not entirely deflated afterwards. We were aware that we had made mistakes and we knew that we could correct them before bumping into the All Blacks again. We also knew that if we clashed with New Zealand again, it would be in the World Cup final – by then, we'd be a much improved side.

Following the match there was a big dinner, which was quite tough for us. We'd had such high hopes, that it was hard to celebrate with the All Blacks, but we did – that's what rugby's about. Even in a World Cup, you have to forget the competition when you step off the pitch, and drinking with the team that's just beaten you is an important part of the sport.

Our other two pool games were much easier than our opener. Italy conceded 37 penalties in their match against us, and we won 36–6. They tried everything to win – tackling from off-side positions, killing the ball in the rucks – but they just stacked up the penalties and ruined any chance they might have had. At one point, 60 minutes into the match, Jeff Probyn went off after a bang to the knee and Judge came on in his place. Now Judge and I had always talked about what we would do if we ended up on the field at the same time, because we both prefer playing loose head. We always agreed that we would have a race for the loose-head spot, and the first one there got to play in that position. So when Judge's athletic physique came ambling into view at Twickenham, I quickly ran round to the loose-head side and was in position before he had time to say a word. Judge just walked up to me and said, 'Fuck off. You're at tight head.' That seemed to clear up any misunderstanding and I played tight head for the rest of the match.

The game against USA was less eventful but equally successful. We beat them 37–9 despite not playing very well. Our handling under pressure was disappointing, and players went to ground too easily – but, a victory was a victory. We had come second in our pool and so qualified for a quarter-final match against France in Paris, knowing that to beat the French we had to up the standard and start playing the best rugby we were capable of.

Before the France game, we had a few days' break in Jersey. The guys' wives, families and girlfriends came out, we relaxed and had some fun. We managed to escape from rugby for a while, but the forthcoming game against France was never far from the players' minds.

Playing France in Paris is one of the toughest matches around, but this is balanced by the fact that beating them is one of the most satisfying experiences in rugby. On the occasion of the World Cup quarter-final there was more resting on the result than ever – it was after all the difference between staying in the tournament and going home. We also knew that Serge Blanco, the full back, was planning to retire after the World Cup so if France lost, this would be his last game. We knew that the whole France team would be doing their utmost to ensure that wasn't the case and the whole of France would be cheering them in their efforts.

There was so much resting on the result that the match itself dissolved into a vicious, cynical battle. The scene was set even before we went onto the pitch, when the authorities decided that France and England should run out onto the pitch together. This meant that we stood in the tunnel for an uncomfortable ten minutes or so, sizing up our opposite numbers and creating more tension than I have ever known before. When the match started, this pressure simply intensified. England managed to stay disciplined and although we played hard, we played fair – certainly a lot fairer than the French did! The real low point came when Nigel Heslop was attacked by Serge Blanco and a couple of the other French lads. It was dreadful. Nige was punched clean in the face and went straight to ground – the whole thing made us all the more determined to beat them and take our place in the semi-final. In the end, that's exactly what we did. At one stage in the match, Will Carling dived over to score from a kick, with Mickey Skinner in close attendance. Will leapt up into the air, so did Mickey – desperate to receive the credit for the score. As the two men hugged each other and argued about who had scored it, Brian Moore ran from the try line to the halfway line, sticking two fingers up at the French fans as he went. Mooro was loving every minute of it. We ran up a 19–10 victory in what was a thrilling, if reckless, game, and there was more fun still to come.

Just after the whistle went we trooped off the field, celebrating the win. Wade Dooley came rushing up and said, 'Fuck me. Did you see that?'

I told him I didn't know what he was talking about.

'Daniel Dubroca has just pinned Bishop up against the wall, and called him a cheat.'

We all went running out to have a look but the incident had passed. We learned later that Wade was right. Dubroca, the former France player who had moved on to become coach of the side, had grabbed David Bishop, the referee, and pinned him up against the wall. Through the evening, the story became more and more exaggerated and ranged from Dubroca having to be pulled off Bishop before he hit him, to him spitting in Bishop's face. I don't think anyone but Bishop and Dubroca knew what really happened, but Dubroca had to apologize.

The day after we had beaten France in Paris, we were on a plane bound for Scotland, to take on the auld enemy at Murrayfield. I had never played at the Edinburgh stadium before and the last time the other players had been there was 1990 when the Scots beat them to take all the silverware, so there were lots of memories of that game and lots of talk of revenge. As far as I was concerned, I knew that only Scotland stood between me and a place in the World Cup final – that was motivation enough without the need to talk about revenge.

Our game against Scotland was memorable for one thing – Rob Andrew's beautiful, perfect, lovely drop goal. Never has a simple kick meant so much. Rob struck it sweetly in front of the posts towards the end of the second half to put us into a shaky 9–6 lead. Luckily, we managed to cling on to that lead for the rest of the game. The other significant factor in the game was that Gavin Hastings, that master of kicking, missed a crucial penalty when we were at 6–6. My lasting memory of Gavin's miss was hearing Rory shout, 'Fuck me, he's missed it.' The boys and I were so shocked at the fact that Rory was swearing that we hardly noticed that Gav had missed his kick.

Beating Scotland meant that we went through to the World Cup final on 2 November against the winner of the other semi-final – Australia v New Zealand. Meanwhile Scotland headed to Wales for the third place play-off match against the loser of the southern hemisphere showdown. We watched the match between the two rugby giants after we had beaten Scotland, which Australia won and so would meet us in the final at Twickenham. Everyone was very excited and once we knew it was Australia that we would be playing, Geoff and Will sat down to plan a game strategy to take us to victory. They thought about what had happened that summer when England had been thumped 40–15 in the Test, and it was generally agreed that the difference between us and Australia was what we did with that ball. We won our line outs, they won theirs, we won our scrums, they won theirs, but once they got the ball – they were more effective.

We discussed one particular move involving Tim Horan that was extremely effective and had led to the Australians scoring loads of tries, knowing that we needed some similar moves up our sleeves that would be as effective. We knew we'd win as much ball as them – what we needed now was a plan for how to use it. At the time, planning more extravagant back moves seemed like a sensible option. Our kicking, line-outs and mauling was already good enough – we'd seen that in the summer. We needed the forwards to provide good ball but then we needed to use it, we couldn't play the percentage game against the Australian backs – it just didn't work. There were players like Lynagh and Campo who could out-kick us, so it would be no use just playing with the boot all the time.

Before the match, Geoff and Will got us together and said, 'Look, we're not in a position of being able to do what we normally do against this side because they'll beat us at our own game, and even at our kicking game – they'll kick just as far as us and it'll be a stalemate. We have to move the ball about, and get it out to the wings.' At the time, I remember thinking, I must admit, 'I don't know about this – we've had no practice at it. Is it a good idea?' The backs had never done it and the forwards didn't like being told that Australia could match them up front.

So the forwards went dragging their feet into the game and we began by spinning the ball from everywhere but, although we moved the ball about, we didn't actually go anywhere – it just went sideways. The backs just ran from one side of the pitch to the other. I remember as the game was going on, the forwards were on fire that day, getting more and more line-out balls and winning more and more possession from elsewhere – but we weren't doing anything useful with it. We weren't scoring either, and Australia were.

We should have changed the way we were playing. We should have gone back to what we were best at. Will has come in for a lot of criticism as England captain for not changing the tactics that were failing so spectacularly on that day, but he still believed that England were doing the right thing. He had Peter Winterbottom and Brian Moore saying to him, 'Come on, we're slaughtering them up front, let's go back to our normal game. We're absolutely killing them up front, we're getting the majority of the ball, but the backs are throwing it about and not getting anywhere.' But Rob and Will insisted that we should stick to the game plan, which has since fuelled the debate about whether the England rugby team is capable of changing its tactics on the pitch.

A lot has been said about it since, because it is the only time that you could argue that Will Carling failed on the pitch. From Will's point of view, he was absolutely con-vinced that was the right way to play. He felt justified in that conviction because just a few months previously we'd been beaten 40–15 by playing it our own way, with lots of physical, driving line-outs and driving mauls.

That is probably the most upset that I've ever been after a rugby game – just to know that we had a chance of winning it. Two of the most often used words are 'if only' – if only we'd played this way. I'm a big believer that you make you're own luck – we didn't, the Australians did. They were the team of the tournament and they quite rightly won. I'm just gutted that we didn't play to England's potential. But I learnt a lot by that – I learnt that if you're in a World Cup final, you just play to win whether it's by one point or a hundred. Once you get to a World Cup final you can think 'We've done it, we made it, let's throw the ball about and enjoy ourselves.' But on the other hand, you think 'We've made it to the World Cup final – let's not throw this chance away. Let's not dare lose this – even if it means winning 13–12.'

In later years, no one remembers the team that got beaten. Even if it's a dull game of penalty kicks, it doesn't matter. I agree with the tactics we took in the game, however when we realized our forwards were dominating Australia we should have reverted to type, but it didn't happen and that's why I've not got a winner's medal – only one for coming second.

CHAPTER EIGHT

A Pain in the Neck

The 1992 season was completely overshadowed for me by a neck injury which I feared might end my rugby career. We won the Grand Slam in 1992 for the second year in succession, setting a new championship points record of 118 in the process. But shortly after the popping of the champagne corks, I was being given the bad news that a major operation was the only chance I had of resuming my rugby career.

I had played through the summer of 1990, the whole of 1991 including a summer tour, the World Cup, then straight into the 1992 season without a break – 19 Tests in 19 months – in addition to club games and England friendlies. For an international prop whose day job off the field was a manual one, it was too much and the pressure started to show in my body. I should have stopped playing as soon as I felt the tingles down my arm but of course I left it until I was practically crippled before I did anything at all about it.

I had suffered throughout the 1992 season from pins and needles in my right arm, but it was only a slight problem and because it wasn't affecting my ability to play I didn't take it too seriously. The problem first really surfaced in our easy victory over Scotland. I could feel pain down my right arm and leg throughout the game and had this numbing pins and needles sensation which wouldn't go away, but of course I didn't come off. I stayed on the pitch and continued through the Five Nations, playing against Ireland, where we won convincingly, 38–9, before the usual fight in Paris where we beat France 31–13.

Then it was home to Twickenham to play Wales for all the honours – the grand slam, triple crown and championship title. We won 24–0 and became the first nation to win back-to-back grand slams since 1924.

I battled through the Wales match with pain and numbness in my right arm that was so severe that I could not lift my arm above my waist. Whenever I scrummaged, Jeff Probyn would have to pull my arm around Brian Moore and lock it in because I couldn't hold my arm up myself.

'Bind me in,' I said to Jeff. 'My arm's buggered, I can't hold it up.'

Such was the attitude of the players at the time, that Jeff's reaction was simple and instant. 'No problem, mate,' and he pulled me in with all his might, holding the scrum straight single-handedly.

By the end of the match, as the whistle went and fans flocked onto the pitch to celebrate our second grand slam, I was in pieces. My right arm was in agony and I knew that something was seriously wrong. The pins and needles sensation which always indicates some nerve or spinal damage was still there, but ten times as bad, so I knew I had to get help. As I came off the pitch I went straight into the doctors' room. Ben Gilfeather, the England doctor, was there.

'I don't know what the hell's happened here, but I just can't move my bloody arm,' I said.

'Let's have a look,' said Ben. 'Try and lift it.'

I showed him my pathetic attempt at moving my arm and he saw the pain on my face so made me sit down. He told me that he'd like to see how it progressed overnight because, at that moment, it didn't look too good.

'I think there's some nerve damage,' he said. 'I'll need to check you out in the morning when you've had time to rest it. I suggest you go out tonight and have a few drinks to help you sleep.'

Never one to ignore doctor's orders, I followed it to the letter, and drank myself into oblivion to cope with it. When I woke the next day it still hurt like hell. I didn't know what to do because if I went to see the doctor, I knew I'd end up in hospital and was still clinging to the hope that it would get miraculously better by itself. In the end, I decided to leave it another couple of days, hoping all the time that it would just get better. Of course it didn't. In fact it got worse so I eventually went along to Harley Street to talk to Jonathan Johnson, a highly respected orthopaedic surgeon who would give me a straight answer and do all he could to help me get back to full strength as quickly as possible.

I didn't have a clue what to expect when I walked into Princess Grace Hospital and asked to see him. I thought the hospital would give me a scan and strongly suspected that he would warn me not to play rugby for a month or so, but I wasn't prepared for the revelation that there was serious damage done to my neck. They gave me a scan which showed that a huge disc was pressing down on a nerve, causing weakness and wasting of my arm. Jon Johnson pointed it out on the scan and sat down with me to discuss what we should do.

He was reluctant to operate unless he had to. He said that if he tried to rectify the problem with surgery, it would be a major operation because of the difficult location of the injury, so he recommended that we refrained from surgery to start with and gave the body time to heal itself. This was my kind of medicine! He explained that he didn't want to open me up unless there was nothing else he could do. Because I was young, my body would be its own best healer – I should try and rest it and, given enough time, it might heal itself. Since the international season was over and there was no summer tour, I knew that I could be relied upon to do this, so I left Harley Street still hopeful that my body would heal itself.

I was extremely grateful to Mr Johnson for trying to repair the injury without resorting to surgery straight away, but in this instance it didn't work. I was in terrible pain for two weeks – I couldn't sleep so had to take sleeping pills. There was so much numbness and pins and needles coming down my thumb and forefinger (which I learnt was due to the disc problems in my spinal nerves C5 and C6) that I used to chew my finger and thumb at night and draw blood without feeling any pain. I'd taste blood in my mouth all of a sudden and think, 'Oh God, I've done it again.' There would be blood everywhere yet I couldn't feel a thing in my thumb.

Through all this, I was getting no sleep and was in continuous pain. I'd practically gnawed my fingers off and knew that it wasn't working out too well. So I went back to Jon, as instructed, and the plan was that he would re-scan the neck to see whether there was any improvement.

'I'm sorry to say that there is no improvement,' he told me. 'In fact, the injury is showing signs of deterioration. I'm afraid we'll have to operate.'

I was in so much pain by this stage that I was past caring – he could have said that he needed to cut my arm off and I would have agreed with him if he had promised me that the pain would go away. Then he told me what the operation would involve.

He would have to take out the disc that was causing the trouble and replace it with one fashioned from bone to be taken from my pelvis. This meant two operations – one to get the bone from my pelvis, the other to insert the bone into my neck. Another problem was the size and musculature of my neck. Jon worked out that the best way for him to operate was by going through the front of my neck, either side of the throat and major vessels. I was suddenly faced with an enormously complicated operation.

I remember ringing my mum and dad to tell them. 'It's nothing serious,' I said. 'But it's a bit complicated because of the way in which the surgeon has to operate. I'll be fine, though. Don't worry.' I don't know whether I was trying to convince them or me.

Jon had to warn me that it was a major undertaking and he could in no way guarantee that I would be able to play rugby again afterwards. However he told me that if I did as I was told and took my time over the recovery, allowing it to heal properly, then I would have a very good chance.

So just a few weeks after first noticing the pins and needles in my arm, I was being wheeled into surgery for a major operation that could rob me of my rugby career. I was in such agony by this stage, and trusted Jon Johnson so implicitly, that I just got on with it and did what I was told.

It was my first major operation and I can remember them stabbing and jabbing at my hand with a needle in an effort to insert a drip of some sort. I said, 'You're having a laugh, aren't you?' The nurse replied that she was trying to be gentle, but I had tough skin on my hands and she couldn't get the needle in!

The anaesthetist said that I should try to count to ten – by the time I got there, I'd be asleep. I was convinced that they would have underestimated how much drug it would take to knock me out, so I started out being very cocky, looking the nurse in the eye as I recited, '1, 2, 3, 4, 5, 6, 7, 8, 9, 10. See I'm still awa---' Gone. Flat out.

Given the skills of the surgeon, the operation was, unsurprisingly, a complete success. I can still vividly remember waking up when the operation was done and the first thing I noticed was that the awful pain which had dogged me for weeks had totally gone from my arm. The only discomfort I felt was a desperate thirst. It was evening when I woke, so I buzzed the porter. I told him that I was starving and thirsty, so he went off to get me some water and some buttered toast with the crusts cut off.

After eating, I felt much better, but as the drugs I'd been given started to wear off, I felt the pain in my pelvis where they'd gone in to extract some bone. There was a piece of tube in there to drain any excess blood and I was all wired up to a drip with a brace around my neck to support my injury.

I had to stay like that for a couple of days and – worse still – put up with rugby visitors who just came in to abuse me! David Pears, a teammate from Harlequins who worked in the City, came to pay a visit after work. I think he completely misunderstood the concept of visiting because he

arrived with nothing at all – no grapes, chocolates or anything – and spent the whole time eating everything I had in
my room. Then, when he left, he buzzed for the nurse and
ran out of the door. I had no idea why he had done this until
the nurse came in, smiled and gathered up the pornographic
magazines that he had left all around the room. At the end
of the bed was a particularly fetching centrefold spread of a
woman with her legs wide open to the camera. Luckily the
nurse just laughed about it, while I lay there, bright red.

Slowly, through my time in hospital, I recovered sufficiently to be allowed to go home, but I was warned, most
severely, that if I didn't take it extremely easy and if I so
much as slipped off a kerb, I'd be straight back in. When I
left I went to stay with Colin Herridge, a good friend from
Harlequins, and his family. I spent the time resting, as I'd
been told to, and doing everything I could to precipitate a
speedy recovery.

I was aware, throughout this period of convalescence, that
I had to curb my instincts to get up and get on with life, and
that was the hardest thing of all. I had been reminded that
there was a bit of bone in my neck that was loose and that
jarring my neck would dislodge it easily because it hadn't yet
had time to fuse properly. As such, I had a stiff brace to walk
around in and a soft one to sleep in.

I missed several club games for Harlequins but luckily
there was no tour that year, so I didn't miss any England
games over the end-of-season and summer periods. Harlequins played Bath in the Pilkington Cup final at Twickenham
on the last day that I wore my neck brace – so I threw it
rather dramatically into the crowd.

After that, I had to spend the summer building up the
muscles in my neck along with England physio Don

Gatherer. He made a neck brace for me, off which we hung weights. The weights increased as my strength built up through the summer. I also had to get my cardio-vascular fitness back, so I began by slowly pedalling on a bike and gently swimming, before going out for my first light run. I did a lot of work to try and rebuild myself after surgery, but years later, I would say that as a result of it I am still stronger on my left side than my right.

As the training progressed and I continued to take it slowly, I became more and more determined that I would play again, never really in doubt that my career would resume. After all, Jon Johnson had said, 'If you follow me to the letter, you won't have a problem,' and that is exactly what I did.

When I first started doing weight training to build myself back up, I was pathetic. The girls in the gym were lifting bigger weights than me. I had these tiny little dumb-bells as they were all that I could lift. But I had a strict timetable of what weights I could lift and when. I knew that there was every chance of me not recovering properly if I tried to progress too quickly. When I was cycling on a stationary bike, it was with the resistance on the lowest setting, and I made sure I sat bolt upright so I didn't jar anything or knock anything out of place.

It was because I had such a good surgeon who gave me sound advice which I made myself follow, that I recovered from the operation sufficiently to get back into rugby training. England didn't go on tour in the summer of 1992 so when I got back into action – in time for the game against Canada at Wembley on 17 October 1992 – I hadn't missed an international! Much was made of this in the press, but the truth was that I was lucky to pick the one summer in which

England didn't have a tour of any description. Any other year and I'd definitely have missed out.

Before the international game, I played just two club games for Harlequins – against Bristol and London Scottish. My first game was the most difficult. It was like coming back to rugby from any injury or illness – until the first tackle, the first scrum and the first line out are over, you can't relax and feel as if everything is going to be OK.

It was quite a slog to get all the way back to full fitness, and my life was not made any easier by the fact that I hadn't been able to work for seven months while I'd been injured and in hospital. As I worked as a freelance carpenter, I had no income at all. I also discovered that the RFU had no insurance policy to help me.

Dudley Wood, the secretary of the RFU, told me, 'We used to insure the team against injury but dropped it because the premiums were too expensive.' How astonishing this seems now. The Twickenham stadium was having a multi-million pound overhaul at the time and the new design of the England shirt was expected to net the RFU around £3 million, yet they couldn't spare the money to help a player who had been in all sorts of pain and was in real financial trouble.

If the RFU had abandoned their insurance policy then they should have been accountable for my injury and the costs that the cancellation incurred for me, but they claimed that because it was an amateur sport, they couldn't pay for the time I'd had to take off. This was an extreme attitude. I was one of England's best players, injured in the line of duty and was finding myself out of pocket by about £10k. I was stuck. I couldn't work because I could hardly lift a hammer, let alone hit anything with it, so I desperately needed support but the RFU were more worried about protecting amateurism than protecting one of their players.

My financial situation was compounded by the fact that we had been told that we would net around £5k from the promotional work that we did for the 1991 World Cup but in the end we were given just £1k each. If you consider the amount of time that we all had to take off work to do it, it was less than I would have earned on a building site.

In all my time as an amateur in rugby, I never minded not being paid. I went into the sport knowing it was amateur and I never worried about money, but it was different when I was seriously injured and lying in hospital, knowing that I wouldn't earn anything for most of the year and that no one would compensate or help me. No one deserves to be treated like that – amateur sport or not.

The fact that they refused to compensate me adequately was a real surprise because when I was first injured I was under the impression they would look after me. I remember talking to the RFU about it as gently as possible at the beginning.

'Look, I've got myself right in a hole here,' I said. 'I'm injured from playing for England and I can't work. I've got no money coming in and my mortgage and bills are going out.'

The RFU said, 'Don't worry, we'll look after you,' so I thought I'd be OK.

But when no cheque arrived, with the bills mounting up and the bank manager on the phone, I started chasing the RFU. I was surprised when they then said, 'Oh no, we couldn't possibly do that. We can't give you money to compensate for lack of earnings – it's an amateur sport. If we pay you loss of earnings, that would make you professional and you'll be banned for life.'

'Right,' I said. 'So how do you suggest I pay the bills?'

'Sorry Jason, we can't help,' they said.

Finally, they agreed that I could have a one-off payment which would be pushed through under some sort of injury clause. When the payment came it was a cheque for £800 towards my medical expenses, which it didn't nearly cover. That's all I received. If I hadn't needed the money so much I would have torn it up and thrown it back in their faces.

CHAPTER NINE

The End of a Golden Era

Playing rugby with Will Carling at Harlequins and England gave me quite an insight into the man who would become one of the most talked-about and photographed people in the country. I'm sure the whole world will think of Will in terms of the tabloid headlines he generated and the allegations about his private life, but he also captained England through a very successful period. He would be the first person to say that captaining England at the time was easy because of all the great players in the side but, nevertheless, nothing should be taken away from him as the impressive leader of a hugely successful rugby team, regardless of what the newspapers may have chosen to say about him.

I knew that Will Carling had a friendship with Princess Diana – all the players did. We knew long before the details of it were dragged through the headlines because we, too, had met her and seen her at rugby matches, royal functions that we were invited to and once at an England training session. It didn't seem strange or seedy in the least – to me and the rest of the players, it wasn't a big deal. In fact, I don't think it was a particularly big deal to anyone until the *News of the World* decided to turn it into the story of the year.

I used to see Will in a gym called Bimal most days. He'd be in one corner and I'd be in the other – then Diana would walk in. She seemed very friendly and would always stop and chat. None of us were particularly surprised by the fact that Will and Diana knew each other as they mixed in the same circles and supported the same charities.

Of course, the fact that they were friends amused us in a childish sort of way! After she'd come to the gym, I'd ring up Brian Moore and say, 'Guess who was in the gym again – there's something funny going on there, you know.' It was just a piss-take we'd laugh about, but we never really believed there was anything going on, and I still don't. Will has continued to deny it and that's good enough for me. Even when he was asked about it by the players and had every chance to talk up the relationship, he never did. He always insisted that there was nothing going on and that they were just friends.

I can clearly remember one time when she came to England training with Harry and William. We were at Twickenham, running through some moves before an international, the line-out had been formed and Brian Moore was about to throw the ball in when we all saw her appear. We looked round, totally ignoring Brian who stood there, poised with the ball, trying to attract our attention. He spun round eventually to see what was going on, and realized that the distraction was the appearance of the most famous and one of the most beautiful women in the world. As nice as Brian is, he couldn't really compete!

One of the things that everyone involved in Diana's visit to Twickenham was most pleased about was the fact that the whole thing had gone ahead without any of the committee getting involved, nor any of the press finding out – a double coup! Everyone was well aware that the slightest hint to the press and the visit would have been off.

In the end, of course, it was the *News of the World* running the story in the way that they did which ended Will's friendship with Diana. It was extremely sad and was a very difficult time for Will, but one of the positive things to come out of it was the way in which the fans at Harlequins rallied round and looked after him. I think it was the first time that Will realized he had a lot of people looking out for him and I felt quite proud of the way the Harlequins supporters behaved. The club has a reputation for being quite cold and formal and the players are thought of as being stars who spend no time with the fans. The supporters themselves are thought of as being terribly well-off City types who come down to the Quins because of the kudos it gives them rather than because of any interest in rugby. They are also seen as 'fair-weather supporters' who have no real passion about the club or its players. I understand where this reputation comes from, and maybe a long time ago the club was like that, but it certainly hasn't been in all the time that I have played there. Harlequins supporters are as loyal and committed as any sports fans, and never did they show that more than when Will was being hounded by journalists. A lot of people at Quins helped him out at that time and shielded him from the press. He's never been the most popular player at Quins because he is seen as being more of an England man than a

Harlequin, so he might have expected lots of hand-rubbing and mickey-taking from the guys down there, but there was none of that. People were saying, 'Come down to my place, stay with me for a while' and advising him where he might go to get away from it all.

I remember one occasion when tabloid journalists turned up at Quins hoping to get some juicy tit-bits and gossip about him, and they got nothing. Again, you would have thought that the fans would have told them a few things, but no one would talk to them – they closed ranks and protected him. I think, in many ways, that the whole thing opened Will up a little bit more to the club – he appeared vulnerable and in need of protection, whereas he never had before and had always seemed supremely in control, self-sufficient and independent. He was closer to the club afterwards.

The Will and Diana story was very strange to live through when it happened, but at the same time it was somehow fitting for the era. At the time, Carling was one of the most famous people in the country and just about everyone in the England team would have been recognized on the streets. We had won back-to-back grand slams, reached the World Cup final at Twickenham and, in Will Carling, we had a captain whose face had moved from the back pages to the front pages. It was all supported first by Roger Uttley, then by Dick Best and by Geoff Cooke, a manager who could genuinely bring the best out of us. It was a great time to be involved in English rugby – a time when the sport was booming and England were winning.

But by 1993, the golden era was already beginning to lose its shine. As we went for a hat-trick of grand slams, something never achieved before, we started to lose our vice-like grip on the tournament. It was the year in which I would experience losing in an England shirt for the first time in the championship, then the following year Geoff Cooke would leave the England set-up, breaking up the successful Carling/ Cooke partnership that had been the linchpin of our earlier triumphs. It was never to be quite the same again.

The 1993 Five Nations campaign opened with another victory when we narrowly beat France 16–15 – they didn't stand a chance! Actually, this was not one of England's best performances, particularly in the first half in which we conceded two tries to Philippe Saint-Andre, the France wing, in a quarter of an hour. The game was Martin Johnson's first for England and he made a huge impact, setting himself up as a ready-made replacement for Wade Dooley. We were disappointed to play badly and only just win but from the team's point of view, it was the win that mattered. If you win in Paris, you're happy – no matter how close the game is. What we wanted, more than anything, was a third Grand Slam. If we scraped each victory by a point, that didn't matter. Winning was what counted.

So we travelled to Cardiff for the second match of the 1993 campaign, and my second match at the Arms Park, an outing which was not as successful as the first, as we went down 9–10. It was awful. We played badly and the papers called for players to be axed straight away. The headlines in the papers called Rory Underwood 'Rory Blunderwood', after he let Ieuan Evans in for the try which won the game. Rob Andrew had a bad time and so did Wade Dooley. What slightly annoyed us was the fact that the number of points for a try had increased to five for the first time. If it had stayed at four, we would have drawn the match. The hard thing to accept was not that we had lose by a point, but that the triple Grand Slam had slipped away by just one point. It would be a huge task to ever get to the position of going for a triple grand slam again.

Our next meeting was with Scotland. Stuart Barnes came into the side for Rob Andrew and made a real impact. Rugby opinion was divided at the time into those who favoured the running, handling Stuart Barnes and those who felt that Rob Andrew's kicking was more effective. There were people who felt that Barnes was a genuinely gifted playmaker who would add new dimensions to the England team. Then there were those who felt that England's power was in the forwards and a fly-half like Rob, who enabled the forwards to dominate, was the best fly-half for the team. I think it's hard to compare such different players. Certainly, England were at their most successful with Rob at fly-half – he kept real control over games and allowed us to dominate. We might have won by more points with Barnesy at No.10, but we also may have won less frequently, because he would have been more of a risk, more adventurous.

Against Scotland, Barnesy played like a dream. We scored three sparkling tries to win 26–12 and were in with a chance of winning the championship if we beat Ireland in our final game. France, the other team who could mathematically take the honours, meanwhile played Wales in their final game. We felt that England's chances of beating Ireland were probably greater than France's of beating Wales and the bookies agreed with us, so we were odds-on favourites to take the Five Nations title, if not the grand slam.

In the end, however, it turned out that we and the bookies were wrong as we were comprehensively beaten after getting just one penalty, giving us only three points to Ireland's 17. France became the new Five Nations champions and our short but glorious reign as champions of Europe was over.

At least we could console ourselves that summer with the prospect of a Lions tour.

After the tour, in November 1993, England played New Zealand at Twickenham – the toughest team on earth, the team that seems to beat everyone. They came to Twickenham on a high after ten wins in succession and England had not beaten them for a decade. We wanted so much to make amends for letting the Five Nations slip out of our grasp and we wanted revenge on the All Blacks for beating us in the opening game of the World Cup. And so it was – from start to finish it was our day. The Twickenham crowd was louder, sang more vociferously and seemed to be more animated and alive throughout the match than I've ever heard them before as we beat the mighty All Blacks 15–9 in a great all-round display of rugby. It was a phenomenal performance of rugby which renewed our excitement and got us all ready for the Five Nations in 1994, the year before the World Cup. Having beaten New Zealand, we knew that anything was possible.

The 1994 campaign began at Murrayfield with a one-point victory over Scotland after Jon Callard put over a last-minute penalty with the final kick of the game to give us a 15–14 advantage. It continued to be an extremely close Five Nations that year because our second game of the season was against Ireland who beat us by a point, the final score being 12–13. However we won our final two games, beating France by four points, 18–14, and Wales 15–8 to deny them the Grand Slam. It was the hundredth game between England and Wales and while England won, we didn't win by enough to stop Wales emerging as championship winners and England the also-rans once again.

The season was followed by a tour to South Africa and by

the news that Geoff Cooke was leaving England to concentrate on his full-time job as chief executive of the National Coaching Foundation. Geoff had been a breath of fresh air for English rugby – a man who understood how to organize and motivate people. He would look to the long term, always planned well and brought in coaching experts to help deal with the detail. Replacing Geoff would be a tough job for anyone, but Jack Rowell – the big, silver-haired man from Bath – was thought to be the best person for the job.

Jack had had extraordinary success with Bath – they really were the dominant club in the country at the time, and he was considered to be the rightful person to step into Geoff's shoes. But Jack was used to being very much in charge and doing everything himself. When he arrived in the England set-up, he was to work with Dick Best, the team coach, John Elliott, the national selector, and Mike Slemen, the backs coach. So the England job was much more of a team role than Jack had been used to. From the players' point of view, it seemed that he and Dick were too similar, too hands-on and too autocratic to work together. From the start they had problems because Jack wanted to be involved in the hands-on work of coaching, not just in standing back and directing. Dick's record as a coach was second to none, so he didn't want to be told what to do. Meanwhile, Jack was keen to establish that the manager was the one who was really in control. He had his opinions on how the side should be coached, Dick had his, and the pair never met in the middle.

When we were on tour to South Africa, it became very difficult to handle the two of them. We would be doing a training session with Dick, then Jack would be throwing some totally different ideas at us which undermined everything Dick had said. I remember being on one of the training pitches and just saying to Dick, 'Hold on a moment. Who the fuck am I supposed to be listening to? Am I listening to you, or am I listening to him?'

Dick said, 'You're listening to me,' in earshot of Jack.

That was that. It was clear then that the Rowell/Best relationship was not going to last very long. In the end, Dick received a postcard from Don Rutherford, the Technical Director of the RFU at the time. It said something like, 'Sorry that we are going to have to release your services. We're going to go with Jack. I'm sure you'll find another coaching job pretty easily because of the standard of coach that you are.'

Dick kept the postcard for posterity. He's probably still got it. What an awful way to treat one of the country's best coaches.

So Jack took over then and it became clear that it was he who had wanted Dick out of the picture so he could be the hands-on coach with the team. I have to say, it did leave a bitter after-taste in some the players' mouths. I and the other Harlequins players felt that Dick had been treated particularly badly, because we obviously knew him well from our own club rugby. It was a difficult time for the players because we had been used to stability. We'd had a few years of Geoff and Dick in charge, but now suddenly they had both gone and Jack, whom none of us knew particularly well (even some of the Bath boys said they didn't really 'know' him), was running the show.

CHAPTER TEN

A Pride of Lions

The 1993 Five Nations had not been one of our greatest successes as a national side. In fact, to be honest, it was pretty dismal. I was thrilled to be back in the England side after my operation the year before, of course, but it was a shock to lose games after being on the winning side for so long. At least we knew that the Lions tour came at the end of the season, and there is no British or Irish rugby player alive who does not covet that red jersey. For me, it represented the pinnacle of the sport and I hoped, more than anything, that I would be picked to tour New Zealand.

I came back from Dublin with Peter Winterbottom after we had been beaten by Ireland in our final game of the 1993 Five Nations. We decided to have a bite to eat when we got off the plane at Heathrow so we headed for a restaurant in Fulham where we ordered food and started having a couple of drinks, like you do. The couple of drinks turned into a couple more drinks and the conversation moved to the Lions team that was to be announced the next week. We debated whom we thought would get the nod while we carried on drinking. We were both desperate to find out whether we had been picked, and after a few more beers it seemed like it would be a great idea to call Dick Best and ask him, because he was on the Lions selection committee with Geoff Cooke.

When Dick answered the phone, I told him that I was with Peter Winterbottom and asked him whether we were in the side. I promised that I wouldn't tell anyone else, but told him that we were desperate to know. Dick was very unimpressed that I had called, particularly as he was in a selection meeting for the Lions. We should have left it there, of course, but we'd had a few drinks, so we didn't! We rang him up again an hour or so later and this time we thought it was all rather amusing – but Dick didn't. He said, 'Will you stop calling me, stop being arseholes.' Of course, the longer we sat there, the funnier it seemed to keep calling him. Finally, by the third or fourth phone call, he said, 'Right, I've had enough of you two now. I can't tell you who's selected, but what I will say is there's only one person in the England pack that's not going and it ain't one of you two.'

'Great,' we thought, 'we're going on the Lions tour. Brilliant news.' We had a few more beers to celebrate, then began wondering who would be the one person left behind. We started to try and work it out and even thought that we might try Dick again to ask him, but something stopped us, thankfully. We eventually came to the conclusion that it definitely, definitely wouldn't be a front-row player. They would surely take all the England front row on tour, so perhaps it was one of the back-row players.

When the team was announced, none of us could believe that it was Jeff Probyn who hadn't been selected. We just couldn't understand why he'd been missed out as he was the best tight-head prop in the country. What were they thinking of taking Paul Burnell and Peter Wright instead? No disrespect to those two for they were good players, but not in Jeff's league. The decision to leave him behind was obviously based on the selectors' wish to balance things up, and not have too many England players in the party, rather than their views on him as a player. That attitude has changed now that it's a professional sport, and there's a real emphasis on picking the best players, rather than balancing out the right numbers of England, Scotland, Ireland and Wales players.

The other loose head who was chosen for the trip was Nick Popplewell from Ireland. Nick and I are quite different players – he's more an explosive, mobile player whereas my forte is in the tight nitty gritty of the scrums, the rucks and mauls. Nick tends to look good with the ball in his hands, while I do more of the groundwork, the unseen stuff.

The tour began with four straight wins – always a good way to begin any tour. I played in the first game, against North Auckland in Whangarei, which we won 30–17 after scoring two tries in two minutes. It put an end to all the speculation in New Zealand that we were going to be stodgy, predictable and unadventurous. The All Blacks knew after that that they had to take us seriously. We continued to promote this view with a 29–13 win over North Harbour in a very aggressive game, a 24–20 win over the New Zealand Maori in which we pulled back from a 20-point deficit and against Canterbury, in which I also played, the Lions winning 28–10.

With just a couple of games to go before the first Test, it was looking good for the British and Irish – then we went to Otago and the Lions suffered their heaviest defeat for 34 years. I didn't play but the feeling of frustration after the match was tangible, even for those of us who had taken no part in it. There had also been injuries sustained in the game, to add to our woes. Martin Bayfield, Will Carling and Scott Hastings had all come off, leaving us in a state of some disarray with the first Test just a week away.

Worse was yet to come. After the game, Wade Dooley was given the awful news that his father, Geoff, had died from a heart attack. Wade would fly home immediately for the funeral, but the New Zealand authorities granted him permission to return when he was ready. This was contrary to the regulations governing tours which said that a maximum number of 30 could be on the tour at any one time. The Lions' authorities planned to call Martin Johnson, the budding England lock, from England's tour to Canada, to fill Wade's shoes in his absence, so when Wade returned, there would be 31 players on tour. It was a kind gesture by the New Zealand authorities to waive the regulations in this special circumstance. They even offered to pay Wade's fare so he could fly back out.

With Wade on his way home, we played Southland and won 34–16, despite it being a flat, boring game which was ill-tempered and lacked continuity.

The next game was the first Test and I wasn't selected which was a huge disappointment. Nick Popplewell won the loose-head spot ahead of me, and Paul Burnell was selected at tight head. It was a frustrating, close game in which the Lions were robbed of victory at the end by a bizarre refereeing decision when the referee, Brian Kinsey, gave a penalty to New Zealand because he said that Dean Richards was preventing the ball being released after a tackle. But the ball was emerging on the Lions' side and if anyone was stopping it, it was Michael Jones. The Lions were a point ahead before that penalty, and they lost by two points as a result of it.

What was clear from the first Test was that Ian McGeechan was not happy with the way the front row was working, but he was happy with Nick Popplewell and what he was doing. Basically, they needed a tight-head prop who was up to the task (in my view they needed Jeff Probyn), which was a bit harsh on Paul Burnell who I thought had a very good first Test. Their solution was to try moving me to tight head for the next match, against Taranaki, to see how I got on. We beat the newly-promoted side 49–25 and my move was deemed to be a success, so it looked as if I would be playing out the remainder of the tour on the other side of the front row. It didn't bother me – I was happy to move over if it would mean winning a Test cap. To be honest, I'd have played fly-half if I thought I would have been picked there for the Test!

After the Taranaki game, a very strange thing happened. It was suddenly announced to us that Wade wouldn't be coming back out to New Zealand because the home nations officials had said that he wouldn't be able to play if he did. Bob Weighill, the chairman of the home nations committee had phoned Wade and effectively overruled the New Zealand invitation, telling him that to allow him to come back out and thus have 31 players on the tour would set a precedent and therefore couldn't be allowed. He told Wade that he could go back to New Zealand and rejoin the tour party, but he wouldn't be able to play. Understandably, Wade decided not to bother. It was an awful time. The players were extremely annoyed with the home nations committee and felt completely let down that one of their key players couldn't return when he had just been through a most awful experience. We had a squad decision not to talk to any committee men who appeared on the tour, something which didn't go down very well, but did nothing to change the situation. Wade stayed away from the tour, and one of the worst, most inhumane decisions imaginable prevailed.

The Lions played two further games – against Auckland and Hawke's Bay – before the second Test and lost them both, going down 18–23 in the first and 17–29 in the second. I played in the midweek match against Hawke's Bay and luckily was one of the only players to emerge with any real credit. The game was a very difficult one because it should have been an easy victory, but most of the guys playing felt they had nothing to prove because most of the Test places were cemented. I was sure that I could work my way in if I played well. Scott Gibbs felt the same way and we both emerged from the game with some credit, which was enough to secure ourselves places in the team for the second Test. For both of us, it was our first Lions cap.

Playing New Zealand is always difficult. Playing New Zealand as a forward is more difficult still. Playing New Zealand in New Zealand as a forward is about as hard as it gets. As I prepared to do just that, with the Lions shirt on my back and in a Test match for the first time, it felt like one of the most important moments in my career. I knew how much it meant to win. If we'd lost, the series would be over, and if we'd drawn, we'd have no hope of winning the three match series. We had to win.

I had a good game in what proved to be quite a comfortable win for us by 20–7, which was the Lions' biggest Test win in New Zealand. The local fans were getting very upset at the fact that the Lions were winning – they really don't like losing at home – and someone threw a beer can at Brian Moore. I didn't see it at the time but when we went into the next scrum, I could smell this awful stench of beer and Brian kept burping. He told me afterwards that when he'd picked the beer can up to throw it to the side of the pitch, he realized it was full, so he opened it, toasted the baying crowd and took a slurp before throwing it aside.

The victory in the second Test meant that we went into the third and final match 1–1 – great for the fans, but not so great for the players of either side who felt enormous pressure in the final week leading up to it. We played a midweek game against Waikato which was a fiasco, losing 10–38 in a dreadful match in which the midweek side were heavily criticized for having an 'end-of-tour' mentality, and not putting their best efforts into the game.

I don't believe that people go out there and play badly on purpose – everyone gives it their best shot, but after an eight-week tour, when you know you're not going to be picked on the final Saturday, it is hard to have the same motivation as when you first arrive. Besides, all that mattered at that stage was beating New Zealand in the third Test.

The deciding Test was to be played in Auckland – the home of New Zealand rugby. We played well in the first half, building up a 10-point lead, but lost our way in the second half and frittered away every advantage so that New Zealand finally beat us 30–13 to take the series.

It was a bitter blow and a horrible way to end my first tour. When I came off the pitch, something which really concerned me was the fact that Craig Dowd, in the New Zealand front row, had been doing his best to put me out of action all the way through the match. Everywhere I went, he was trying to kick and punch me at every opportunity. I don't claim to be whiter than white myself, but Craig was being outrageous, targeting me from everywhere, seeking me out and punching me – it was as if he had a personal vendetta against me.

At the dinner after the game, I walked down the steps into the main dining area and saw Craig sitting there at a table full of players and wives. The attractive, blonde girl next to him was staring at me, and he was obviously nudging her and pointing at me. She was shaking her head. He suddenly stood up and came over to me.

'Look, I've really got to apologise to you,' he said.

'Don't worry, it's all part and parcel of the game,' I replied magnanimously.

'No, I was out of order, and there's a reason for it,' he explained, going on to tell me that his fiancée had been staying in a hotel in Auckland a couple of nights earlier with some friends when a group of guys swaggered in and introduced themselves as Lions. One of them said he was Jason Leonard and they set about chatting up the girls. Craig's fiancée wasn't interested, so she decided to head back up to her room, but the 'Jason' guy followed her into the lift and tried to force himself on her. She managed to get away from him and run up to her room, where she phoned Craig straight away – he had a fit and decided to take his revenge on my face in the Tests!

It was when he was sitting with his fiancée afterwards and I walked down the stairs that he pointed me out she told him I was not the one who'd grabbed her in the lift!

Fans pretending to be players are fairly common on tour because the locals don't necessarily know what the players look like away from the pitch, yet the girls are normally very impressed by meeting the Lions. I remember going out with Peter Wright for a drink once. We were in the bar and a group of young girls came up and asked us whether we were following the Lions' tour. We said, 'Yeah, yeah, we're following the tour.'

One of them said, 'You know some of the Lions players are in here tonight, don't you?'

'Really?' we both said, looking around, unable to see any of our teammates. At the time we were shielded behind a pillar, so whilst we could see round the bar, few people could see us. 'Where are these Lions?'

'There,' said the girl, pointing at two drunk blokes in their twenties, both wearing kilts. 'That one's Rob Andrew, and that one's Jason Leonard,' she said.

Peter Wright just cracked up. 'Do me a favour, love,' he said. 'We'd love to buy them a beer. Point us out to them.'

'Sure,' she said, without a clue about who we were.

The two guys jumped up at the offer of free beer and came round the pillar to meet us. When they saw us, their faces were a picture – I've never seen anything so funny.

'Oh, Jesus Christ,' they said, and left the bar very quickly.

I enjoyed the social life when touring and still do, although that has slowly eroded on the three tours I've been on because the sport has become increasingly professional. My first Lions trip was a fascinating experience although it would have been much better if we'd won, of course. What I found particularly enjoyable was the tour mentality – everyone sticking together, the cross-nation banter and the breaking down of national stereotypes. Even as a player, you end up believing what's written about other players a lot of the time, so when you meet them and tour with them for eight weeks, it can be a real shock to discover they're actually OK. It's also good to get to know some of the non-England players in a friendly environment because, routinely, we tend to see people only when we're about to play them, or have just played them. You're all on the same side on tour, which produces much tighter bonds and allows you to get closer to other players.

Tours are also good because the team stays together in victory and in defeat. After an England match, some guys go back to their families, some want to meet up with wives and girlfriends, and others feel obliged to talk to sponsors or officials. On tour, we all stay together, do the same things and go to the same places. It may sound claustrophobic but it engenders great team morale and brings you very close to your fellow players.

Lions tours are more special than any other, because of the history and tradition and because of all the amazing players in whose footsteps you're following. When you even see the red jersey, you think of all the greats that have worn it. It's a very proud time.

Ian McGeechan once said that if you are part of a successful British Lions tour, you'll always remember those who were with you. He said, 'You might be walking down the street thirty years later, and you'll see one of your tour teammates on the other side of the road. You'll look at each other and you'll just remember what you've been through and what you did for each other. No one else will understand because they weren't in that position. You'll just see someone and nod and you'll both know.'

Where I think we went wrong on that tour was that no

matter how well the midweek side played, they felt that they weren't going to get in the Test squad. If you have a happy squad, you'll have a successful Test team – that's the way it works. If your midweek side is winning, that also helps the Test team.

CHAPTER ELEVEN

Hello, Mr Lomu

I could have been England's captain for the World Cup in South Africa. It could have been me bravely leading my country into the biggest sporting event of the year. It could have been my face on all the T-shirts, tea towels and front pages. Forget Bum Chin – I was offered the job of England captain in 1995.

I was flattered when they first offered me the job, of course. Who wouldn't be? I felt like the chosen one – picked out from the team as the natural leader. But unfortunately my feelings of joy didn't last long before I discovered that every other bugger in the England team had also been offered the job. In fact, by the end, I wondered why they had taken so long to offer it to me!

The year was 1995, and Will Carling had the captaincy taken away from him just months before the World Cup because of his now infamous comment that rugby was being run by 57 old farts. He murmured the remark quietly off-camera, but it was picked up by a microphone, broadcast over the credits at the end of the programme and quickly leaked to the press in advance of the programme being aired. Dennis Easby, the President of the Rugby Football Union, reacted strongly to the comment and stripped Will of the captaincy.

The whole episode is as daft to think back on now as it was to live through at the time. We had just won the grand slam in the 1995 Five Nations championship with a strong and settled team and the World Cup in South Africa was hovering on the horizon – the biggest event, sporting or otherwise, ever to be staged by South Africa. They had been admitted back into the sporting fold a year previously because apartheid was abolished and Nelson Mandela, one of the most highly respected figures in world politics, was in power. It was a new dawn for South Africa, a new chance for them, and it was a competition in which we had great hopes. After getting to the World Cup final in 1991 and coming so close to victory, we all felt confident that this time we might be able to go all the way. Our wins over New Zealand in 1993 and South Africa on tour in 1994 gave us additional confidence – we'd proved that we could win when it mattered and that's what World Cups are all about.

The incident with Will and the old farts would have been hugely distracting at the time, if it hadn't been so comical! I don't think any of the players actually believed that he would stay sacked for more than a few hours because it was so ludicrous. When the affair dragged on into the next day, and particularly when the RFU started phoning around the other players to offer them the captaincy, we were all very confused. It was a complete nonsense. Of course Will had to be the captain for the World Cup.

The first players approached and offered the England captaincy were Rob Andrew and Dean Richards – the obvious ones. They realized what was going on straight away and said they couldn't take the role on. I think the speed with which the offer was turned down must have shocked the RFU a little. They clearly expected other players to leap at the chance to replace Will, but that's simply not how things work in a team sport. Loyalty is more important than self-advancement, so everyone steered clear of the role they were being offered – everyone, that is, except for Ben Clarke. In his defence, this was because he didn't know what was going on. No one had been able to get through to him to warn him about the situation. As a result, when he was asked whether he would like to be captain, he said, 'Of course I would.' When he heard what was going on, he backed out straight away, having to put up with massive amounts of abuse from the rest of the players. We made his life misery for two or three weeks with all our mickey-taking!

Will eventually apologized publicly with a smile on his face and the whole matter was dropped. If they hadn't sorted it out, there would have been no England captain in the 1995 World Cup because it is an absolute certainty that none of us would have taken the role on. Anyway, Will was reinstated and the England team headed off to South Africa for the World Cup with a captain and a fiercely loyal team.

The problems of playing a World Cup in South Africa were more than compensated for, as far as I was concerned, by the thrill of the tournament and the important political and social messages which were bound up in every aspect of the competition. There were pertinent reminders everywhere that the corpse of apartheid was still warm – shanty towns and dismal accommodation laced the more affluent suburbs, there was a lot of violence and we were aware that there were many areas that were simply too dangerous to venture into.

There was also the trouble of altitude and heat for us to contend with. To try and offset some of the effects of them, we trained in all-in-one suits like the ones divers wear, including on exercise bikes to get used to the oppressive heat. We must have looked bizarre with those bloody things on with their enormous black hoods which featured a glass flap that you looked through, but we were persuaded that it would all help with our performance. We were also given special fluids to replace all the minerals and salts lost through exercising in the strange outfits. We took the foul-tasting solutions for about two weeks and felt rotten, so we decided that it had to stop so we put the ridiculous space-man outfits away and refused to take any more of the drink. I think we all felt much better after that.

The England team was based in Durban for the start of the tournament, in a beautiful hotel and near to great training facilities. There was a real buzz about the place as the whole country was taken over with the excitement of it all, and South Africa's transformation into the Rainbow Nation. It was an exciting time to be in the country – you felt as though huge social and cultural changes would be cemented by the successful running of this major sporting event. The eyes of the world were on South Africa and no one wanted anything to go wrong.

We began our campaign with two victories that were much harder fought than we'd anticipated, beating Argentina by six points (24–18) and Italy by seven points (27–20), but we made up for it by beating Western Samoa 44–22 to top our group and move on to the quarter-finals, but the opening games had been a lesson to us in how far the world had moved on since the last World Cup in 1991, when Italy were an easily beatable side. We were not worried about the fact that our performances were rather average in the opening games for we knew that we were conserving ourselves for the big test – the knockout rounds. South Africa had beaten Australia in the first game of the competition, so we knew that we were likely to meet our old friends the Aussies in the quarter-final.

Looking back now, I would say that the game against Australia was like our World Cup final in many ways. We gave so much in that match that we were utterly exhausted by the end. The intensity of the match was obviously higher because of the history of the 1991 World Cup final – we really didn't want to be knocked out by Australia again, whatever else happened. Also, we hadn't played Australia since that 1991 meeting, so it was our first chance of revenge. In the end, it was Rob Andrew's drop goal which appeared to sail over the posts at half the normal speed which won the match. There are some great pictures of the entire England team staring up at the ball as it flies through the air, willing it to go over! It was a momentous kick and an exhilarating experience.

The relief that we felt was amazing. Not only had we got our revenge on Australia, we'd beaten them to a semi-final place. But more importantly than all that, we'd avoided having to play extra time, something which none of us could have faced! If Rob hadn't kicked the ball when he did, the whistle would have blown and we'd have been faced with another 20 minutes of rugby. If we'd had to do that, I don't think we'd have been much good – it was such a hot, humid day and we had worked so hard that we were absolutely knackered.

The quarter-final was so all-consuming that it was difficult to get up and reinvigorate ourselves to face the All Blacks. New Zealand are always strong, but we researched their particular strengths in 1995 and discussed them at length. I remember at one team meeting, one of the players – I can't remember who it was – said, 'What are we going to do about Jonah Lomu?'

We all decided that we wouldn't have a game plan geared to counteract one player, because that would be exactly what the New Zealanders would love. If we put three men on Jonah, they'd be breaking through and scoring all over the park. So we decided that we would play our own game, making sure that we defended well all over the field. I think that with hindsight (what a great thing that is!) we simply underestimated the impact that Lomu would have.

New Zealand went into the match looking for revenge on us, in the same way that we had wanted revenge on Australia, because the last time we had played the All Blacks was our victory over them in 1993. The New Zealanders don't take too kindly to losing and they certainly don't take kindly to being beaten twice.

They started the match in a blaze of glory. No sooner had the game started than Jonah had the ball and ploughed through four or five of us to touch down. For at least 20 minutes of that game they played some of the best rugby

I think New Zealand have ever played – it was quite stagger-ing to watch it unfold around us.

I thought our players of the match were Will Carling and Dewi Morris. Will had a great game – he chipped, chased, caught well and scored, but he didn't have a chance against a rampaging New Zealand pack, their bright athletic backs and the greatest scoring machine world rugby had ever seen – Jonah Lomu.

New Zealand were the team of the tournament in 1995, even though they went on to lose to South Africa in the final. They were a phenomenal force – an all-time great New Zealand team which would have won any other tournament on any other occasion.

When South Africa won the final, there were lots of rumours about the lengths they'd gone to secure their vic-tory. There was much talk of the All Blacks being given food poisoning the day before the game. Ten of the team were ill on the day of the final – some of them being sick on the morning before playing. Rumours like that always concern me because there is no evidence that the poisoning was deliberate. However, I remember being in South Africa a year after the World Cup and the security guard who'd been with the All Blacks team in the World Cup was promoting a book that he'd written about the event. He said in his book that he went into the doctors' room on the Friday night before the final and it was full of players being violently ill. He said they all had food poisoning and he was convinced that they had been given it on purpose.

Of course, all such allegations aside, the reason that South Africa beat New Zealand in the World Cup final was that they managed to contain Jonah Lomu – they realized exactly what a threat he was and they snuffed him out of the game.

When South Africa won, the country went mad. The whole place was in a state of complete celebration. Cars stopped in the streets and started blaring their horns, people danced and sang – there were major celebrations.

I didn't go to watch the final, although some of the players did. It felt like a non-event to me because we'd just played our worst match ever – losing to France in the third place play-off to come fourth overall. I just wanted to go home, to be honest. I'm not a great watcher of rugby at the best of times, and certainly not when we'd just lost to New Zealand and France on the trot.

Our third place play-off game was on the Wednesday after we'd been beaten by New Zealand. It doesn't feel like there's anything much to play for in those play-off games – the difference between third and fourth is the difference between having to qualify for the next World Cup, and not having to qualify, but when you've just lost and are out of the tournament, it doesn't seem like too much of an incentive, I'm afraid. Especially since most of the team won't be there by the time the next tournament comes round. The defeat was the first time that I'd ever lost to France, and I think the repercussions of losing to them went deeper than just that one match because we gave France some of their confidence back.

But while we mourned the fact that we'd finished in a miserable fourth place, the eyes of the rest of the world were on South Africa – the newly-crowned world champions at the first time of asking. The images of Nelson Mandela turning up at the stadium in François Pienaar's shirt and handing him the trophy afterwards were among the most potent of the century. The white man and the black man embraced and the whole of South Africa cheered. It was a very special time. Rugby is very big in South Africa and the tournament took over the entire country. It felt like something momentous was happening.

While we were there, in the best traditions of Lions tours, we went out to see the country and meet some of the people. Some of the England players, including me, went out to the townships to coach the rugby-mad youngsters who were desperate to play like all the stars they'd seen in the World Cup.

I had an idea about how poor the children would be, but it was a real eye-opener to see how utterly desperate some of them were. It is hard going into the townships, but at the same time it is very rewarding. I went for the first time on tour in 1994 and I put my trainers down for five minutes and had them stolen. I suppose it was silly of me to put them down, but these kids were all so tiny, I couldn't imagine any of them walking around in my big shoes. I had put them down because all the kids tend to run around barefoot, so I kicked off my size 11s and got stuck in to playing. Of course they were lifted straight away.

In 1995 it was even worse. That's when I discovered how desperately poor some of those kids were. We had our packed lunches in one of the coaches, so when we'd finished coaching, we climbed onto the bus and started eating our lunch. As soon as the children realized there was food around, they swarmed all around the coach with their noses pressed up against the windows, begging for scraps. There must have been 200–300 children gathered around us and there were only 30 sandwiches on the bus for the players. One of the guys, I don't know who it was, couldn't stand it any more, so he threw his packed lunch out to them which was obviously the wrong thing to do because it ended up with ten or so children madly fighting over it.

We all started to throw our food out, but there were just too many children and not enough food. The children started desperately fighting each other for the sandwiches. We realized what a mistake we'd made, throwing 30 sandwiches out to 300 kids, but it had been so difficult to sit there and eat with them begging that we thought we'd done the right thing. The children were clinging on to the side of the bus as we drove away, tears in their eyes as they begged for food. It was terrible. Really awful.

As I looked back at the children, barefoot with no trainers or shoes, dressed in their school clothes and playing rugby in the dirt on broken glass, stones and all manner of things, I was almost heart-broken. It was one of the most unhappy occasions ever but it taught me what real poverty is about.

CHAPTER 12

Professionalism? It'll Never Last

I never took up rugby to become rich. To be honest, I never expected to make a penny from the sport. I just wanted to play the game at the highest level possible. But the game has slowly changed while I've been involved. From 1987 when the first World Cup took place until it finally went professional in 1995, rugby union grew beyond all measure, becoming more commercial, much bigger and, as a result, far richer than ever before. The pressure on players got greater and greater until England players were effectively doing a full-time job as rugby players without getting paid. Holding down a job in addition to playing rugby at the highest level was becoming more and more difficult. The demands of playing, training and promoting the sport and the national team were becoming all-consuming. While players struggled to do jobs outside the sport to pay their bills, everyone else in the sport was thriving. Involvement in rugby was a licence to print money . . . unless you were a player.

The players were put into a more and more difficult position as the amateur regulations started to be loosened and the concept of 'amateurism' became more and more meaningless. The England players found it particularly difficult at this time because the International Rugby Board left the interpretation of their regulations up to the home unions. It was blatantly obvious to us that the regulations were being interpreted differently in the southern hemisphere, where it became clear that, whilst they might not be being paid to play, they were certainly earning money from rugby.

I had realized this back in 1993, in New Zealand, when on my first Lions tour I saw Sean Fitzpatrick on television promoting a tractor in his full New Zealand kit. None of the Lions players could believe it, because we had been expressly barred from promoting anything while wearing our rugby kits.

The officers of the Rugby Football Union were desperately clinging to amateurism while the rest of the world was clearly semi-professional. There was no way that a national team captain, standing there in his kit and advertising a commercial product, was not being paid. In England we weren't allowed to do anything in our England shirts because it would deem us professional. In fact, we couldn't do anything in pure white jerseys and shorts because of the implication that we were in rugby kits. We were once told that we could only wear white shirts and shorts if they clearly weren't rugby kit – for example, we could wear the England football kit in an advert if we wanted to, because that was recognizably non-rugby. Of course, this was no help at all, because no marketing manager in his right mind would want a group of rugby players to advertise his product while dressed as footballers. Where was the sense in that?

We tried to make money for the squad where we could, of course, and within the tight boundaries of the RFU's ungenerous interpretation of the amateur regulations. During the 1991 World Cup campaign we ran a promotion called Run The Ball through which we hoped to make £5k each. It wasn't much, but it would at least reimburse us for the money we lost through time taken out of work for the tournament. In the end, such were the constraints put upon us that we only made £1k each. After tax, it was barely worth having considering all the work we'd done.

The 1991 efforts really fell apart because everything we tried to do was blocked by the RFU. 'Oh no you can't do that,' they would say. 'Oh no, you can't use that wording,' or 'You can't do your picture like that.'

There was one quite famous incident where Timberland wanted to get a group of players together in their gear for an advert. Some of the players got involved – Paul Ackford, Brian Moore and Rob Andrew amongst others. They weren't wearing rugby kit in the photos, so it was all above board and legitimate, but Timberland wanted to place the ad in one of the Five Nations programmes in the 1991 season. Suddenly, the advert was pulled by the marketing department of the RFU. They wouldn't let it run in the programme and yet it was at their discretion to allow it to. They chose to make things as difficult as possible for the players, and that's why there was such a strained relationship between the union and the national players for the first part of the 1990s. There was a sense at the time that the committee actually believed they were the boss, even though they had nothing at all to do with the national squad and were just there to keep the administration ticking along.

I remember one player writing to a committee man – a very polite letter – to ask a favour. The committee man wrote back and said he wouldn't address his concern until the player wrote back addressing the letter properly, giving him his proper title. The player concerned tore the letter up and didn't bother to pursue his request.

I had the impression that it was very much them and us between the players and the RFU. We just didn't want to be with them and they were unable to help us. I never felt that these people were there for me and when I desperately needed the RFU's help – when I was injured and couldn't work – they weren't able to be there for me.

It is obviously not like that now. The whole thing is run much more professionally and the committees are smaller and more disciplined. Back then it was appalling. It seemed like they were having all these trips around the world for themselves and their wives while we struggled to get a few hundred pounds in expenses.

When rugby finally went professional, despite all the advance warnings, despite the fact that just about every other mainstream international sport was already professional, and despite the fact that it was quite obvious that it was going down a professional route – the whole thing seemed to totally surprise the RFU. The announcement was made and the RFU's reaction was complete disbelief. While the rest of the rugby world, the media and the public at large were discussing the dramatic way in which rugby was set to change as a result of the new professional game, my memories of it are of being invited to a meeting with Don Rutherford in his office at the RFU. Don was the technical director at the time and he had gathered together some of the more experienced England players together to discuss the way forward for the sport. Don is a decent rugby guy, a man whom I grew close to, but the RFU's stance was rigid and they refused to believe what was happening, let alone to believe that it would grow still further.

'This professionalism,' said Don. 'We'll give it six months and it'll fold. There's not the finance in the game. It won't last, so we're not going to sign you up and put you on contracts because it will just go belly up. Any fool can see that.'

What? More like: any fool could have seen professionalism coming a mile off and would have prepared properly for it – except the RFU. As a result of their incredible hesitation in the early days, the clubs contracted the players, signed them up to long deals and began a power battle with the union that is only just being resolved now – years after professionalism was installed in the game. All the club versus country battles, the rows about the length of the season, the structure of the season, and how many games we should play, are all based on the fact that the RFU didn't react quickly enough at the beginning, and the players ended up being contracted to the clubs, which resulted in the national game losing some of its power.

Everyone else in the major rugby-playing countries had one foot in the door already when the sport went professional; they were on the move and caught the ball going forward and ready to attack, whereas we weren't ready to catch the ball at all, and as soon as we saw it coming we were told to go back inside and put our tracksuits on. Is it any wonder that we had problems?

It's frustrating when you look back. The amateurs of the day were so short sighted, for example, that people like

Dudley Wood continued to believe, throughout his time in office, that because he was never paid to play, no one else should be. I would try to offer some context by explaining that I trained twice a day to get to the level of fitness that was necessary to compete in international rugby then, but most of the arguments were futile – the opinion would never change. It never did.

Professionalism should have meant us all being signed to the Rugby Football Union on central contracts because in rugby union that is where the money is. Everything should be geared to the national game which is the shop window of the sport. I believe in the clubs – they have a very real role, they unearth any new talent, get the youngsters in and turn their raw ability into world-class performances. The clubs work on them and invest in them and they are essential in the mix that makes up rugby union, but the England team must be perceived as the most important area of the game.

It's amazing to think back, and realize that if a few people had looked at professionalism more sensibly, all the subsequent problems we've had would simply not have happened. The foreign players that have come over to England to play rugby are astounded by the mess we've managed to get ourselves into. Players like Ian Jones, the New Zealand lock, and Jason Little, the Australian centre, couldn't believe it. Both of them have said, at some point, 'How's your body?' My reply 'How do you think?' would be answered by something like, 'It's amazing. How can you play an international on a Saturday when you're playing a club game on a Tuesday night? We would never have to do that back home. I've only just got here, but I feel as if it's the end of the season. I can't believe we're not even two-thirds of the way through it.'

After deciding, in their wisdom, that professionalism wouldn't stay very long, the RFU were made to realize that the money needed to support the game would be found when millionaires like Sir John Hall came into the clubs, and they were forced to do something. They called for a one-year moratorium during which time the sport would not be fully professional, so that they could get used to the idea and put some systems into place to cope. It seems that most other countries in the world already had systems that worked but, as ever, we had to start from scratch.

The moratorium year was a case of the RFU panicking and holding the flood waters at bay. It may have seemed like a good idea at the time – to hold fire and think about things for a year – but it meant that the rest of the world and the clubs moved ahead of England. It meant that while all the world's leading nations had centrally contracted players, and had begun working on a way forward for the sport, we were all sitting around waiting to see what would happen. I think the reason that the RFU were shocked by the announcement – soon after the 1995 World Cup – that the sport would go pro was that there appeared to be few signs that it was going to suddenly turn. The reason that the sport very suddenly bolted towards professionalism was because Vernon Pugh, chairman of the International Rugby Board, made everyone realize that in many countries the sport was already effectively professional. The other reason was that the rugby administrators' hand was forced by the arrival of Kerry Packer, who expressed an interest in buying up rugby union and making it into a glamorous spectator sport. His timing could not have been better – in 1995 there was a World Cup on the horizon, huge amounts of money in the sport and players who were giving up everything but were not getting anything back. He appeared like an angel on the horizon, offering riches beyond our dreams.

I was approached and was made an offer to join this new rugby revolution. The offer arrived on my desk through Rob Andrew, Brian Moore and other senior players who were liaising with Packer. I remember that I had all the contracts in the back of my car at one stage as I was looking after them for Brian Moore and every time I drove in and out of the RFU, I'd think, 'Oh, no, I hope to God no one wants to put anything in the back of my car, or peeks in there when I'm not looking.' Eventually I rang Brian and said, 'Can you come and pick these damn things up?'

Most of the England players signed contracts with Packer because the possibility to earn big money seemed amazing – hundreds of thousands of pounds and a much higher profile for doing what we were already doing for nothing. When players saw the number of zeros on the contract, they couldn't get their names down fast enough.

From a player's point of view, professionalism meant huge changes. Suddenly, I didn't have to work for a living which was a massive relief. I could train at the best times for me rather than in the early morning and evening to fit around work, which made a huge difference to the quality of my training and quality of life. When we first went professional, I found that we all just trained all the time. No one understood what professional meant at the time. We all thought that because we were professionals, we should spend all our time training. The players and coaches thought that professional rugby players should be running around a rugby field from 9 a.m. to 5 p.m. – a normal working day – but of course that doesn't work. If you train relentlessly, without stopping to think what you're doing, you just get absolutely worn out, and it really doesn't do you much good at all.

The club coaches were experts in rugby but knew nothing about how to coach professionals because the sport had always been amateur, so they carried on doing what they'd done in the old amateur days, but did more of it. Players were absolutely exhausted by the time the matches came round. Slowly, a year or so after the sport had gone professional, coaches, fitness people, masseurs and other experts came into the sport from outside. They had worked with professionals in other sports and understood what being a professional was all about. Rugby union had to learn some lessons quickly. Professionalism meant using your time sensibly and to the best advantage, and not necessarily training all the time. Rest, relaxation, mental training and physiotherapy all had to be part of the mix.

It was when we started training properly, and not killing ourselves, that the game started to change. We were all fitter and stronger than ever and we had experts in all areas of play that we'd never had before. We understood all about defence and attack, we could run faster and for longer and the whole game shifted up a gear, becoming more intense and being played at a much higher level.

You need to develop slowly in rugby union, pushing each of the areas of your game on a bit every day. There are so many different facets to the modern game – scrummaging, ball in hand, running, defence, attack, line-outs, mauls, rucks, kicking and chasing. In the old days, props didn't have to get involved in half of this but, increasingly, once the sport had gone pro, they had to be able to run with ball, pass it and handle it. You stopped being able to specialize in one area and had to be more of a total player. Rugby union slowly became a different game at the highest level. The days of the big-bellied props went for good. I saw this coming and whilst I was never a pot-bellied prop, I knew I had to get extremely fit to compete in the new era, and to stave off the opposition from the new, younger props who were coming into the game and going professional straight away.

I remember Steve Redgrave coming to talk to the team on one occasion, and one of the things he said was that in all his years of training, he had one clear goal – to make that day's training session just a bit better than the day before's. If he could make tiny improvements every day, he would improve enormously over the course of the weeks, months and years.

This is exactly what is now happening in rugby. It gets slightly tougher every season, thus widening the gulf between the fast-growing professional game and the amateur sport. Every area of the professional game is becoming more and more professional, and all these small advancements in every area are creating a very different game over the course of the months and years.

It's not just the action on the pitch that has been changed by the arrival of professionalism. There's a brand new medical centre at Twickenham now, to make sure that players are treated as quickly and efficiently as possible when they come off the field. You can be x-rayed, have an accurate diagnosis and be flown to hospital afterwards. It's a world away from what's happening in junior rugby where they still rely on the faithful bucket and sponge to cure all injuries. The two groups of players – amateurs and professionals – aren't playing the same game or under the same conditions any more.

The big changes that happened on the international stage were mirrored by changes at Harlequins. Dick Best, director of rugby at Quins and fresh from his stint as England coach, was eager to make changes. He was determined that the club needed a transformation. We needed to become more aggressive, commercial and more successful. I think Dick was right. We did need to be a much better side. We were in a prime position to make the most out of professionalism, but we had to be considered seriously and we had to start winning. Dick's way of doing this was the same as Dick's way of doing everything else – he worked us harder and harder and bollocked us more and more. This didn't bother me. I'm fine with hard work, my life was devoted to the game and I wanted us to be the best. But not everyone felt like that. Players started to resent the way we were being treated, and as one of the senior players, there was pressure on me to intervene. I tried to explain to Dick that the players were getting fed up, and that it would be well worth him easing off them for a bit, but he simply didn't understand.

I remember going up to his office after he'd upset one player, and saying, 'Dick, you can't say that.'

'Yes I can,' he replied.

'You can't, Dick. You've just crucified that bloke – his confidence is already low. You've upset him.'

'Well, he's no good any more,' was Dick's response.

'Look, you can't say that, because you're going to need him at some point. You're going to have to pick him off the floor and make him go and do a job for you. He won't be able to you if you've smashed his confidence to pieces.'

'No I won't. I'll get someone else.'

Dick wasn't being cocky. He genuinely believed that and once he gets into that mode, he's a very hard bloke to reason with. Having said that, I liked him a lot and never had a problem with him because his coaching was quite brilliant and that's what really matters. He has an amazing track record – 13 wins out of 17 games with England. It's a record that is better than any other coach's.

The players held various meetings to discuss how they felt and eventually senior management figures were brought in to the debate. Edwin Glasgow, the chairman of the trustees, wanted to know what was going on, as did Roger Looker, the chairman of Harlequins. Suddenly a localized players v coach conflict had escalated into a major club issue. Players started saying that they had no desire to play for Dick, and our results became less and less impressive. All the blame for this was laid at Dick's door, and in the end he was axed by Quins, which was a bit unfair.

Probably the best coach in the country, Dick was sidelined and thrown out of Harlequins, but it was never about his coaching ability – that was never questioned. It was his management skills and the way he treated and spoke to players that led to his downfall, which was a pity, because I can't help thinking that something could have been done about that. If you've got someone who has the ability to be the greatest coach ever, you would have surely spent some time working on his personal skills, however lacking they might be thought to be.

Perhaps Quins could have been more proactive and sent Dick on a management course. He can't be the first person ever to be talented but with a manner that didn't particularly suit all the players. I remember suggesting this course of action to a couple of the trustees but there wasn't a wholly positive reaction back. They said they'd see and the next thing we knew was that Dick had gone. It may have been that he was offered a chance to work on his management skills and there is every likelihood that Dick said something like, 'That's the way I am – you either take me or leave me.'

I don't know, but I do hope they tried. I hope they didn't just take the easiest solution, and just get rid of him and get some one else. It wasn't a particularly nice episode and there were people involved with giving Dick the sack who had been friends with him for over 20 years, so obviously they didn't like the situation.

When Harlequins got rid of Dick, they confirmed everyone's worst fears about the way the club is. People won't let go of the image of Harlequins as a club with a 'buy 'em in and chuck 'em out' mentality where everything and everyone has a price. After Dick left, Andy Keast, his deputy, took over as Director of Rugby and many of the problems continued. He was very much like Dick – a good coach and very analytical, but the way he spoke to players was unbelievable. The ideal image of a coach is someone you would walk barefoot over broken glass for – people like Sir Alex Ferguson or Sir Alf Ramsey – men who are revered and loved for their skills allied with persuasive natures.

Andy was headstrong like Dick, so Quins got rid of their second Director of Rugby in two years. All the time, the club officials were saying how eager they were to get rid of the club's image of 'if it's not working we kick 'em out'. Next in was John Gallagher with Zinzan Brooke. Gallagher went, another lamb to the slaughter and Zinny became coach without ever particularly wanting to. It was foisted on him and he stayed in the role for a year before he, too, was shown the door, on New Year's Eve 2000.

CHAPTER THIRTEEN

Captain Leonard

The relationship between Geoff Cooke and Will Carling was the bedrock on which England's victories in the early 1990s were built. But when Geoff left, Will never managed to re-create that close relationship with Jack Rowell. From the start, they didn't get on. There was a power struggle between the two of them which just got worse and worse. After the 1995 World Cup, their relationship really deteriorated.

Will had been used to having discussions with Geoff about the team and the way things were going, but with Jack everything tended to be presented to him as a fait accompli. There were few discussions – instead of making suggestions and talking over the best way forward, Jack would be more likely to say, 'This is what we're doing.' This way of doing things managed to antagonize Will in the same way that he had alienated Dick – he simply couldn't work with other people. He was used to saying what was going to happen, without discussion.

I think Will felt that his authority was undermined by the arrival of Jack because England's new coach felt the need to assert himself as the overall boss. This led to huge animosity – Jack would say, 'You're only the captain. I'm the coach, and this is what's going to happen.' Will didn't like this because he was used to having a greater input and because he'd been with the team for a long time he felt that he should have a much bigger say in what was happening. Eventually, it became obvious that it was either going to be Jack or Will that left, but Will got in first. He announced that he was stepping down from the role and thus initiated country-wide speculation about who should take over. As one of the more established players in the side, I found my name on the shortlist.

The speculation surrounding the appointment of Will's successor was quite fun but, to be honest, I never expected it to be me who was chosen. There were players around with experience of captaincy whom I thought would be more likely to get the job. I also felt that Jack would be eager to appoint someone he knew he could work well with, so I suspected that the new captain would either be from Bath, and thus known to Jack for a long time, or be someone Jack got on very well with, I didn't really fit into either of these categories. Meanwhile, I was appearing as a likely candidate in the papers. My captaincy credentials were mulled over and my character analyzed. One day they were saying that I was definitely in the frame, the next day it was definitely someone else. I was even asked my opinion as to whom it should be and I said I thought it should be Tim Rodber, because he was Jack's kind of man – big, strong, no nonsense. The other guy whom I thought might get the captaincy was Ben Clarke, because he was one of the few people who seemed close to Jack. The two of them had worked together at Bath for a number of years and I knew that Jack respected Ben. Ben was also pack leader at the time, so would have made an easy transition.

There were five of us who kept being mentioned as potential captains – Clarkey, Lol Dallaglio, Rodders, Phil de Glanville and myself. There were debates on radio and features on television looking at the candidates and treating it a bit like a general election. Some shows had phone-ins apparently, with readers voting for who they think should be captain. I don't think I came out top in any of them, but I don't think any one character came top all the time. It became clear that no one knew who was going to get the job – it could have been any one of us.

Even the individual players who were rumoured to be in the frame didn't have a clue who was going to be the next captain. We'd talk amongst ourselves, but no one knew who was going to be appointed, because I don't think any of us knew Jack well enough to second-guess him.

It was an interesting time for me because I was absolutely sure that I wouldn't get the captaincy, so I could watch the whole drama unfold and was as intrigued as anyone else to find out who it was going to be. I remember one day, there were a few of us 'captaincy candidates' at training, and I said, jokingly, 'We should all have a punt on who will be the next captain. If we all put some money together we could stick it on one of the guys, and make a bet at the bookies – we'd make a fortune.' We were always joking about this and trying to work out how much money we'd make.

Lawrence and I went out the night before the new captain was going to be announced, knowing that the RFU had pulled out all the stops to announce the new name – they were going to have the new captain dressed in the all-new England kit, and stepping out from behind some sort of curtain to meet the press. Lol and I knew that we hadn't got the job because neither of us had heard anything and we figured that the future England captain must have heard by now. So we went out for something to eat at a little restaurant in Kingston, owned by mutual friends of ours.

It was quite busy in the restaurant that evening because I had invited some of the French players, including Laurent Cabannes and Laurent Bénézech. As we walked in, they ordered champagne and started toasting us, saying that one of us was definitely going to be the next England captain. Lol and I sat down and started talking about whom it might be. I still had it in my mind that we should put some money on this, because I was convinced that we could find out who had got the captaincy, and if we put £5,000 each into the kitty, we'd have £25,000 to put on – then split the winnings.

We were both aware that the captain-elect would have been warned, on pain of death, not to talk to anyone else, so they might take some convincing, but we'd all known each other for a long time and I was sure that whoever had got the job could be persuaded to own up. We were in that restaurant until about 5 or 6 a.m. planning this great wheeze and the more we drank, the more convinced we became that we'd be able to retire off the proceeds.

Eventually, I said to Lawrence, 'Look, I've got Clarkey's number in my phone. I'll give him a bell and find out if it's him.'

Ben answered straight away. 'I don't know, mate. I haven't heard anything.'

I made him promise, and he said, 'Yes, I can tell you now – on my mum and dad's life – it's not me.'

Right, so it wasn't him then, and I ticked him off my list.

Lol had Rodders' number in his phone and as we both thought that it could well be Tim who'd got the nod, we decided to try him next. There was no answer, so Lol left a message. It's really funny looking back now, but with Rodders' answerphone on, we thought it must be him. We were just about ready to run down to the bookies and stick a huge bet on when Lol's phone rang and it was Rodders on the other end.

'Is it you?' was Rodders' first question.

'No,' we both said. 'We were ringing up to see if it was you.'

'No, it's not me.'

Another name to tick off on the list, and you don't have to be a mathematical genius to work out that four names out of five had been ticked off, therefore it was either Phil de Glanville who was going to be the captain, or one of the people we'd talked to was lying. Lol and I looked at one another like gangsters in an old black and white movie.

'He's gotta be the one.'

'Gotta be,' said Lol.

I picked up my phone and entered Phil de Glanville's mobile number. It went straight onto answerphone, so I left a message. Then I tried his home number – no reply. He was the only person that we couldn't get hold of.

'It doesn't matter whether we talk to him or not – it's got to be Phil,' said Lawrence.

'I know, but what if one of the others is lying? I don't think we can stick twenty grand on Phil without talking to him. What if someone's lying because they've been warned not to tell anyone?'

We kept trying to call Phil – ringing every number that we

had for him, but there was no answer. Obviously, I realize now that he had been told just to switch his phone off and come to London for the announcement.

So we abandoned our hopes of making a fortune and had a few beers.

It wasn't until the next morning, when I wandered onto Twickenham Green where I was living at the time, and popped my head into the bookies, that I realized how much money we could have made. I couldn't believe it – Phil De Glanville was 18–1. Luckily, the guy in the bookies didn't recognize me. I got on the phone to Lawrence straight away. 'You won't believe this,' I told him. 'De Glanville's only eighteen to one.'

'Then you won't believe this,' said Lawrence. 'De Glanville's just been announced as the next England captain.'

I could have cried. But it's probably a good job I didn't put the money on because just imagine the trouble we'd have been in if anyone had found out! I suppose, thinking about it, it was obvious that it was going to be Phil, because he's another guy that's very close to Jack – they'd worked together at Bath and he played in the centre with Will, so knew a lot about the way Will captained. Also, Phil was a bright, good-looking young centre in exactly the same way as Will was, so the public would take to him, and his tenure wouldn't be seen as a huge departure from the extremely successful Carling era that had preceded it.

In many ways, this would prove to make things quite difficult for Phil, because he was always seen as being in the shadow of Will and Jerry Guscott. I suppose that would have been true of anyone coming in after Will – one of the most successful England captains in the history of the game – but it made it doubly hard as Phil played in the same position and could so easily be compared to him. I thought he did very well in the circumstances and was a good players' captain. He knows the game and how to play – he's very bright, astute and thoughtful. But there were lots of questions asked about whether he should really have been there, because many felt that Jerry Guscott and Will were the best centre partners. Phil got a lot of stick in the press because of his play, which I always felt was quite unfair because he's a very brave man – which is why he's had more stitches and more broken bones than anyone else in the England squad. His nickname at one time was 'Paper Face', because his face was just covered in cuts. He used to throw himself around like no one else. As a captain he was everything we could have hoped for and I was surprised that they didn't stick with him.

The next captain after that was Lawrence. I think that the reason he was selected was because he was this dynamic young player who was going to be around until the next World Cup, so it's ironic, really, that he ended up losing the captaincy just before it. Lol is a good friend and he made a great captain – he's a natural in the job and it was nice to have a forward in the role. But I've been lucky in that most of the captains I've played under have been good, all with their own distinctive qualities – little things that differenti-ated them from previous captains. There are things that every captain does that can be either good or bad. Will, for example, was very serious, especially when he first started, as a terribly earnest, serious young man. I think he felt it was a huge task because of the standard of the players around him – players that he was supposed to lead and organize into a team. There were people like Rob Andrew, Rory Under-wood, Brian Moore and Peter Winterbottom, a group of players who were more than capable of organizing and looking after themselves. Rob would say, 'Right, this is what we're doing' and Will knew he was right, so he had the common sense to let people share the responsibility. Will has a sense of humour and is ready to take the mickey out of himself. When people talk about what a great captain he was and refer to him as having captained the British Lions, he always says, 'Yeah – to their biggest ever defeat!' He's nowhere near as precious as people tend to think that he is. All the players in the team were like-minded, strong individuals, and as much as you could say that Will was lucky to have guys like those around him, the fact that he was able to cope at that level – and pull all those strong individuals into one of the most successful teams in English rugby – says much about his abilities as a captain.

Phil followed Will. Easy to talk to and astute, he was more vocal as a captain – that was the main difference that we noticed straight away.

Lawrence was the next captain and he, more than the other two, really wore his heart on his sleeve. A very emotional bloke. He was more vocal than the other two put together, and would get pumped up and start screaming on the pitch and at the players.

After Lawrence, Martin Johnson took over. He is quieter and doesn't say many words – but the ones he does, you listen, because he's got that aura around him. He's the sort of bloke that would walk over broken glass for you if you're in the same shirt as him. He really is the bloke that you want on your side rather than playing for the opposition. He doesn't rant and rave, but has everyone's respect.

The way these guys are as players tends to be the way they are as leaders, to be honest. Will used to joke that in the early 1990s, all he had to do was toss the coin and decide which end they wanted to play – the coaching and management team had sorted out the side that was to be on the pitch, and the players were able to look after themselves once they were out there. But it would be a mistake to underestimate the power of a good captain.

I don't think I would have enjoyed the role, looking back. It's a tough job and so much bigger than the work you do on the pitch. The modern captain needs to keep totally on top of his game because he needs to ensure that he keeps his place on playing merit, while at the same time he has much more to do than any other player, and not just on the pitch. He has to involve himself in selection, motivating players and making sure that those who aren't selected or are on the bench are OK. Then there's the match itself, and however much of a hands-on captain you are, or aren't, you know that you'll be blamed for everything that happens between the whistles. After the match, you have to go back to the changing room and make sure everything's OK. You want to stay with the players and go off to meet all the families, but while the other players are doing that, you have to go up for the press conference – which, obviously, isn't too bad when you're winning, but quite tough if you are disappointed at having lost a game.

When you eventually get back to your family, it's practically time to go off to the formal function in the evening, where you have a key role to perform in making a speech, hosting the opposition captain and not getting blind drunk (you see, I could never have done it!). Even when your formal duties are over at around midnight, if you venture out of the hotel to have a few beers, you'll be greeted by several hundred fans or opposition fans wanting to share every last detail with you about where you went wrong, or where you could have been better. It means that you have these stop/start conversations with family whom you haven't seen all week while guys try to perfect your game for you after they've been drinking non-stop for most of the week.

I just don't think I would have enjoyed it that much if I had been given the captaincy. It would have affected every area of my life, because at the time that I was in the frame for the captaincy, it was a period of my life when I was just going out and enjoying myself all the time – with not a care in the world. I was never one to avoid having a night out and a few beers with the lads.

I have captained England, though, and it did have a very positive effect on my game because I scored my only try on the occasion. It was against Argentina – the country I had played against in my England debut. Will Carling was my vice-captain for the match, running the backs. The back line wasn't going that well, so in the last 20 minutes I said we would take it in the forwards and that's when the try came. We had a line-out and the ball went to Martin Johnson who drove it forward and through the defence with the rest of the England pack attached to him. All of a sudden I came round and found my hands on the ball. I had Mark Regan at my side and we drove for the line. As I'm not one to celebrate – I'd never jump up and down or anything like that – the cameras got it wrong. I scored and Mark picked the ball up, so everyone thought he'd scored. When we came in, all the press were asking who'd scored. I said it was me, but Mark Regan said it was all of us – a forwards' try. Sorry, but I can't let that one go. It was me – I had my hands on it!

CHAPTER FOURTEEN

Lions Roar

Ian McGeechan, the man who had done such a great job as coach of the 1989 and 1993 Lions tours, was announced as the man who would lead the Lions again in 1997. This time he would be joined by Fran Cotton, the former England prop, who would be the manager of the tour party.

The 1997 Lions were different from previous tours – we were told from the beginning that this was the first professional Lions tour and that winning matches would be the out and out priority. There would still be time for other tour activities like meeting local communities and having our traditional kangaroo courts, but the focus would be firmly on winning the three-Test series in South Africa.

The first move the new management made was to release a list of 62 names of players who had been selected in a preliminary squad. This group would be whittled down to 35 who would be taken on tour which was five more than had been taken on any previous Lions tour and was based on the New Zealand model of touring in which you took sufficient players to enable you to have two teams – one for midweek games and a totally fresh side for the weekend games. The New Zealanders had always taken 36 players on tour, allowing them 21 players for each Test (the team plus 6 on the bench) and a separate 15 for midweek matches.

We were all called to a meeting at the Metropole Hotel in Birmingham in March where the management talked through their hopes and expectations for the tour and ran through how the plans would proceed until the party left for the eight-week tour. What struck me straight away was how well-organied and disciplined everything seemed to be. They were taking the 1997 tour very seriously and said that the management team would be comprised of 12 people – bigger than on any previous tour.

The 35-man squad was announced at the beginning of April, and we were all invited to Sky's offices in Hounslow where the formal announcement of the squad would be made. The Leicester players could not come to London for the announcement because they had a match at home that evening, so when Martin Johnson was announced as captain, he was linked to the studio by satellite from the clubhouse in Leicester.

I think some people were surprised by the decision to make Jonno captain when he wasn't the England captain at the time (Phil de Glanville was), but none of the players were very surprised. We had all seen Johnno do a wonderful job for Leicester and knew that he'd be great in the role – some-one who would lead by example. I naturally really liked the idea of having a forward in charge.

Before heading off to South Africa, we all assembled at

Oatlands Hotel just outside London. It's a great hotel where a lot of the touring sides stay when they first come to England, and it was where Fran gave his first speech – welcoming us all, and reiterating how much they wanted to win this tour. Following the welcome speech there were lots of mundane practicalities to be taken care of, such as visiting the doctor for a health check-up and to be given the all-clear, and picking up all our kit from Adidas, the team sponsors. As usual, there were bags full of it and I knew that by the time I came back to London, most of it would have been lost, discarded or stolen.

Some of the time at the Oatlands Hotel was spent working with Impact, the management company on various team building and motivational exercises. These involved the usual tasks – working in pairs and teams to complete tasks in order to prove the importance of teamwork and communication. Luckily, I love all that sort of thing so was quite happy with the idea of spending a week doing it. We also started our rugby training and began the long discussions of South Africa's strengths and weaknesses, and how we would overcome them. In between the rugby sessions, which became more difficult as the week progressed, we battled on with the Impact training sessions which included canoeing down rivers, learning how to deal with the media and continuing to bond as a group.

In the final session, we looked specifically at the tour ahead of us and pulled together all the training we'd been doing, to look forward to the coming weeks and what we wanted to achieve. We were asked to consider the 'Lions' Laws', as they were called. These were just a series of words which related to the tour in some way – words like discipline, identity, cohesion, support, trust, openness and honesty – then we had to get into groups to discuss them. I was with Jonno, Jerry Guscott, Jim Telfer and Barry Williams and our task was to discuss the disciplinary committee and how we thought it should work. I don't think there were any startling, bright or original ideas, but it was good to think we were all involved in the structure of the approaching weeks, and had some say in the way in which it would be managed. If it did nothing else, it was a good PR exercise and pulled us together as a group.

The flight to South Africa was great. The tour was sponsored by Virgin, so we were flying first class which makes an enormous difference because there's so much more room and with shoulders the size of mine, you need it. The air hostesses and crew on board couldn't have been any nicer to us and the pilot had even managed to get permission to fly over Ellis Park on the way in.

The first game of the tour was against Eastern Province in Port Elizabeth and I was chosen to captain it because of my previous Lions experience. It was an important game as you have to get tours off to a good start, and I knew that I had been selected because they needed someone who understood what they were doing, to get out there and ensure us a win. Even though it was just the first game of a long tour, I knew that for the sake of the rest of the tour it was vital that we came away with a victory.

When we first arrived in Port Elizabeth we discovered that half our luggage had gone missing, the hotel was scruffy and unpleasant and the food was nigh on inedible. Fran ordered huge plates of sandwiches to keep us going and made it clear that he would do everything he could to get our luggage to the hotel the first thing the next day.

The game on Saturday, at the Adcock Stadium, started

well for the Lions. We played some good rugby in the opening quarter – throwing the ball around and looking as if we wanted to play a wide and entertaining game. Things started to go a little awry when the South Africans came back at us, and at one stage we went 10–11 down in the second half, but tries by Will Greenwood, Doddie Weir and Tony Underwood, added to a first-half try from Jerry Guscott, gave us an impressive 39–11 opening victory.

I was pleased with the way I had captained the side, we had stuck to our guns and had played the sort of rugby that we had wanted to – the sort of rugby that we believed would beat the South Africa side in the Test matches. One of the best moments for me was when Scott Quinnell tackled Kobus Wiese, the huge South Africa lock, and sent him flying. Those moments are very significant in the forward power battles that take place in a game. Scott's tackle showed them that we might have just got off the flight and we might have a long tour ahead of us, but we weren't going to back down from anything. I had played at tight head the previous season, leading up to the Lions tour, which is obviously not my favourite position, but I was prepared to play it on tour if it fitted in with the team's plans. Tom Smith was a strong loose head so he played in the number one shirt for the opening game, and I played as tight head. Keith Wood, the Ireland hooker, made up the front row.

The next match I played in was against Western Province in Cape Town, which was another victory, by 21–38, but as it was Johnno's first match, he took over the captaincy. I played again, against Northern Transvaal, in one of the two defeats that we suffered on the whole tour (the other was in the third Test). We lost 30–35, and I did not play again until after the first two Tests, against Northern Free State.

I captained the side to a 67–39 victory in what was my last game of the tour.

From a personal point of view, it was a disappointing tour. I didn't make either the loose-head or tight-head spots my own, so I found myself firmly established in the midweek set-up. But Lions tours are not about the vanities of individual players – they are team occasions and despite not playing as much as I would have liked to, I still felt very much part of the tour, and as if my contributions were as valid as everyone else's. It says much about the way in which the tour was run that I felt part of the squad even though I didn't play anywhere near as much as I would have liked to because I was overtaken in the selection by Paul Wallace, a man who totally justified his place at tight head, with Tom Smith at loose head.

But my woes at not having a great tour paled into insignificance besides those of players like Paul Grayson, who found themselves on the way home, unable to stay on tour because of injuries. Paul first noticed a groin injury flaring up when we were at the hotel in Weybridge, but he thought he would be OK and decided to come to South Africa in the hope that it would clear up. It didn't, and after the Western Province match he made the dreaded one-way journey.

Fran worked out that an average of six players return from Lions tours with injuries, but that doesn't make it any more bearable if you're one of them! Jerry and I took Paul to Oscar's, a dreadful looking late night bar, for a few bevies to send him on his way.

Lions tours are not about Test caps, despite what it may seem like from the outside – it's about a big group of players going away together and between them doing what is necessary to win. Players have bad days and I didn't have a great tour, so it was right that Paul and Tom were the Test props, which didn't mean that I didn't support them every inch of the way, and do all I could to help them in training.

I am as competitive as the next person but Lions tours are different. I knew I wasn't going to make the Test side so I decided to try and help the other front-row players as much as possible. I did everything I could, whether it be scrummaging sessions, line-outs or rucking and mauling sessions. On the 1997 Lions, it really felt like our small, close-knit group of players and managers against however many millions of people there are in South Africa. It felt like us against the whole world and you felt as if there was a role for you whether you were playing in the Tests or not.

I know Jim Telfer was very pleased with my attitude because he said afterwards how much I had impressed him, but I think all the players would have been the same in my position – knowing that they wouldn't make the Test team but feeling, nevertheless, that they had much to contribute in a very specialist area. I'm sure most of the players on the trip would have been in there and helping.

Those outside a tour may not understand that it is not just about you personally being in peak form, but also about doing what you can for the team cause, for when you're on tour you want the side to win even if you're not playing. You want the guy who takes your place to do well because you want the Lions to win – that is the most important thing.

Geech said after the tour that it was the comradeship and the closeness of all the players in the party that made the tour the success it was, and I think he was right. He said that some of the most important people on that trip were the midweekers because they won their games, and helped the Test team prepare for theirs.

I know I started off as first choice but slipped down through the ratings, although I never stopped wanting to play – I'd bust my back training, but when it didn't happen, it didn't happen. The first Test team was to include Tom Smith, Keith Wood and Paul Wallace in the front row, with Jonno and Jeremy Davidson behind them. One of the most hotly debated subjects after the team announcement was whether the Irish combination of Wallace and Davidson was a good idea, or whether they would have been better with Simon Shaw and me in the pack. Shaw and I were bigger, and obviously I had a lot of experience. I try to keep out of discussions like that – you can debate for ever the merit of one set of players over another, and I'm sure the selection committee did that and came down on the side of the lighter Irish boys. I never feel it is my role to moan and complain once a team's been announced. The time to make your presence felt is on the pitch.

There was some consolation from the fact that Geech and Fran admitted how hard it had been to make the Test selections, and that it was the toughest selection they'd ever been involved in because everyone in the squad was vying for a place in the team. The 1997 tour was the ultimate 'squad tour' – we were all made to feel part of it from beginning to end. This continued, even on the day of the first Test, when Geech played a video that had been put together and featured all our best moments from the tour to date. There was a small section on everyone in the squad, not just those due to take the field in the first Test – a nice touch.

There was a tremendous atmosphere at Newlands, with

the number of red shirts among the spectators matching the number of green and gold shirts. There was a real buzz in the air for the evening game in the beautiful stadium, with Table Mountain sitting authoritatively in the background. It wasn't a great game of rugby, looking back, but it will be for ever etched into the minds of all those Lions supporters who saw it because of a blinding five or so minutes of play from Alan Tait and Matt Dawson which won the game for us. Daws's try was something else, especially since no one expected him to be in the Test side. Everyone had mourned the injury to Rob Howley which we thought would hamper our chances, but there was Daws, throwing an outrageous dummy and racing over the line to win the game.

The two props had a very good game, so I knew that there was little chance that I would make it back into the side for the second Test, and once the Lions had won that – thanks to that memorable drop goal by Jerry Guscott in the Durban sunshine – I suppose I knew the management would stay with the same faces for the final outing in Johannesburg, and rightly so.

Once the Lions had won the second match of the three-part series, they had effectively secured victory, so it was time to start the celebrating. First on the list of things to do was the shaving of Geech's head. In a rare moment of madness, our head coach had alluded to the fact that he would shave all his hair off if we won. By the time we'd finished, he looked like Roland Rat, and that was the nickname that he was stuck with for the rest of the tour! We went out and celebrated that night – drinking, eating and dancing the night away in the knowledge that nothing could take the series away from us. It was disappointing to lose the third Test but that did little to cool our excitement over the victory. The trip to South Africa had been hugely successful and immensely rewarding, even for a player like me who had certainly not played as well, or as often, as I would have liked.

CHAPTER FIFTEEN

England Move Forward

The arrival of Clive Woodward was like a breath of fresh air. He immediately wanted to change things, make everything better and think of new ways of doing things. He was never constrained by the way things had been done in the past and he moved English rugby a long way forward.

He came in with a mission to run rugby like a business, being convinced that you could apply the same strategy to rugby as you applied to successful businesses. He would talk about how to maximize what he was doing, how to get the best out of everything and how to involve everyone. It took some getting used to and at the beginning it didn't work very well because there were too many people involved in making every decision, but after Clive had settled in to the job, it worked perfectly.

When Clive started work with the England team in late 1997, he brought specialist coaches with him and the players were unclear as to what role they were all to play. We hadn't had backs, forwards, defence, attack, scrummage and kicking coaches before, let alone throwing in coaches, tactical analysts and all the other people who suddenly became associated with the team. I realize now that it was the right thing to do but, at the time, we were a bit alarmed at how quickly everything was changing and what all these new and varied coaches were going to do. Some of the players had visions of the coaches all wanting to have their input, and us having to train ten hours a day to allow them all to contribute. Luckily the whole thing was managed by Clive, and he made sure that the coaches all had their input and that we got the most out of them.

Clive's theory was that we should find a way that worked best for England and not copy what other rugby nations were doing. We should establish the England way of doing things, and let other countries copy that. In the past, we had tended to rely on southern hemisphere models of how to coach rugby. I remember that when the New Zealand team put together a booklet of their training drills, coaches in England got hold of it and we all copied it slavishly for years. They relied on warm-up and ball-handling set-ups called Auckland grids. Soon, every rugby player worth his salt was doing Auckland grids at every available opportunity, because we all figured that if it was good enough for the All Blacks, it was good enough for us. I had no problem with that, because New Zealand were the best team in the world, yet there might have been something better that we could have been doing, but we never even considered anything else because we were determined to copy the New Zealanders at every turn.

At least Clive wanted to create a model of good practice

that was different and that he was convinced would work for us. I'm not saying that it was perfect and I have to admit that we lost games where we should have won – notably Wales at Wembley and Scotland up at Murrayfield – but I think any side has to go through learning phases.

When Clive first turned up in the England dressing room, we didn't really know what to expect. Very soon it became clear that his coaching would be much like his playing – a bit different and slightly off-beat. He was unconventional as a player and we would soon see that he would be very much the same as a coach.

I remember the older players saying how he used to warm up for internationals at Twickenham by standing behind the posts, facing Dusty Hare as Dusty practised his goal kicking. When the ball came through the posts, Clive would let it pass over his head, then at the last second, catch it behind his back before it hit the ground. He was always relaxed when he was a player – the forwards would be banging their heads against the wall and getting very uptight while he remained calm and confident. The good thing about Clive, and where he differed from Jack, was that he wanted to change things, stir things up and take some risks.

He would also make us switch on to the opposition and try and read their minds, instead of just predicting what formations they would play in. I remember him saying, before England versus Scotland, 'If I were Scotland, what would I be thinking? I'd be thinking England are going to keep the ball in the forwards as much as possible. They'll imagine lots of rolling mauls and tight, defensive play and that's what they're training for . . . so we won't do that – we'll do something completely different.'

So, under Clive, we started to do things a bit differently.

We broke the tradition of English forward play; we became unconventional and unpredictable. Because Clive had played as a back, he was always keen for us to get the ball out to the backs as much as possible. He advocated an open, running game of rugby which he particularly liked because nobody would be expecting it.

I once said, 'Oh, no, you can't do that' when he suggested just getting the ball straight out to the backs. 'Why not? Tell me why not?' he replied, straight away.

He does this all the time and to be fair to him, if you've got a good argument, he'll say, 'OK, we'll think about it.' He's very good at challenging preconceptions and making you think about why you are doing things. 'We've got great, explosive backs. Look at them. Why don't we just give them the ball?' he would say.

It does make sense, but not until you sit there and think, 'Why don't we give it to them straight away? We've got some of the best broken field runners in the game.'

So that's what we started doing. We started changing our game and doing what our opponents didn't expect – we started thinking differently and playing differently.

Backing Woodward up was John Mitchell, the New Zealander, who was assistant coach when Clive first started. He was very, very good and extremely competitive. When he went back to New Zealand, he was replaced by Andy Robinson, who was another keen competitor. Even if you play tiddly-winks with either of those two, the pair of them are desperate to win. Brian Ashton was brought in to work with the backs and he was also very good. He is credited with being just a backs coach, but he also did a great deal of work with the forwards as we all tried to become more complete, more 'total' players. Under Clive, there was no room for 'forwards' and 'backs' – we were all players who had to get out there and do whatever it took to win. The forwards had to break down defences as well as the backs, but we always used to do it by barging through the middle. Brian would say things like, 'Why do you have to run through someone, why can't you run round them? Why can't you find some space to run in? I can't understand why you would want to run at a bloke who's sixteen stone when you could just run round him.' After some training with Brian, the forwards realized that they didn't have to go barging through all the time.

Then there were the other experts – Phil Larder came in as the defence coach as Clive broke the game down into small components and built it back up again, better than ever. Nothing was left to chance, and all the time we were aware that, even though it was two years away, Clive was already building for the 1999 World Cup. That was the one he desperately wanted.

Our first Five Nations tournament with Clive was in 1998 and we went into it feeling positive after a 26–26 draw against New Zealand at Twickenham. But any confidence we had soon evaporated as we got off to the most inauspicious of starts, losing 17–24 to France in the first game, thereby setting them on their way to winning a second consecutive grand slam. The French played with such blistering pace and panache that we were much further behind them than the scoreline suggests. Losing that opening game was extremely disappointing, especially since we went on to win the following three, overwhelming Wales 60–26, Scotland 34–20 and Ireland 35–17. We followed the tournament with a summer tour to the Southern Hemisphere, which I did not go on. It was, in every respect, 'a tour too far' and was effectively an

England third team because so many players were either injured, due to have an operation or resting before the 1999 season which had the World Cup at the end of it. It meant that England fell to a dismal defeat, losing 0–76 and earning the wrath of a nation as Australian coaches and officials lambasted England for sending over an inadequate team.

In 1999 we prepared for the last Five Nations Championship – Italy would join the tournament in 2000 and make it the Six Nations. It was also the last competition before the World Cup, so England were eager to do well and set down a marker to the world.

We did just that for most of the championship, beating Scotland 24–21, Ireland 27–15 and France 21–10 to make up for their victory over us the previous year. All we had to do was beat Wales in the final game to win the grand slam. The world seemed to think that the England colours were all but tied to the trophy because the match was a home game for Wales but would be played at Wembley because the Millennium Stadium was being completed in advance of the opening World Cup game. Not being able to take us on in Cardiff would rob Wales of their traditional strong home advantage, which meant that the win was as good as in the bag . . . or was it? The Welsh rugby fans managed somehow to recreate Cardiff at Wembley Stadium that day. There was a sea of red scarves, shirts and flags – it was amazing, and the Wales team responded. They beat us 32–31 and suddenly it was Scotland at the top of the table and winning the championship – the white ribbons were torn off the trophy and blue ones were added on.

Afterwards, we all felt devastated by the loss and its implications – losing the grand slam, the triple crown and the championship. I can remember asking myself all these questions: could I have played any differently? What was my preparation like? Should I have done more? Did I take the Wales team seriously enough? The answer to all of these was that I had worked hard, I thought I'd done enough and I definitely took Wales seriously. It was just one of those things. We had to learn from it and move on. The World Cup was coming up. There were plenty of opportunities for us to excel in the coming months.

The period from the end of the Five Nations in 1999 until the start of the World Cup in October was dominated by the news that Lawrence Dallaglio, one of my closest friends, had been in a tabloid sting. Lol found himself spread over the front pages of the *News of the World* after being tricked into 'admitting' that he had taken drugs on tour. He came clean afterwards and said that he had lied to the undercover reporters. He said that although he hadn't taken drugs on the 1997 Lions tour he had pretended that he had in order to further his relationship with the reporters, who had told him they were advertising executives who could land him a massive sponsorship deal.

It was quite a shock to open the papers and read about it, especially since I was on that Lions trip and I can honestly say that I never heard about, or saw, anyone with drugs. When I read that Lawrence had admitted taking them, I couldn't believe it. I just thought it was ridiculous. Yet there was more to it for there was supposed to be this half a million pound advertising contract up for grabs. The whole thing brought home to me that anyone could get caught up in this way, but that it was grossly unfair that it should count against him – it wouldn't in a court of law.

As far as the allegations that he actually took drugs go, I remember John Bentley seeing the article and saying, 'I was

with Lol that night in South Africa. I don't remember anything like that. I would have seen if he'd taken drugs and
I didn't see anything.'

What the whole incident did was bring home to the
players how vulnerable they are, and how they have to be
careful of the tabloids. We've always read things about footballers and the hard time they have with the press, but
rugby players had never been treated in quite the same way
before. From then on we all realized that everyone had to
be extra careful.

I'd only ever known an incident once before when a player
was set up. It was when we were on tour to South Africa in
1994. A girl came up to Will Carling in a Union Jack blouse
with the shoulders cut off. She was chatting away and all of
a sudden tore the shirt off to reveal she had nothing on
underneath. A guy behind her produced a camera and tried
to take a photograph of Will with this topless girl. Had it
been reproduced in the tabloids, it would have looked
extremely incriminating and would have made a particularly
good piece for some newspaper because Will was due to
get married soon after the tour. I remember Mike Teague
grabbing the photographer and throwing him out. That was
about the only time before the Dallaglio affair that we'd
come across any tabloid journalists trying to stitch players
up. In the 1995 World Cup we heard that certain tabloid
papers offered a bounty of £10,000 for a couple of prostitutes to sleep with some of the players, being told that by
our own rugby press who disliked sensationalist tabloid
reporting as much as we did.

After the Lawrence Dallaglio episode, there was a story
going round about a woman employed by a newspaper to sit
in the bar of the Petersham Hotel, hoping to be pulled so she

could get into a player's room and subsequently sell the story. Apparently she only did it once for although she sat there all evening the rugby players were absolute gentlemen and at the end of the night she was left on her own in the bar.

After the *News of the World* incident, Lol stood down from the England captaincy, and pulled out of the summer tour to Australia. Meanwhile the rest of the England team headed Down Under. While we were there, we had a call to say that some tabloid journalists were on their way out to see what we were up to. We thought this was hysterical because we were on a daft island called Couran Cove in the middle of nowhere off the coast of Queensland – we couldn't have caused any trouble, or got up to anything we shouldn't have, even if we'd wanted to. Yet we were being warned that journalists might start following us around. Hello? Following us where, exactly? It would have been nice to have the company – I've no idea what they thought they might catch us doing!

It was a disappointing summer tour and we returned having been beaten by Australia again. For the third year in succession they had retained the Cook Cup and we had to regroup in time for the World Cup.

CHAPTER SIXTEEN

Gifts from God

In the summer of 1999, while the rest of the country went about the business of enjoying blissful, sunny holidays, I became a father for the first time.

I'd always wanted to have children – like most people – but I never knew when I was going to fit it all in around my rugby and the massive commitments that come with playing international sport. In the end, Sandra had Harry, our first child, just before the World Cup, and Jack shortly before the Lions tour – both of them choosing to enter the world just before the two most important events in world rugby. The timing couldn't have been worse, but none of that seemed to matter when they arrived.

Harry, our elder son, was born on 19 June 1999, the day that we all met up for pre-World Cup training camp. It was the morning that we were supposed to be going to St Mary's College for fitness tests, so of course the boys were convinced that I was just telling everyone that Sandra had gone into labour in order that I could get out of the tests. Sandra had first thought that she might be going into labour the night before, so she and I stayed up all night watching *Friends* videos and waiting to see whether the pains were real. By about 3 a.m., she decided that we ought to go to the hospital, so the two of us got into the car and I drove slowly and carefully to the maternity ward.

Harry was eventually born at 1 p.m. and weighed in at 7lb and 12oz – I was there watching every minute of it. You don't realize, until it happens, just how emotional it all is. I knew that I would love being a father, but being around other people's children doesn't prepare you for how you'll feel when you see your own for the first time. It was amazing to look at this little person that Sandra and I had created together. Of all the things you ever do in your life, that is the most important. I felt immensely proud of the achievement and so pleased that he was healthy and that Sandra was well and happy.

When she passed Harry to me, I felt more terrified that if I'd had Jonah Lomu racing towards me at top speed. Harry looked so vulnerable and delicate that I was scared of harming him. I think Sandra thought it was hysterical that I was so worried. She's used to seeing me running around, unafraid of anything, then there I was with this new-born baby and I'd never been so frightened.

Once I'd handed Harry back to his mum, I strolled round the room, thinking of all that lay ahead, knowing that while I was enjoying my new family, all my England teammates were involved in pre-World Cup fitness work. I looked at Sandra appealingly. 'Do you mind if I sneak off now?' I asked.

Sandra didn't look in the least bit surprised by my request. In fact, she said afterwards that she knew as soon as Harry was born that I would want to get back to the team, and she'd been waiting for me to say something. It wasn't easy to leave, but I knew Sandra needed to rest and there wasn't much I could do there and then to help with the baby, so I eased myself away and went back to my car.

I drove from the hospital in Kingston, through Richmond Park, to meet up with the team without having slept at all the night before. When I got back to the England guys, they were great – full of congratulations and really pleased that everything had gone so well. Jerry and Lawrence were already both fathers, so they were particularly thrilled. They were also amazed that I'd managed to produce a boy because the trend among rugby players is to have girls – Jerry has three and Lawrence has two.

It was obviously very difficult to leave Harry and Sandra behind, and focus on the team's preparations for the World Cup. I'd just been through a most emotional, life-changing event, and now suddenly I had to change my focus from the creation of a new life to fitness testing and rugby training. It was quite a transition.

I returned to see Sandra that evening, then went to Kingston the following morning to pick them both up and bring them home. Because Sandra and I knew that I would be away a great deal for the first few months of Harry's life, we had already decided to employ a maternity nurse to stay with Sandra and help her through the difficult early days. When I caught sight of the nurse, I couldn't believe it – she was a huge woman from New Zealand and a passionate All Blacks fan. Every time I saw her, she wanted to talk about New Zealand's chances in the World Cup. We were in the same group as the All Blacks for the preliminary stages of the tournament and faced our most crucial game against them, so that was the last thing I wanted to do! I tended to try and keep out of her way whenever I could.

Our pre-World Cup team building was done at the Royal Marines Base in Lympstone in Devon – the same place that my brother had passed out as a Marine. I had always had a great deal of respect for the Marines, and by the end of our week there, I had even more!

For rugby teams, the training sessions that military personnel put themselves through are a good test of how strong the team is as a unit and how confident and communicative the individuals are. There may not be much similarity on the surface between the Marines and the England rugby team, but the reality is that within every good team there are core values which are the same whether you're fighting a war or playing a match – for example: trust, determination and communication.

One exercise that we did was on a mock-up of a sinking ship. The Marines had a half-boat on hydraulics which gently rocked to simulate the movement of a real boat at sea that is slowly being filled with water and sinking. I was the leader for this exercise and it was my job to direct my group of men to save the boat by plugging all the holes which were emerging in its side. As water started slowly seeping through holes, I organized the guys to fill them to prevent us from sinking. As I had men concentrating on one hole, another would appear, so I'd have to redirect them to fill a hole in a different part of the boat. All the time, the water level was rising and more holes were appearing. There was real pressure to get the job done as quickly as possible, because the vessel was sinking and no time could be wasted. I really felt the urgency of the task as the water started to rise and rise. Soon the players were treading water while they tried to repair the holes, waiting for my instructions to abandon ship.

I managed to get everyone off the boat safely, but it sank and so I thought I had failed the exercise, until I found out afterwards that it always sinks, and the exercise is not how long you keep it afloat, but how well you cope with the impending disaster and how safely the troops are taken off the boat. The whole exercise was about reacting under pressure, comradeship, assertiveness and staying calm – just the sort of skills we would need in the World Cup.

The exercise was developed by the Marines after the Falklands War, when so many men had lost their lives because they drowned, not by gunfire. The Marines always use this exercise now to train their men to cope and survive on a sinking ship, and to prevent such a disaster in the future.

We stayed in the same teams for the whole week and competed against the other players who had formed rival teams. I had Danny Grewcock, Matt Perry, Richard Cockerill and Neil Back with me – we were the dream team and ended up winning the overall competition. As we completed tasks we were observed by assessors who specialize in analyzing how cope under pressure. They were looking to see who the team players were, who were not great team players, who was willing to listen and who was willing to give advice. In life it's no different to rugby – there are some people who are open to new ideas and responsive to instruction, whilst there are others who will not listen to what they're being told, acknowledge blame or seek to improve. Under the pressure of an alien environment and in potentially life-threatening situations, these characteristics come to the fore very easily. The guys who analyzed us after watching us for just a comparatively short length of time apparently got our personalities down to a tee. These people knew nothing about rugby, but were able to pinpoint characteristics and how they might affect our ability to perform in a team environment. They said that I had leadership qualities and was prepared to listen. They said I was very good at talking to other people and would volunteer to do whatever was needed.

Most of the players enjoyed the course and found it beneficial in some way. The only person who didn't was Jerry Guscott, who made no secret of the fact that he absolutely hated it. Apparently, when the assessors looked at him, the first thing they said was, 'How is this bloke playing a team sport? He doesn't care.'

I don't think that's entirely true or fair. Jerry does care, but he was typically Jerry on the course – he couldn't see the relevance of what we were doing, and thought that our team-building time would be better spent warm weather training in Portugal, or doing fitness work. He never wanted to be a soldier and could see no reason why climbing up walls and jumping off sinking ships was going to help him when it came to the World Cup.

Jerry is a team player but he's an individual as well. He's very much for the team, but he's also a very dominant person within that team and likes to be an individual. The idea of a game where you rely on your teammates to save your life did not appeal to him in the least. No one really surprised me on the training week because in a team sport like rugby you get a chance to see what people are like all the time, so you're fairly sure you know people anyway. It was a close squad before we went on the trip and it was a closer squad afterwards. Everyone enjoys each other's company – that's always been a big thing in the England squad. We do tend to socialize and get on quite well.

One of the most significant exercises we did was a race in which we had to really trust the people around us. We were all blindfolded and had to walk along in our groups, keeping in touch with the person in front (a hand on his shoulder). We wore breathing apparatus with the masks blacked out with masking tape so we could see nothing. It all made us feel very claustrophobic and a little scared of what we were going to go through. We had no idea where we were being taken or what was ahead of us. The Marines walked us into a building where we could see nothing, so we were totally reliant on each other, particularly the person standing directly in front. Teamwork and communication were the only ways of surviving. We had to go through an obstacle course in the pitch black. We were aware that we were walking through water but we had no idea how deep it was going to get or what was in it. I remember thinking, 'hold on a second. How long have I got to go under here for?'

Of course, the person who's just gone in front of you is waiting for you so you've got to go through it quickly or you hold everything up. You have to trust that he's gone through, so you'll be OK. A few people apparently freaked out and just ripped their masks off because they hadn't got a bloody clue what was going on. It felt like we were in this awful, terrifying place for hours then, when we were allowed to take our masks off, we saw that it was just a few chairs and a little water about two yards long – nothing scary about it at all. Yet it had felt so frightening when you couldn't see or hear anything and had the gas mask on which made you wonder what noxious gases were around.

I thought they'd put us through an obstacle course of some sort and couldn't believe it was just a bunch of chairs that we had been going over, through, round and behind. The fear had been created by people bashing and rustling papers, books and small drums by our ears. These sounds were muffled because we could hardly hear anything and they appeared all the more ominous. I thought we must be in the middle of some life-threatening scenario.

We learnt through the week that trust, comradeship and communication were the keys to surviving the tasks. On one occasion we had to put a fire out on a ship involving the use of extinguishers which just filled the whole room with foam so you couldn't see in front of your face. When you put your hand out, it was gone – into the foam. There was no way of knowing where the fire was or where your teammates were unless you kept hold of someone in the group, so once again we were walking around with our hands on each other's shoulders, totally surrounded by foam. Suddenly I'd realize that I'd just lost someone behind me. That's where the element of teamwork and trust came out – the person that I'd just lost had to know that I would find him.

I thought it was all very good. I'm a big team player anyway and I always put a big emphasis on the team, so it suited me. It was great to go off playing soldiers, and it definitely brought us together as a group as the biggest tournament in the world loomed closer.

The fourth rugby World Cup kicked off on Friday, 1 October with Wales v Argentina at the new £120 million Millennium Stadium in Cardiff. The tournament lasted five weeks and matches were spread around the nation. There were 20 teams competing – four more than in 1995 – and the countries were divided into five pools of four teams with play-offs for the quarter-final places meaning that 41 matches were played. England were in Pool B with Italy, New Zealand and Tonga. We were fairly confident that we could beat Italy and Tonga but right from the beginning of the competition, we were aware that the match against New Zealand was crucial, because if we lost it we would come second in the group, necessitating a play-off game, then we would have to face South Africa in the quarter-final. Whereas if we won the group, the road to the final stages was much less treacherous. The winners of Pool B went straight through to the quarter-final and a likely match against Scotland. In other words, beating New Zealand meant we had a chance of going all the way to the semi-finals. Losing to New Zealand meant having an extra game, then a very tough quarter-final fixture. Of all the teams, in all the world, why did it have to be New Zealand that stood in the way of our preferred route?

In our opening game we beat Italy 67–7 and in our final pool game we beat Tonga 101–10 – two easy victories. But sandwiched between them was the crucial one – New Zealand. I think that in some ways we were so concerned by the New Zealand game that we became a little overawed by it, never relaxed and therefore failed to play the standard of rugby that we all knew we were capable of. It was so important to win it that common sense went out of the window.

I think that forward-wise we played as well as we ever have. I certainly enjoyed the match, but it was difficult playing such a big game early on, and it was difficult to accept the implications of the loss. In many ways that New Zealand game was our final. It was them who, effectively, sent us out of the tournament.

After the All Blacks game, there was a real sense of disappointment in the England changing room. We all knew how hard it would be for us to come back from there. We played our quarter-final play-off match against Fiji and won, entitling us to a quarter-final spot against South Africa in Paris.

It was very difficult going over to France, but there was still a feeling in the side that we could do it and win ourselves a semi-final place. After all, we were just two matches away from the World Cup final so anything was possible. On the day of the match we were still optimistic and confident that we had what it would take to send the reigning champions out of the competition, but alas, that was before we were confronted by Jannie de Beer, the former London Scottish player, and his 'gift from God' – his kicking skills. His five drop goals blasted England out of the tournament. I tried to charge them down along with everyone else, but to no avail. The South Africa coaches had worked out that England's real strength was defence, and they knew they would have a hard time penetrating it, so Nick Mallett, South Africa's head coach, decided that drop goals were the way forward, because you can't defend against them.

For us, this was definitely a case of a game too far. We'd played Tonga in the final pool game, Fiji in the play-offs and South Africa in the quarter-finals – all within a week of each other, and after a tough and exhausting match against New Zealand. There was nothing left to give and we could only watch in amazement as De Beer's kicks sailed over the posts and sent us reeling out of the 1999 World Cup.

It was extremely hard after that match, as it always is in World Cups, because not only have you lost the match but you're out of the whole competition, and you have to watch the tournament going on around you when you're not involved. Suddenly four years' work and the big pre-tournament preparation stint has amounted to nothing. It was also difficult because our finishing position meant that we had got progressively worse in the past three tournaments – in 1991 we finished second, in 1995 we finished fourth and now we were ranked between fifth and eighth.

I went home from Paris to be greeted by the joys of fatherhood. It was lovely to be home with Sandra and Harry, but it took some adjustment for all of us. Sandra had just about got used to the idea of the two of them being there and, suddenly, I came back into the picture and the three of us had to work out a way of all living together. Much of the onus for the care of Harry was on Sandra in the early months, when I was flitting in and out, going to training, matches and the World Cup camp, so I had to get stuck in and take some of the burden off her so she could get some time to herself.

At least looking after a baby stopped me from moping around the house and thinking of the lost chances in the World Cup. Sometimes it can feel almost like a bereavement when you are knocked out of a major tournament – it's as if a part of you is missing. Suddenly the huge event that you had hovering on the horizon, and were training non-stop for, has gone and you're left with this empty feeling inside.

I did stay involved in the tournament a little bit after England were knocked out, because I did some corporate hospitality on the day of the France v New Zealand semi-final – meeting people, talking about the rugby, that sort of thing. Jerry was there too and there was a strong Kiwi

element at the lunch – all of whom were convinced that the
All Blacks would win the match easily.

I remember talking to one bloke and saying, 'What do you
think, then? It should be a good game.'

He replied, 'It'll be easy – all we've got to do is turn
up today.'

Of course, France's form before that day had been shock-
ing, while New Zealand had been in good shape, but still – I
wasn't as convinced as he was.

'You should never say that. You should never bet against
the French because you never know with them. They pull
great victories out of nowhere. There are no certainties in
rugby.'

'OK, let's have a bet,' he said.

'A tenner,' I replied.

'OK, done.'

It was all said in a light-hearted way, but I wanted to
make the point that nothing is ever a foregone conclusion in
rugby – not even where the All Blacks are concerned. Once
the match began, New Zealand tore France to pieces in the
opening phase of the game and I started to fear for my ten
quid. I think they were 20 points up in the first 10 or 15
minutes. But then the match turned was turned on its head
as France started scoring. Because they were the under-dogs
and because they're our European neighbours, I suppose, the
Twickenham crowd were completely behind France and
cheering like mad every time they got the ball.

After the match, I saw the guy I'd had the bet with. He
was devastated, shell-shocked.

'That's the easiest £10 I've ever made,' I said, as if I'd been
full of confidence that France would win.

The reality is that the best thing and the worst thing about the World Cup is that it's a knockout competition. Anything can happen – it's all about getting that win on the day.

Harry was just 11 months old when Sandra discovered that she was pregnant again. I was thrilled, but I'm not sure whether Sandra was quite so pleased when she first found out because of the timing of it. She looked at the calendar and realized straight away that the due date would fall perilously close to the next Lions tour. Since Sandra would have Harry, a toddler, to look after as well, the thought of me possibly being away wasn't a happy one! In the end, we discovered that the due date was before the Lions tour, during the Six Nations championship, which was slightly better – at least there was a chance that I'd be in the same country when the baby arrived.

I went through half the matches in the tournament in 2001 unsure whether Sandra would go into labour while I was on the pitch. I had always been clear about the fact that I would miss an England game if the baby came, and everyone in the England management was aware of my feelings on this. I told Sandra to call one of the coaches or RFU officials if she went into labour while I was playing and I would come straight off the pitch.

But, as it turned out, Jack kept us waiting until the very end of the Six Nations. I got through the tournament to the final game, England v France at Twickenham, and both Sandra and I were praying that the game would be done and dusted before the baby appeared. I remember in the week leading up to the France game, some of the papers had cottoned on to the fact that I would pull out of the match if Sandra went into labour. She said that when she walked down the street in Twickenham, people used to shout, 'Keep your legs crossed, love' – she got a bit fed up of it by the end.

We decided that I would proceed as usual in the week leading up to the game against France even though Jack was, by now, overdue. But I reiterated to Sandra that as soon as the baby came – whether I was training, sleeping or playing at Twickenham – she was to let me know and I would come straight to her.

We got all the way through the week, and I phoned Sandra before the game started. She seemed fine and there was no sign of the baby, so I took to the field while Sandra stayed at home in Twickenham.

'I thought I'd be fine,' Sandra said later. 'Then, I was sitting at home, watching the match on television and there was this strange feeling like I was going into labour. I decided that if it got worse, I would go to hospital and I would ring someone in the England set up and tell them I had gone into labour, but ask them not to tell Jason until after the match. I really didn't want him to have to come off. If he'd come off and the team had lost, I'd never have heard the end of it from the fans!

'It was while I was thinking about what to do, that it suddenly occurred to me that I would never be able to get to the hospital through all the Twickenham traffic, so I'd have to ring an ambulance. I was busy worrying about how the ambulance would get through the crowds when the pains died slowly away. I was so relieved that I wasn't going into labour at such an inopportune moment.

'Jason phoned me when he came off the pitch, I told him what had happened and asked him to come home as soon as he could.'

It was quite funny because the players had a small function at Twickenham after the match which I couldn't get out of, so I went to it, then got on the coach with everyone else to go to the Hilton for the formal dinner, but the bus dropped me off at the corner of my road on the way through. I shouted – 'Right, I'm off to have a baby' and ran home. The next time the players saw me – at the Hilton the next day – I was carrying Jack!

Our second son came into the world at 4.50 a.m., after Sandra had been in hospital for just a couple of hours. He was 9lb 6oz so I have a feeling that he's going to take after his father. And then came Francesca. Having the three kids is tremendous fun and it adds a whole new dimension to my life. I go home after training, pick up the kids and it makes me feel instantly better.

I must admit that the work involved with children is much harder than I ever thought it would be. I remember getting up one day when Sandra was worn out. She hadn't had time to get dressed properly, Harry was still in his pyjamas, the house was a mess and she looked tired and fed up. 'Go and have a morning to yourself,' I told her. 'I'll get Harry dressed and get this place tidied up while you go and enjoy yourself at the gym.'

It took Sandra about five seconds to agree that that would be a good idea and she was quickly out of the door. When she came back home, the house was more of a mess than when she'd left. I hadn't even managed to get my trousers on, Harry was starving and was still in his pyjamas.

'See?' she said. 'It's not so easy, is it?'

'No,' I said. 'I haven't had a minute to myself.'

'Now you understand how I feel every day,' she replied.

It's extremely demanding, but very rewarding. I want four children altogether, but I think Sandra will take some convincing!

Harry made his first television appearance on *This Is Your*

Life – he was brought onto the set at the end after I'd endured what must be the biggest shock of my life. Having to face the haka is nothing compared to having to face Michael Aspel and that red book of his. I was at a function at the Royal Bank of Scotland to launch my testimonial year with a lunch when they got me. It was totally unexpected. As I turned round to thank everyone who had helped with the planning and organization of the function, I could see people smiling, then I saw him standing beside me with that damn book tucked under his arm and a grin on his face. I just looked at him, and all I could think was 'Run, run, and keep on running.' The trouble was that we were deep inside a high security bank, so if I'd done anything of the kind, I'd have been immediately tackled to the ground by dozens of security men.

Looking back, I should have known that something was going on because all week Lawrence and Jerry hadn't been returning my calls – maybe they were worried about accidentally letting it slip that they were involved with *This Is Your Life*. But these things only seem obvious when you know the facts. The truth is that I had no idea at all. It was a complete surprise – and I hate surprises.

Once you've been 'caught' you're supposed to go straight back to the studio where they are all waiting for you, but I had to have a pint first, so I persuaded them to come with me round the corner for a couple. I ended up having four or five pints before we got there, and the production girls and researchers were getting a bit worried. I think they were panicking in case I arrived at the studio too drunk to stand. But I really needed that time to relax a bit and I'll always be grateful to Jerry for calming me down a bit. He told me that he'd had *This Is Your Life* done to him a few years earlier, and it was great fun.

He said, 'There'll be a few surprises there and people that you haven't seen for quite a while, and then afterwards there's a great party. That's all. You'll enjoy it.'

When I thought about it, I relaxed a bit and realised that it was going to be OK. As it was, there were surprises all the way through – school teachers, old friends and family friends were there, many of whom I hadn't seen for years and years. My mate from Canada came over which was great, and afterwards we all mingled together and had a party. I don't know what the people at the BBC thought, though, because – whether it was the rugby boys or my family, I'm not sure – we drank the bar dry three times!

CHAPTER SEVENTEEN

Lions in Australia

I am of the strong belief that while a Lions tour is in progress, what is happening on it should stay a closely guarded secret. It might be an old-fashioned view, but when you are part of a close group you should respect team members enough not to speak out, and – most importantly – what goes on tour, stays on tour. Matt Dawson and Austin Healey were wrong to have written what they did during the 2001 Lions tour and they know it. Having said that, Matt apologized to everyone over his column and it was immediately forgotten about. The players accepted his apology and he was as much part of the team after the article as he had been beforehand. There was no problem at all within the team.

I think most people accept now that it was not the content of Matt's article, but the timing of it that was wrong. He shouldn't have written it while the tour was still going on and he shouldn't have allowed it to be published on the day of the first Test – that was the mistake he made.

On the positive side, he was honest, and he highlighted in his piece that this was not a perfect tour. I agree with him – it wasn't. But many of the problems had nothing to do with the personnel in Australia. Graham Henry and Donal Lenihan have come in for considerable criticism – some of which is valid, but much of which isn't. Problems like the length of the tour (the shortest ever) and the fact, therefore, that we were trying to pack too much training into too little time, were not the fault of Graham and Donal.

I think the only criticisms that I have fall into two areas: pre-selection and communication. Pre-selection was a big issue because we all felt, throughout the tour, that the Test team had been selected before we had even left Britain and, no matter what you did, you would not get into it if they hadn't mentally picked you. This had a real downside to it because it meant there were several players on the tour, myself included, who felt that, whatever they did, they would never be first choice in their position. I found this difficult because I honestly don't believe that any of the props had a fantastic trip – we were all about equal. I do not query at all the selections that were made, but I know that some players were never made to feel as if they had a real chance of getting into the Test team – I think the management had made their decision and that was that.

This feeling of pointlessness was compounded by the fact that midweek games were played on Tuesday. By the time we had travelled to the destination of the midweek game on Sunday, after the Saturday match, there was time for just one quick training session on Monday before we played on Tuesday. This, obviously, made it even more difficult to pull off a team performance that was good enough to challenge the pre-conceptions of the selectors.

My other main criticism of the tour was communication which manifested itself in several ways. Most poignantly for me was watching the lack of man management when players were told they had been dropped from the side, or were not required. I will come to the details later. The other aspect of communication was the inability of the management to tell us precisely and accurately what they were planning for us. Every training session that was due to be an hour and a half long would end up being two and a half hours, and we never had rest days despite being promised them. I can remember now as we all sat round and Graham Henry announced that the next day would be free. We all looked at each other and smirked because we knew that a note would be pushed through our doors the next morning saying 'Team meeting at 3 p.m., line-out practice at 4 p.m.' or whatever. It was not that these were very strenuous sessions, but that not having a rest day when we could have taken a complete break is a mistake. You need to be able to go off, play golf, have lunch and just get away from things, or you start to become stale, fed up and all toured-out. To be told that you have a day off, so that you make plans, then to be told that you can't have it after all is annoying. When it happens throughout the tour it leads to resentment – which is exactly what happened, and why players spoke out.

The 2001 Lions tour started like they all do – with speculation in the media about who would be selected, who would be captain and which famous names would be missed off the list. Various journalists rang me to ask me what I thought, since I'm friendly with both Keith Wood and Martin Johnson – the two guys who were leading captaincy contenders before the tour, but I had no idea who was in the team, let alone who was destined to lead it. I said I thought that either of them would be good, but that I had not heard even a whisper about who was going to get the nod. This was quite different from previous years when I had always been able to coax information out of selectors in advance. The reason for the change in 2001 was simple – the management were desperate for information about the team not to be leaked to the press in advance of the formal announcement, so it was decided that we would all be told at the last minute, and that no advance hints would be dropped. In the end, I heard via a letter which was delivered at home in St Margaret's as the announcement was being made to the media.

Every time you are invited to play for the Lions it is an honour that is almost too great to describe. The first time I was selected, in 1993, it was wonderful because it was the first time – always special. When I was selected again, to go to South Africa in 1997, it was wonderful because we would be facing the world champions back in the country that we had visited two years previously for the World Cup. In 2001 it was special because it was my hat-trick. The Lions only tour to three countries and my selection meant that I have now toured all three in succession – this time against the reigning world champions.

It is odd but, despite the fact that a Lions tour is one of the most romantic and highly respected trips in the whole of sport, the letter inviting you to take part in it reflects none of this – it is quite formal and deals with all the contractual and practical issues that need to be sorted out before a professional tour can proceed.

There is much to do before you can leave on tour –

various dinners and profile-raising events to attend as well as the traditional kit fitting and visa organization. One of the great delights of going away on the sponsored tours is all the kit you get. At Tilney Hall – the place we went to for our pre-tour team-building – we were handed more shirts, shorts and track-suits than we could ever possibly need. It was when we were given the gear that you could first tell who was new to touring and who was experienced – those of us who had been on a few Lions tours before knew that taking piles of shirts away was a huge mistake. It may seem a good idea to take whatever you're given, but you have to carry everything you take. Considering that the Lions itinerary involved us flitting backwards and forwards across Australia and jumping onto aeroplanes every few days, I knew it would be a case of: the lighter the bag, the happier the man. I saw some of the new guys – like Simon Taylor – jumping at the chance to get their full quota of gear as they jammed their bags full of the stuff, whereas I just took about half what I was offered, and smiled knowingly as they trundled out with about six bags of gear in addition to what they had brought from home. I had turned up at Tilney Hall with nothing but a toothbrush and at the end of the day managed to head for Australia with just two bags. Neil Back had five when he started, but he soon realized his mistake and started shedding shirts as he travelled round the country!

The events at Tilney were run by Impact, the same company that had organized events prior to the 1997 tour. It was, essentially, a big team-building exercise with us split into small groups and given various challenges, like trying to get across planks of wood while blindfolded. It was about building up trust and developing friendship with players that you had only ever played against in the past. In my group were Andy Robinson, Rob Henderson, Rob Howley, Dafyd James, Neil Back, Will Greenwood and Colin Charvis.

The day that I can remember most clearly was a climbing day, when we all had to swing around on ropes and climb up the walls. We were 20–30ft off the floor, and although we were supported by pulleys and safety harnesses, it was quite scary. Will Greenwood and Rob Henderson had particular problems with this because to say they were scared of heights would be an understatement – they were terrified! We had to pull together and look after them, yelling encouragement and offering all the support we could to get them through the living nightmare. It was completely the opposite with Neil Back, who is totally fearless – he wanted to be the first to do everything. Nothing at all seemed to faze him.

It is the process of learning these small things about the guys that you will be working with for six weeks that make these team-building sessions special. You learn about the individual characteristics of your teammates while building team spirit and trying to have a laugh in the face of adversity. It may not be relevant that Will Greenwood (nickname Shaggy because he looks like the Scooby Doo cartoon character) hates heights, but it is relevant that we were all able to pull round and work as a team to get him through.

Obviously, we were doing all this in between sessions of heavy rugby training so by the time we got on the plane to Australia, some of the players were already feeling exhausted. I think, though, that those early training sessions were crucial because we had to break down the national characteristics and the relationships that had been built before the tour. Just because something always works with the England pack doesn't necessarily mean it's going to work with the Lions. We had to start again and look at the strengths of the individuals and at what sort of game we were going to play. I think, for these reasons, that we could have done with longer in the pre-tour phase to get our rugby and our team-building right. In fact, if the tour had been the nine weeks that it usually is (one week before going, then an eight-week tour) all the criticisms of the tour would not have been expressed, because we would have had more time to train and some spare time to relax. I would advocate that for future Lions tours there should be more time together as a group before leaving so that there is no panic during the actual tour. A couple of weeks in camp before a six-week tour (with the possibility of families coming to visit you in camp) would enable you to gel as a group before leaving.

In the time at Tilney Hall, before leaving, we also worked on a few playing options because the problem with going on tour to another country and playing solidly for weeks, is that by the time the Tests come along, everyone has seen what sort of rugby you're playing. We knew that we needed to have several options and variations in our armoury before leaving.

Our first stop was Perth, where we played Western Australia. It was an ambitious team, full of players from amateur clubs looking to be spotted and picked up by Super 12 sides – it was a good opening fixture that gave us a much-needed practice without worrying about losing. I think, with the exception of the Tests, the first game of a tour is the most important one. If you arrive on the other side of the world and lose your first game, it affects everything – you've got a huge mountain to climb because confidence goes and team morale starts to dissipate. That's why tour organizers insist on a gentle introduction to the tour. Our 116–10 victory over Western Australia was a nice boost.

Next it was on to two games in Queensland, against the Queensland Reds, but first against the Queensland President's team. This was a harder game because many of the players were in Super 12 squads, but were not regular first team players. It was harder for us in the first half because we simply tried too hard. Buoyed by the great win the week before, we tried to play too much rugby – most of it in our own half! At half-time, Robbo just said gently, 'Get it in their half, then start playing.' It seemed to do the trick.

People are always fascinated about what goes on at half-time in the changing rooms, especially when players come out and have a blinding second half. The truth is that there's not much time for very much to happen. By the time you've had a drink, re-bandaged or re-taped anything that hurts, had any niggling injuries seen to, put some ice on your sore bits, had a bite to eat and possibly gone to the loo, your ten minutes are practically up. Coaches never say anything magical or inspiring at half-time – it's not a team talk, but the best coaches are able to put to you succinctly and quickly what you are doing wrong and how to put it right. Sometimes when you're on the pitch, focusing on your own game, you can't see the bigger picture. As a forward, you often can't work out why you're not scoring when you seem to be getting so much ball. A little word from an insightful coach can go a long way to explaining what's going wrong, and help you put it right.

Andy Robinson is exceptionally good at this. He can assess the first 40 minutes and pinpoint exactly where the problems are. It worked in this game – the Lions put 50 points on the board in the second half and pulled off another convincing win (83–6). I was on the bench for this game and for the next one against Queensland Reds which the Lions won 42–8.

We were all training exceptionally hard at this stage – sometimes three times a day. It was also becoming clear by this time that Donal and Graham had a clear idea of who was going to be in the Test team, and who wasn't. I felt that being on the bench for the early games of the tour didn't help my cause, and whilst this didn't stop me training as hard as I could, it didn't make it any easier. Everyone's competitive and everyone wants to play in the Tests. If you feel quite categorically that you aren't going to play in the Test team, it doesn't make the three-times-a-day training sessions very easy to bear.

The players were represented on the tour by the Senior Players' Committee which was originally designed to include one player from each country, plus Martin Johnson, the captain. Lawrence Dallaglio, Dai Young, Keith Wood and Rob Howley were the chosen ones because the Scottish lads were a bit shy and didn't fancy being on the committee. The purpose of the committee wasn't all negative – they weren't there just to complain to the management, their role being to make sure that the players' interests and views were expressed. When the committee complained about all the hard work we were doing, the management responded that they needed to get hard training in for the first few weeks, but that there would be less of it as the Tests drew near. To be fair to them, that is exactly what they did, although the mammoth training routine continued until just before the Tests, including doing a two-hour run on Fridays – the day before playing.

By the time the fourth game of the tour came round, I still had not started, which I found difficult, and so it was a huge relief to hear that I'd been selected to play in the next game, against Australia A – our biggest match outside the Tests.

Hot and sweaty – England training at Bisham Abbey in 1996.

On the charge – I show the astonished All Black cover defence
a clean pair of heels in 1993.

As good as it gets – Ieuan Evans and I are mobbed by delighted fans
after our victory over New Zealand in 1993.

Spreading the word in the townships – I love the chance to share the joys of rugby with youngsters, but unfortunately, shorter professional tours often prevent it.

Gotcha! . . . Argentina's Jose Santa Maria is stopped in his tracks by me and the lads in 1995.

Now watch this carefully, lads . . . Johnno and I explain the finer points of the game.

He went thata way – you-know-who leaves Tony Underwood stranded as he heads for the try line.

Poised and ready for action against Argentina in 1996.

A great honour – captaining England against Argentina in 1996. I also captained the Lions in South Africa in 1997.

Such grace and balance – I could have been mistaken for Jerry Guscott.

It's just all work and no play on these modern tours – me in South Africa in 1997.

Talking tactics – Geech and I
find a nice spot in Umhlanga
Rocks to talk tactics on the
1997 Lions tour.

Leader of the pack – Johnno and
Lawrence listen attentively as I
try to sound impressive!

The greatest feeling in
the world – winning
the Lions series 2–1
in 1997.

On the charge – Lawrence, Phil Vickery and I against New Zealand in our first game of the 1999 World Cup.

Keeping my head above water – army training before the 1999 World Cup.

The end of our hopes – Matt Dawson gets the ball away in the 1999 World Cup. South Africa went on to win this match 21–44 and knock us out of the tournament.

On our way to a 46–12 victory over Wales in 2000.

Another Scottish win – ten years after they beat us at Murrayfield for the 1990 Grand Slam, Scotland do it again in 2000.

How many Aussies does it take to stop Jonny Wilkinson on his way to the try line in the first Test on the 2001 Lions tour.

It was a difficult tour, but an enjoyable one with people like Rob Henderson. Here we celebrate victory in the first Test.

Jack burning off some
energy in Richmond Park.
It was taken just before I
left for the World Cup.

The World Cup final – 22nd November 2003.
The greatest moment of my rugby career.

Simply Stunning. We
were overwhelmed by
the thousands of people
who turned up in
London to celebrate our
World Cup victory.

Once more unto the breach. England play their first
Six Nations game since the World Cup, beating Italy
in Rome in February 2004.

This was the first I saw of Francesca.
She was born on 27 October 2003,
while I was in Australia.

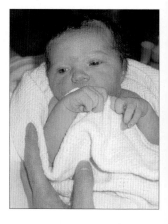

I hoped that it would offer me the chance to shine and contend for a place in the Test team.

The training after the Queensland game was done in two groups, with those who'd played against Queensland allowed to rest a little and just do some personal fitness, while those of us selected tried to get ourselves sorted. Since the game against Australia A was to be played on a Tuesday, we only had the Monday to really prepare for it because Sunday was a travelling day. The Monday was spent ironing out any difficulties – running through all the moves and all the links between forwards and backs. We made sure that everyone understood the various line-out calls and that the forwards were working well together, then we relaxed and just talked things through.

The day of the Australia A game was very difficult because it was an evening kick-off, so we had the whole day to get through, knowing that we couldn't do anything too strenuous, or stray too far from the hotel.

By the time 7 p.m. came, we were all raring to go, and I think that might have hindered us a little bit. I feel, looking back on the game, that we might have tried too hard because so many of us were hoping to put ourselves in the running for Test spots. We turned over far too much ball in the match and gave away far too many penalties around the tackle area. All in all, our weaknesses were enough to lumber us with our first defeat of the tour – a horrible experience, even if it was by just three points (25–28).

I know that after every defeat, the losing side is looking for someone to blame, but I genuinely feel that we weren't helped by the referee in this match. Indeed, I have to say that we didn't get a decent referee throughout the tour. The essential problem is the age-old one of the differences between the southern hemisphere's interpretation of the laws and the way we view those laws in the northern hemisphere. You would really have thought that professionalism would have brought an end to such differences – with referees encouraged to take a uniform approach to the laws. It is a global game now, after all. But there are still differences and we definitely suffered on the tour because of them. The main ones are in the scrum and in the tackle – the areas that we fell down on in the Australia A game.

In the northern hemisphere we're far more competitive in the scrums, and we start pushing straight away, whereas in the southern hemisphere referees like the pack to wait until the ball comes down the tunnel before pushing (which makes it almost uncontested as far as I can see). In the tackle, there has been a real turnaround. In the past, southern hemisphere referees insisted that players should always stay on their feet. Now, they seem to think its acceptable for a player to secure the ball on the floor, whereas northern hemisphere players get straight to their feet because our referees are less tolerant. The whole thing took some getting used to on tour because hitherto it was the other way round, and southern hemisphere referees had been the strict disciplinarians.

The defeat took some getting used to. The first game lost on tour is always a shock. It reminds you that you're miles from home, with limited resources, one game's gone wrong and they're getting harder all the time. It also gets you thinking about the tour more generally and about people at home. I had never been on a Lions tour before with children back at home and Sandra having to cope with them on her own. Jack was just a few months old and I knew that Harry was old enough to miss me, and to be asking Sandra when I was coming back.

NTL, the tour sponsors, organized a video link-up with Harlequins, so that Sandra and the kids could go down there, I could see them on the screen and they could see me. Sandra said that Harry thought the whole thing was amazing – every time he saw me playing on television after that, he couldn't work out why I wasn't talking to him like I had on the TV at Harlequins.

As we prepared to face our final two games before the first Test – against New South Wales Waratahs and New South Wales Country – we were determined not to lose again. Losing in a Lions shirt hurts – more than losing in any other shirt. We wanted to put things right. I was a water boy for the Waratahs game so my contribution was limited to rehydrating the guys, but it must have done some good because we won 41–24 to put us back on track!

Then disaster struck. First, on the Sunday after the game, some of the guys went out on a boat to go whale watching, and on the way back they dived into the water to cool off and swam to shore. With them was Anton Toia, working with the team as baggage man and one of the most important men on tour. Everyone wonders what baggage men do – well, they just sort out all your problems! Whether we needed new boots, a stud or a tie, Anton would be there, getting whatever was required and sorting out anything that was causing trouble. He was also the man who made sure all the training equipment we wanted was available – from balls to scrummage machines, cones and pads.

The first I knew there was a problem was when I couldn't find James Robson, the team doctor, anywhere. I had wanted to have a chat with him and stood around the reception area of the hotel for ages, waiting. Eventually, I was told that he had been seen running off towards the beach where Anton was in trouble. I learned later that Anton died from a massive heart attack which happened while he was swimming back from the boat.

It was extremely hard for everyone to focus on something as meaningless as a rugby match after the incident, so the evening meeting was called off. I heard that I'd been selected to play against NSW Country, the game before the first Test, so I knew I had to be impressive. But even as I heard the good news, it seemed rather overshadowed by what had happened on the beach earlier in the day.

Following the tragedy of Anton's death, there was more bad news, though not half as serious – Lawrence Dallaglio was injured and had to go home. He had been injured before leaving for the tour, but we all thought he'd be OK. Certainly the doctors had thought he would last the trip and be fine. But he wasn't and was told he could take no further part in the tour; he was to fly home after the first Test. The Lions won the final pre-Test game 46–3, but the match was marred for me by an accidental kick in the face which meant me leaving the pitch before the end.

The Test team was announced the very next day and I was extremely disappointed not to make the starting line-up, but at least I was on the bench which, in modern rugby, almost guarantees you some action. This is an area that has changed a great deal since my early days when it used to be very much a 15-man game, and no-one would leave the pitch unless they practically had a limb hanging off! These days it's a game for 22 players with regular technical and tactical substitutions made. We no longer think of the bench boys as replacements for injuries – they're there now to add a new dimension to the team as the match progresses. At least, that's what I tell myself every time I find myself on the bench!

There were some amusing moments on the tour when we got to Sydney, and a couple of daft ones. Among the daftest was the fact that we opted to do our final training session for line-outs on a patch of grass that we did not realize was overlooked by the Australian team hotel. We don't know whether any of them were watching, but if they had been they would have seen us run through every top secret move that we planned to do in the first Test.

It was at that session that I had to run through all the line-out calls and scrum signals that we had devised with Dorian West, a newcomer on the tour. Line-out calls are quite complex now – they determine not only where the ball's going to be thrown and how it's going to be caught or tapped, but also what is going to happen afterwards. Poor Dorian had much to learn, very quickly, knowing that he would have to put it into action in a noisy stadium under the pressure of the first Lions Test, if required.

Back at the hotel, there were some funny moments such as Jason Robinson being put into the same room as Rob Henderson. Clean-living, early-to-bed, early-to-rise Robinson was not at all interested in sharing a room with the all-night-television-watching, snoring Henderson, so he appealed to the management who moved Hendo out and into a room of his own.

It can be quite tricky on tour when players are rooming together. I was with Malcolm O'Kelly, who is the world's messiest man. It wasn't too much of a problem because I'm not the tidiest person myself, but I should think the hotel management must have had a fit when they saw the room after we'd been there. The tidiest people on tour were Neil Back and Colin Charvis who had their immaculate bags neatly packed and their rooms spotless. We were convinced that Backy cleaned up before the maids came round, and washed his glasses before sending them back to room service!

The team was at fever pitch before the first Test. The atmosphere was fantastic, there were red shirts everywhere in Brisbane and the Lions wanted to win. I did some light tackling with Rob Henderson before the game, to help him get warmed up, and he nearly cut me in two. He was so focused he was bouncing off walls. They all were.

If anyone needed any extra help, there was Willie John McBride's speech beforehand which was fantastic. He handed out the jerseys and you could see the emotion in his eyes when he recalled the great games he'd played for the Lions. As he looked round the room at all the players and wished us luck, you could tell that he'd give everything to turn the clock back and come out on the pitch with us. We all realized that day that we were part of something very special, with a great history. It was a moving speech from a very special player.

The noise in the stadium hit us all as soon as we walked out. It created a real buzz and I think everyone in that team knew we had to win. On the bench we kept leaping up and down and shouting so much that the fourth official had to come along and tell us to sit still. The victory seemed much simpler than any of us had anticipated – 29–13. We had scored over twice as many points as them and had dominated the game but despite this, the atmosphere in the changing room was subdued afterwards. This was just the first stage of a three-part battle and until we had two victories under our belts, there was nothing substantial to celebrate.

The Matt Dawson 'incident' was not nearly as dramatic an occurrence on the tour as it was in the papers at home. I managed to miss the bus back to the hotel after the match because I was chatting with my mates, and by the time I got back to the hotel all the press were eagerly talking about it. I didn't know anything about the column he'd written, so Paul Ackford, who writes for the *Sunday Telegraph* these days, filled me in on Saturday evening.

The fact is that Matt realized he had made a mistake, stood up in front of the group on Sunday and apologized unreservedly. The apology was accepted and it wasn't spoken about again. There was no residual anger or resentment. Matt had apologized and as far as we were concerned, the episode had passed.

Before the second Test, we played our final club match of the tour against ACT. This was significant for the fact that Matt kicked the winning conversion and we all mobbed him to show how pleased we were and how everything had been forgiven and forgotten. The match was also significant because it was where Justin Harrison and Austin Healey continued the war of words that had started in the Australia A game. It all began when Austin scored and Justin pointed out that the Lions were still losing. Austin said, 'That's just one try.' When Austin scored for a second time, he said, 'Oh, look. My second try,' whereupon Justin threw his scrum cap at Austin.

I was on the bench again for the second Test. It was disappointing not to be in the starting line-up once more but it is the team that matters, not individuals, so I quickly got down to helping the front row prepare. One of the fundamental changes that professionalism has brought has been the move from a player-centred approach to a team-centred approach to rugby. Today we realize that the most important thing is team victory.

The Lions had moved from being underdogs to favourites between the two Tests, so suddenly the pressure was on for the guys to repeat the standard they had reached in the first international. But Australia had woken up to the Lions. They realized how well they would have to play to win and had worked hard on cleaning up their game since the first Test. They looked weak again in the first half but by 60 minutes into the game, they were playing good Test rugby and were firmly in the driving seat. Their defence was great, they had stopped playing the fancy rugby that had lost them the first Test and worked on slowly building their score. The result was a 35–14 victory for them, meaning that we went into the third Test at 1–1, providing all our fans with a winner takes all finale to the tour.

I found myself off the bench and out of the team altogether for the third Test. This was a huge disappointment, not only because I was dropped, but because of the manner in which I was told – just five minutes before the team was announced to everyone else. The lack of man management that I spoke of earlier had reared its ugly head.

On the morning of the team announcement, I had breakfast with Graham Henry and he said nothing to me about what was going to happen, chatting to me casually while knowing that in an hour he would be announcing that I was completely dropped – yet saw no reason to tell me. It was when I was going back up to my room, just before the formal team announcement, that Robbo came up to me and told me I was out. I was grateful to him for telling me face to face and being honest about it – it's the bitterest pill you have to swallow. I just wish I'd had more time to get my head round it.

Once the team was been announced, I congratulated the

selected players, wished them well and I meant it. I would swallow my pride and do everything I could to help the team win. That's what the sport's about – no player is bigger than the team and I wanted those guys to go out and win as much as I wanted to play myself. I would give them every encouragement possible.

Before the third Test we went out for a big squad meal in Sydney to a Ribs'n'Rumps restaurant – it was the social event of the tour, the one time that we all got together and had a great night. We had had a night out in Perth, at a Chinese restaurant, but the food took so long to arrive that half of the guys ended up going out for McDonald's while they waited! Luckily, at Ribs'n'Rumps you didn't need anything else to sustain you – it was a restaurant for big meat eaters. I headed for Robbo as soon as we walked into the restaurant because he's a vegetarian, so I figured on having his share. In the end I found myself next to Phil Vickery who is about as far from vegetarianism as it's possible to be. We sat there eating huge chickens and lumps of meat with our hands. Proper food – lovely.

The third Test was a bitter disappointment. Watching from the stands was frustrating and seeing the guys lose after everything that had happened was awful. I was almost in tears as I walked on to the pitch to shake hands with them after they had lost 23–29. There were only six points in it – one converted try and the whole six-week tour would have looked totally different. It's amazing how a long tour can come down to just a narrow margin of victory like that.

I heard later about Austin Healey's article in the *Guardian*, in which he'd been rude about Justin Harrison – calling him an ape – and also about Australia and Australian men. As I said before, he shouldn't have written it but I think it's a mistake to think that it motivated the Australians – they were motivated regardless of what he had to say. To think that Australia were provoked by Austin's words is to seriously underestimate the psyche of the Australians – their motivation comes from within.

Once the tour finished, there was a great deal of talk about the management of it, and the way in which the players had related to Graham Henry – the first foreign coach. I don't think there were too many problems about him being a New Zealander. The only slight criticism might be that he didn't understand anything about the ethos of a Lions tour. The fact that we played rugby, rugby, rugby all the time had a lot to do with the fact that this was the shortest Lions tour ever, but it was also because Graham treated it like any other tour, and had us playing and training all the time. In this respect, it was totally unlike previous Lions tours I have been on, and I think that was a shame.

To have the honour of touring to all three southern hemisphere countries as a Lion is fabulous – the greatest honour in the game. In two of them, I saw the country, met the people and was able to put something back into their rugby to thank them for their hospitality. In one country, Australia, I didn't, and whichever way you look at it – professional sport or not – that is a real shame.

CHAPTER EIGHTEEN

The Triple Grand Slam . . . Not!

Three times it has happened. Three times! How can any team get to within a match of winning the Grand Slam on three successive occasions, then lose everything in the final game, each time? After losing to Wales at Wembley in 1999 in the final game of the last ever Five Nations, we were sure that we weren't going to let the same thing happen in 2000 in the first Six Nations tournament. The last game was against Scotland, on a cold, wet and windy day at Murrayfield. This was a victory that we desperately wanted and one which the whole world appeared to believe that we would get. But it was not to be. Scotland won and we were forced to fly home as Six Nations champions, but without the big prize once again.

Surely, surely, the same couldn't happen in 2001. After the experiences of Wembley and Murrayfield, we were a wiser outfit. The players had learnt how games can be lost, and they'd been reminded how painful that can be. In 2001, the same thing would not happen.

Of course, in the end – for a number of reasons, including Ireland's ferocious attacking play – it did. Having played some special rugby early in the competition, in which we'd scored over 40 points in every outing, we found the six-month break enforced by foot-and-mouth disease to be too much. We were slow, disorganized and full of mistakes in Dublin, whereas Ireland, keen to become the third Celtic team in succession to floor us, were vibrant and committed.

There were numerous post-mortems after the game as rugby fans and press alike tried to work out what had gone wrong. Some thought the England team was too complacent – expecting to win the match without any trouble – but that simply isn't true.

We rated the Ireland team highly, especially after their victory over Wales the week before. We knew how much passion we would encounter and we felt well prepared as we went to Dublin to play them.

There were those who said that the England side was not 'tough' enough to win in high-pressure situations, and people said that we lost because the England players were in a comfort zone and didn't feel the need to push themselves. I didn't believe that was true.

When you're a professional player, devoting your life to perfecting your game, you are more likely, not less, to feel the need to win than someone who is just playing for enjoyment. And there is no question that the players are in a comfort zone. We all know that there is a squad of players queueing up behind us to take our places. I know that there are good, young props coming up behind me all the time, and that I need to continually prove myself to keep my place.

There was no question of England sitting back and not giving everything in Dublin. I think the players who had lost in 1999 and 2000 were desperate to succeed, as desperate as any England player has ever been – professional or amateur. They don't take to losing easily, and they were all devastated to miss out on the Grand Slam. As for those of us for whom it was the third time we had missed out – it was particularly hard to bear, but all credit must be given to the Irish. By the end of the 2001 campaign, England had won every Six Nations tournament ever played, but they had never won a Six Nations Grand Slam.

Six nations – England, Scotland, Wales, Ireland, France and Italy – competed in the annual competition in the first tournament of the millennium in 2000. Much was made of the fact that Italy was joining the competition and to the outside world, the changing of the Five Nations to the Six Nations seemed to be a big deal, a much bigger deal than it ever was to the players. We thought it was great that there would be a Rome leg to our international trips, and we thought that the Italy team was up to it – despite their poor showing in the 1999 World Cup and despite what many in the press appeared to think of them. They had got themselves a new coach, Brad Johnstone, the former All Blacks player and Fiji coach. We knew that he would be demanding of the Italians, get them fit and get them organized. There were good players in the Italy team – if they could be sorted out properly, they would be a competitive side.

There was also no truth in the speculation that Italy were an entirely unknown quantity for us. We had played quite a few times against them and they had tended to be hard games, so we didn't expect them to be a walkover, or a 'banker'. We had also seen Italy play some close contests against some of the biggest sides in the world. Indeed, eighteen months before they joined the Six Nations, they beat France, when France were Five Nations champions.

I never thought that Italy would be the pushover everyone claimed they would be, and I don't think any other players did – a view that was borne out when they beat Scotland in their first game. The crowd in Rome went mad and Italy had officially joined the party.

Having another foreign-speaking team in the Six Nations served to remind us all how much more competent and civilized the other European nations are when it comes to speaking other languages! The French can normally speak English and some Italian, all the Italians can speak English and most of them a bit of French, but most of the England team speak nothing but English and most of the time, pretty bad English!

If the Italians and French did not continue to make the effort they do, then communications would grind to a standstill. Luckily, unless they lose badly (when suddenly, it's 'non parlez Anglais, non parlez Anglais'!), their English is very good, and they are happy to stand at the bar and do their best to join in with the banter. Since many of the French players now play for Premiership teams, their language skills have improved even more, and I find I chat away to the French guys without even thinking that I'm not speaking to them in their first language.

The relationship between the teams in the Six Nations is very good, whereas in the past, there was more friction between the sides when they came together for the annual tournament – not so much with the players as with the fans who only saw the rival team once a year. But the Heineken

European Cup and the movement of players from club to club throughout the world, has led to fans of all sides knowing more about the players representing different countries. This has meant less bitterness and direct hostility when the national sides play one another.

One of the interesting things about having played rugby for so long, and through such an interesting period, is that you can see how much things have changed. Years ago, at an England v Wales game, everyone used to keep away from each other because we felt we had little in common. We'd only see each other once a year so there was never enough time for a proper relationship to develop. Now we play against each other all the time. I have played alongside Welsh, Scottish and Irish players at Harlequins, as well as countless Australians and New Zealanders. For example, Keith Wood, the Ireland hooker, was a close club mate of mine and I saw him all the time. I feel I have as much in common with the other professional players from Six Nations sides as I do with my mates in the England team, so there is no question of us not socializing after the games.

Indeed, it is only the minority of fans that let everyone else down now. The Wales players are very sociable and friendly, whereas the fans still harbour some of the resentment that used to exist between the two countries. In the Wales/England game at Wembley in 1999 a few of the Welsh supporters were spitting at the girlfriends of the England players. Natalie, Matt Dawson's girlfriend, was spat at when she turned her back to walk out of the stadium. I'm not sure where this attitude comes from, because the players don't act like that. I know for a fact that if I had been standing with Scott or Craig Quinnell when something like that happened, they would have throttled the blokes concerned.

In the Six Nations of 2000, our first match was against Ireland, and we got off to a cracking start, moving 40 points away from the visitors before they had a chance to claw their way back into the game. We beat them 50-18 in the end. It was a particularly good game for me, not only because England won convincingly, but because I managed to keep up a favourite personal record of mine – of knocking Keith Wood unconscious whenever I play him at Twickenham. For the second time, I knocked him spark out in that game. He got straight up and carried on, but he knew perfectly well who was behind it!

The year previously, I had suffered against Ireland, at the hands of the Ireland pack (no doubt led by Woody). We were playing at Lansdowne Road and they absolutely kicked the shit out of me. I left the pitch somewhat dazed, battered and bruised afterwards, and – to be fair to Paddy Johns – he came up and apologized, much to the amusement of Woody who had relished every crunch and every smack. Being an absolute gentleman, Paddy Johns came up to me in the bar and offered his sincere apologies. I told him not to worry, saying I was on the wrong side, and shouldn't have been there anyway. While Paddy was saying sorry, Keith was standing beside him, saying, 'It's all right, Paddy. You don't have to apologize. It's really all right, Paddy.'

'No, I want to apologize to Jason,' Paddy kept repeating. 'I want to apologize. I feel bad. I just want Jason to know there's no ill feeling meant.'

Woody was right – there was no need to apologize, and there was certainly no sense of ill feeling after the match, but how nice of Paddy to make that effort and feel the need to talk to me. He is known the world over as a cracking, hard rugby player and an absolute gentleman. It's not hard to see why.

After our victory at Twickenham, we moved on to Paris for a match in which we held off France, in the dying moments of the game, to win 15–9. We had players sin-binned for the last ten minutes, while the French made charge after charge at our line, determined to exploit our lack of numbers. Even though we were exhausted, we kept them at bay. There was a great picture in one of the papers in which the entire pack was lined up, American football-style, all on three pins, just ready to dive at anything which came near the line. There was no way that a ball was going over that line – we would defend it with everything we had. We won that game because of our defence and tackling. There was one particular tackle that I will always remember – Jonny Wilkinson felling Emile Ntamack. Jonny was inches shorter but he went at the Frenchman like a bullock and sent him powering backwards. That sent a warning out to the French. We were prepared to play a hard, physical game – not just in the forwards. They would have to put up with us knocking them down all over the park.

After two victories, much was expected of England in their next game, against Wales at Twickenham. Before the match, there was much talk about the fitness of the Wales players. Neil Back had said the Quinnells were fat, which led to much debate about their ability to match us on the field. Because of the insult from Backy, the papers speculated that we would be in for a needling, nasty game but, in the event, it was actually a very clean match and, in some ways, a bit of a damp squib. We beat them 46–12 in a game which started to show what England were capable of. We threw the ball around and people began to sit up and take notice.

We played the Italians in Rome for the first time, in a tiny stadium which was bursting with support. It was great to see how many England supporters had made the journey, frantically waving flags and singing. We won the match 59–12 and prepared for the final game, in Edinburgh, against Scotland.

We worked extremely hard before the game against the Scots. The England players wanted to win but, equally, we knew that Scotland wanted to stop us in our tracks just as they had done ten years previously. The 1990 match at Murrayfield had gone into Scottish folklore after they beat us in the Grand Slam showdown, so the prospect of repeating the feat a decade later appealed to them enormously.

We knew that Scotland would be up for it on the day, and we also knew how much they could raise their game when playing England. They play a good 15–20 per cent better against us, so we knew we needed to raise our game to beat them. There was no complacency, no sitting back and thinking that the win was ours. We worked hard and we trained for the match expecting a battle.

We spent a week in Scotland preparing for the game and I remember the Scots buttering us up in much the same way as the Irish did in Dublin a year later. They would say, 'Careful of our boys – don't hurt them. You're only going to stick fifty points on us, aren't you? You have to give us a chance.'

Whilst we all knew that they were trying to lure us into a false sense of security, I think that for some players, being continually told that you have practically won before you even walk onto the pitch can have a negative effect. For us this wasn't the case but you have to be aware that if you relax too much and take too much for granted, then it can be a terrible shock come 3 o'clock on a Saturday afternoon when the opposing team throws everything they've got at you.

I know that at Murrayfield, and the year previously at Wembley, some of the younger players were surprised by the ferocity of the games. The desire to beat the English is still very strong. Even though much of the bad blood that existed between Scotland and England, and Wales and England, has now gone, there is still a great desire, on the part of the Celtic nations, to beat England.

The Scotland team came out with great passion, desperately wanting to win and deny us the Grand Slam again – they beat us 19–13 in one of the most disappointing games I've played in. All credit goes to Scotland for the way they played and for winning the match, but I do think the bad weather played a part – the rain absolutely hammering onto the pitch. It's something I've never seen before in my life and it stopped us playing the game that we wanted to. It limited us. It shouldn't have, and we should have been able to play in any weather, but there's no doubt that it did limit us. I remember saying to Matt Dawson and Lawrence Dallaglio, 'It ain't working, let's just keep it tight, kick it into the corners.' We needed to adapt to the weather conditions because playing in conditions like that – with rain followed by sleet, then snow until we could actually see water settling on the pitch – we should have kicked the ball the furthest we could up to the other end of the pitch, let Scotland have it and then defend against them. It is easier to do that when the ball is like a bar of soap. I think the players got a big wake-up call that day. In an ideal world, you want to play textbook rugby. You want everything to be perfect. But, in reality, you can't always do that. Sometimes you have to play a very ugly game of rugby to win. I take nothing away from Scotland that day because I think they played the conditions right and their players played well. It was our match to lose, and we did just that.

Once the match was over, I stayed out on the pitch and applauded the Scotland players as they left. They had played well and it never occurred to me to do anything but clap them off the field. I was singled out, afterwards, for doing this, and praised for staying behind. As far as I am concerned, that is what you do in rugby. You have to put the disappointment of not winning to one side, to do the decent thing, because if you're not big enough to take losing on the chin, you don't deserve the plaudits when you win. I hope that, whatever disappointments might come my way in the sport, I will always be the guy on the pitch at the end, clapping the opposition. That sort of behaviour is extremely important to me.

After the match, we were all a little subdued at the official dinner. I felt like sneaking off early but, in the end, I went for a few beers with Mattie Stewart because – much like applauding the opposition – that is what rugby is about. We spent the evening talking about everything except the game. When people came up and tried to talk to Mattie about the match and how well he'd played, he just politely told them he wasn't talking about the match, he was having a drink with me. That was a decent thing to have done. However much I try to be decent and honourable in defeat, I didn't want to relive every second of the game with a dozen Scotsmen!

Although losing to Scotland and losing the Grand Slam were disappointing, there is a very professional edge to the England squad and the focus moved quickly to the tour to

South Africa that summer. Playing South Africa in South Africa is one of the big rugby challenges, and the England players were eager to notch up a victory over one of the world's biggest sides, to atone for the miserable defeat in the Edinburgh rain.

Just before the South Africa tour, the England management had a reshuffle when John Mitchell headed back to New Zealand. It was a great disappointment to lose Mitch, but he obviously made the right move because he went on to become the All Blacks coach. Mitch's greatest strength was his ability to get on well with all the players. He was a real players' coach and we were gutted to see the back of him. Mitch had a hard New Zealand edge to him that was a real attribute to the England side. He was a well-liked guy, hard nosed but fair. Once Mitch announced that he was leaving, Andy Robinson came in as coach and Clive Woodward's job title was changed to manager.

I was pleased that Andy moved in so quickly to take up the reins where Mitch left off. Someone of the calibre of Andy Robinson is always an asset to a team, and as a forward I was very pleased that he was coming on board. He'd obviously worked with Clive before as they were both coaches to the England Under-21 team and both at Bath, so there was none of the trouble that there had been with other coaching set-ups that I'd played under, where someone new comes in and a power struggle ensues. Robbo is quite a practical person. He said before the tour of South Africa that he didn't want to change everything that Mitch had done, but that he'd just tweak certain areas. Andy is no fool and knows the game well – a little bit like Mitch. He is also extremely competitive and doesn't like losing. He can be very serious, very intense, in the same way that Martin

Johnson is. You can look at Andy or Johnno and see the deep concentration and intensity etched on their faces. Andy's brain is on the go, constantly.

The South Africa trip was a two-Test tour. We lost the first 13–18, but won the second in a magnificent 27–22 victory that was one of the toughest matches I've ever played in. Looking back at that tour, we should have made a clean sweep of them – we only lost the first Test because of a debatable decision by the video referee.

Luckily, Andy and Clive both retained confidence in us going into the second game and, even though we had lost the first Test, they didn't dramatically change what we were doing. They both believed that the game we were playing was the right one to beat South Africa. The second Test was a vastly different game. We got the chances that we wanted, were able to create and our defence was good. We came away with a win in Bloemfontein where South Africa had lost only twice before.

After that game, we were all absolutely shattered. I think pure adrenalin carried us through for most of the game. I remember the humidity and the continual physical confrontation with the South Africans. After the match, some of us could barely speak as we slumped in the changing rooms trying to digest the fact that we'd beaten them.

After the tour, we returned to England to face Australia in November, and we beat them 22–19. But despite our successes, we still hadn't got a contract with the Rugby Football Union that we were happy with. We had tried to arrange to sit down and talk to them but they had been evasive and unhelpful, so after months of fraught debate with them, during which they refused to move one inch to accommodate us, we decided to go on strike.

It sounded a bit dramatic – to refuse to play for England, particularly since it is a great honour to be selected, and the pinnacle of a player's career. But whatever else the players are, they are also human beings, and they deserve to be treated with respect. Just because playing for England is an honour, it doesn't mean that you should be treated badly. It may be the greatest honour to play for your country, but it is also the way in which the RFU make a lot of money. We all knew how much was in the Union's coffers, so we were determined that we would make them negotiate with us and stop running the organization of the team like a dictatorship. In any dictatorship you're going to get rebellions, and that's exactly what happened – basically, the players said 'No'. They told the RFU that they would not accept the contract that was being offered and withdrew their labour until a compromise was reached. It was not about the money per se, but about establishing the players' rights. Throughout the conflict I felt very strongly that I was acting for the stream of players coming through the sport behind me. This is their future that we're taking about.

We sat down to discuss what to do, with Lawrence, Johnno and Matt leading the discussions. They were wrongly accused of being ringleaders when news broke of our plans to strike but that simply wasn't true. They were experienced players so they acted as the voice box and got things organized. In a group of twenty-odd, you can't all run the show or it would degenerate into an RFU meeting!

The three guys leading the debate made sure that every avenue was explained and explored before the option of striking was mentioned. There was a secret ballot where players handed in notes, little bits of paper with a yes or a no on, and every single one was a yes. We thrashed everything out in detail twice. It wasn't a rash decision – we knew exactly what we were doing. We were there for hours debating the likely consequences of our actions. Then, once we were all decided, we withdrew our services for the game at the weekend. It was particularly hard for me because the upcoming game against Argentina was the one in which I was going on to beat Rory Underwood's record and become the country's most capped player but, at the time, you don't think of yourself, you think only of the team as a whole.

The strike was not about me and my ability to break a record, it was about the young players in the squad who were working hard at the peak of their profession and had still not signed a contract. If we didn't act, the whole thing could have gone on for another five years.

In the end, the RFU agreed to negotiate with us and the strike was called off. We returned to the team hotel, resumed our preparations and I duly led England out to beat Argentina 19–0 and became the most capped player in the history of English rugby. The year culminated in a 25–17 victory over South Africa. It meant that we had twice defeated the team that had knocked us out of the World Cup. To beat South Africa twice in a row – home and away – is a phenomenal achievement and we all felt very proud. Suddenly our slip-up at Murrayfield felt like a lifetime away.

The 2001 Six Nations started extremely well, with a victory over Wales in Cardiff. As we beat them 44–15, with Will Greenwood scoring a hat-trick, I thought back to my first years as an international, when Cardiff was the place where the England team hated playing. Some of the younger players in the squad would never realize how difficult Wales were to beat back then. They would have laughed at the thought of us all listening endlessly to the Welsh national anthem in order to lessen the impact it would have on us on match day! How long ago that all seemed.

Italy travelled to Twickenham for our second match of the tournament and we beat them 80-23, before Scotland visited and gave us the chance to avenge the previous year's defeat, by beating them 43–3. Even France were no real match for England as we beat them 48–19 at Twickenham – it seemed that nothing could stop us rolling on to a Grand Slam finish to the tournament. Nothing, that is, except for a national epidemic.

When foot-and-mouth broke out and our game against Ireland looked to be in doubt because of the Irish Government's decision to restrict mass movement in and out of the country in order to reduce the chances of the disease spreading, there was no-one in the England team who thought of the disappointment of losing out on the chance to win the Grand Slam. Everyone understood that the plight of the farmers was far greater and more important than our own inability to play a rugby match. The game was rescheduled for October and the players' focus shifted to club games, and the fast-approaching Lions tour.

By the time the Ireland game came around again, the England team had not played together for over six months. This was, undoubtedly, a factor in explaining why we fell apart in Dublin, after we had looked so solid earlier in the year.

It's impossible to know exactly what it was that lost the game for us. Certainly, having Phil Vickery, Lawrence Dallaglio and Martin Johnson out did not help the forward effort and a few of us had a bad game, myself included. There were lots of errors in that match – enforced handling errors in the backs and problems in the line-outs for the forwards. The Irish capitalized on every chance they had, and while we fumbled the ball and lost possession, they were making ground and moving towards the try line. England also gave away too many penalties – far too many. We turned the ball over too much, lost possession and allowed Ireland to dictate play and they kept the scoreboard ticking over. It was all too much to expect to win from such a position and Ireland were worthy winners.

Luckily, modern rugby is fast moving and there are always new challenges around the corner. We knew, after the Ireland defeat, that games against Australia, Romania and South Africa were only a few weeks away, so there was no time to dwell on the loss. After that, there would be the Six Nations championships, a summer tour, then – the year after – a World Cup in Australia. There is always something new to move on to in rugby – a bigger prize and a new challenge. I have achieved much in this game, but there is still a great deal that I would like to do. Even when my playing days are over, I hope to remain closely attached to the sport that has enthralled me for most of my life. People ask, 'Do you see a future in coaching, or maybe a role in the media?' – who knows?

CHAPTER NINETEEN

Jason Leonard MBE (More Beer 'Ere)

I get a lot of post – invitations, requests and even some fan mail. It all arrives at Harlequins and I go in and sort through it every so often. I tend to read through the letters as quickly as possible and get the job done with all the speed I can, to enable me to get out on the training park without delay. So, there I was, perched on the edge of the desk with a pile of post, when I ripped open an envelope and stopped in my tracks.

'Would you consider being honoured?' the letter said. Honoured? Me? I read it again and the words were still there – a letter asking me whether I would accept an MBE if I were offered one in the Queen's Birthday Honours List. Um . . . yes, I thought. It took me about half a second to decide that I'd be extremely honoured and flattered to have such a prestigious award bestowed on me. I'd never dream of turning something like that down, but even if I wanted to, I never could – imagine what my Mum would say!

Discovering that I was to be appointed an MBE was a great surprise and a great honour. It was quite an emotional and humbling moment – to realize how highly thought of I was. I knew that I had to tell Mum straight away because she would be really thrilled and she was – she almost dropped the phone. She was saying how great it all was but, I have to admit, I just kept thinking that I wasn't worthy of it. I kept thinking of all the people who are helping charities and working with kids to give them a better life. I only play rugby – why was I being honoured?

Once I'd come to terms with the fact that I was getting the award, all sorts of practical questions ran through my head: could I take Harry and Jack with me to the Palace to collect the MBE? If so, could they actually come into the Palace with me? I knew that I desperately wanted them to be there for my big moment but, at the same time, I just had all these terrible images in my mind of Harry running off and climbing all over the expensive furniture, knocking over priceless antiques and having to be escorted out of the building. In the end, I decided to just stop worrying about the whole thing and enjoy it. Certainly, it was about time something enjoyable happened. We'd had an exhausting and frustrating year – England had failed to win the Grand Slam again, I'd found myself sitting on the bench for much of the international season and Harlequins had narrowly survived relegation.

The 2001/02 season had not started well, of course, because the Ireland game had been delayed and slotted into the new season. If we had won that Ireland game, it would have got the new season off to a great start but, in the end, it meant we began on a bit of a downer. For a start, there was a massive clear-out after the Ireland game as Clive sought to address the problems and try some new players in the side for the autumn internationals. I was relegated to the bench in the process, which was obviously upsetting but it certainly didn't kill my morale as people tend to think it does. When you're on the bench in modern rugby, there's a very good chance that you'll come on to the field and you always have to remember that while you're on the bench, you're in with a chance. You've been put on the bench because Clive wants you involved in the match in some way You just have to rise to the challenge – it simply makes you work that little bit harder to prove that you should be on the field.

The first international that autumn was against Australia – we approached it with a certain amount of trepidation, as we did all the autumn internationals after the defeat to Ireland, because we knew that we needed to get back into a winning habit. We were also aware that doing that against the world champions would be extremely difficult especially with the recent memory of the Lions tour over the summer. A lot of the England boys had played in the second and third Tests, which the Lions lost, and it was still at the front of their minds, so Australia represented something of a major challenge. They were on the sort of winning streak that we craved – as World Cup holders, Tri Nations champions and on the back of the Lions victory, they would desperately want another win.

I knew that because I was on the bench I would have to watch problems occurring without being able to do anything about them. I found myself trying to follow the game and work out what needed to be done with regard to my specific role so that, if I was called on, I would know how to put things right. Obviously, this was made difficult by the fact that I didn't know when, or if, I was going to be summoned. I just had to make sure I was alert, and mentally ready to go on the pitch the whole time. It was made doubly difficult in my position because I cover both sides of the scrum, and would only have about a minute's notice of which side of the scrum I have to cover when I come on.

England beat Australia 21–15, which was a tremendous experience, but after the match there was an air of relief more than anything else. There was no mad partying. We all knew that we were back in camp on the Monday and we had to beat Romania the following Saturday and then follow that with a victory over South Africa, or we'd have the newspapers telling us we were hopeless again.

For the Romania game, I was not only selected to play, I was also asked to lead the team on to the pitch to celebrate becoming the most capped forward of all time. It was my 93rd appearance in an England shirt. Sean Fitzpatrick, the great New Zealand captain, had worn the black shirt 92 times. I had a great reception from the crowd when I appeared on the pitch – it was powerful and emotional and really humbling, as 75,000 people stood up and cheered. It was quite breathtaking. I've always had a great reception from the Twickenham crowd but this was something else. The whole experience of getting the 93rd cap was very special. Fitzy had called me during the previous week to wish me luck and congratulate me on passing his record, which was nice of him. Fitzy is a guy whom I respect and like enormously and I was delighted that he took the trouble to call.

After the rousing reception, it was time to get on with the game. It was an unusual match because there was never any question that we would win – we just wanted to make sure that we played the best we could. The worry was that we would just relax because the pressure wasn't on, and not produce anything approaching a decent performance. It was also difficult because we were in a lose/lose situation – we were expected to win by 100 points or everyone would have said that we didn't have the killer touch. Yet, if we did win by 100 points, we knew everyone would say, 'What was the point in that?' In the end, of course, we won 134–0 and the reaction was just as we had predicted – everyone said it was a waste of time. For the players, though, it was far from a waste of time; the game was completely worthwhile because it allowed us to play against a team who were thrilled to run out at Twickenham and it continued our winning streak leading into the game against South Africa.

Afterwards, there was a brief reception at Twickenham, at which the Romanians went about trying to swap everything they possessed – they wanted to change not just shirts but socks, shorts, ties, jumpers – everything they could see. This didn't bother me at all; I happily handed over everything I had!

Once the Romanians had headed off home with their newly acquired stash, it was time to play South Africa. This was seen as a big test for England because we were thought of as a team that could not string wins together. We needed to prove that we could – and that we could do it against the best teams in the world. I was back on the bench for this game but watched with a big smile on my face, while England ran in a 29–9 win. It was only at this stage that the players decided they could socialize a little bit. We all went out for a few beers together and celebrated what had turned out to be an excellent three weeks' work. We had all been cooped up in camp for almost a month, so it was nice to forget about the rugby for an evening and hit the streets!

Even so, I'm afraid that when we went out, we found ourselves discussing the match for most of the evening, and analysing the way the three matches had gone. First, there had been the Australia match, which was a tight thriller – very closely contested – and a good win. The Romania game was a real try-fest with an incredible number of points per minute. It was the match in which all those of us who'd been on the bench for the Australia match tried to push the selectors as much as possible to pick us against South Africa. In the final game, we played a style of rugby that we were generally happy with. It was not as good as the Six Nations the year before, but it was certainly on the way there. We came out of the match with a lot of enthusiasm for the forthcoming Six Nations and the idea that if we pulled everything together then this, at last, might be the year in which we finally won the Six Nations Grand Slam.

While the situation with England was looking extremely positive, the same could not be said of Harlequins. John Kingston had come in as Head Coach of the club at the beginning of the season, which was great news; all the players knew him from his time at Richmond where he was highly thought of by such players as Ben Clarke, so we were all pleased that he was coming to Quins.

Unfortunately, we made a disappointing start, losing our first two games – to London Irish in the opening game, then to Bristol the week after. Since they were both home matches, this was a particularly disappointing start. We had no idea, at the time, how much worse things were going to get.

In the early part of the season – we were very up and down – our first victory was against Wasps, and we won our opening game in the Parker Pen Shield against Bridgend. We even beat Saracens but then we'd lose other games that we really should have won. We slipped down the table and players and management were beginning to worry. Our lowest point was between November and February – the period between the internationals, when we should have been able to play well with the full complement of internationals in the team Instead, we had at least half the team injured at any one time. By the time we lost to Northampton in February, it was our sixth successive defeat in the Zurich Premiership and our fifth league defeat at home. Just when we thought things couldn't get any worse, we lost to Bath the week afterwards and Gloucester the week after that. We were, by now, at the bottom of the table with eight straight defeats in the Premiership.

While we were struggling in the Premiership, we did OK in the Cup, reaching the semi-final, but losing to London Irish. What really mattered, though, was staying in the Premiership. If we'd gone down it would have been terrible for Harlequins – the club would have undergone substantial changes if we'd had to cope with the cuts in income and prestige resulting from life in the lower divisions. But it was proving difficult to win matches because the squad wasn't strong enough to cope when key players were out injured One reason for this is that if you have so many injuries at one time you are not able to field the same side on consecutive weekends so you can't achieve the continuity you need at this level. With injuries to leading guys like Keith Wood, Will Greenwood and Dan Luger, any team in the Premiership would struggle and we were no exception.

This period was extremely difficult for players, coaches and supporters. We were getting close to winning in some matches, then we'd lose by one or two points. The trouble is, losing is a habit. Your confidence gets lower if you keep losing, so you lose even more and players begin to lose their confidence. A player who would usually make that pass or kick doesn't make it because he's nervous about messing up. Suddenly, you're motivated by fear of failure rather than by trying to win; players stop being expansive and going for it and they close in and simply don't play good rugby. The only way to break the cycle is to start winning some games – a real catch-22.

Confidence was really low in the side and heads were down. A rut was developing and Mark Evans, the chief executive, sensed that he would have to do something fairly major to change the way everyone was feeling or the season would be over and Harlequins would be going down. Mark decided that he would take over coaching the side, as well as retaining his position as chief executive. John Kingston was made assistant coach while Mark moved to the helm to try to guide us through some fairly choppy waters. All that mattered now was notching up victories and squeezing any points we could out of games to ensure the team's survival in the top flight.

There were some significant moments when our luck changed and we started to move in the right direction to save the team from disaster. Beating Newcastle 33–19 in mid-March would go down as a major moment because we scored four tries and so won a bonus point, giving us a maximum five points. We were off the bottom of the table. At this stage we still hadn't won away from home all season.

Then, at the beginning of May, when we were beginning to panic, we pulled ourselves out of the relegation zone with a 40–16 victory over Leeds Tykes. It was a tough game, in which the loser faced relegation. We won it comfortably and the wave of relief we all felt was incredible. I never actually thought we'd go down – I thought we'd pull games out of the bag when we really had to, but it had been a worrying few months.

The hardest thing about our run of defeats was the awful atmosphere down at the club. Everyone – office staff, groundsmen, management and secretaries – they would all have been out of a job if we had gone down, and probably never work in a rugby club again. There was a great pressure on the players to win matches in order to keep the club together. It wasn't so bad for the players – they could easily play somewhere else, but the staff might be out of work for a long time, and all because we weren't playing well.

I wouldn't have chosen to leave the club if we'd gone down but, the question was, would they have been able to keep me on the payroll? Probably not. If you move out of the Premiership, the money you get from television, the RFU, sponsors and gate receipts is all reduced, so you can't afford to pay the top players and they leave. Without any top players, how can you hope to get back up into the Premiership again? It's very difficult.

After the Leeds game we moved out of the relegation zone, and then we finally knew that we couldn't go down. Later we heard that Rotherham were not going to be promoted from National League One because their ground didn't meet requirements, so no club was relegated from the Premiership. There was a lot of debate about how long the RFU had known that there was a problem with Rotherham. Did they already know that no team would go down while we were panicking about trying to win a match at all costs? Did the RFU keep it quiet in order to make the end of season fight for survival more exciting for fans? Everyone involved – from Quins, Leeds, Bath, Sarrics and Rotherham – had given it their best efforts at the end of a long, hard, season, so it was cruel not to have promotion and relegation after that.

The club it was cruellest to, of course, was Rotherham. I think that what happened to them was unforgivable – never mind the repercussions for us. The team – including players like Eric Peters whom I know well – worked extremely hard for promotion and they should not have been denied it on some technicality. I appreciate that rugby is a business as well as a sport, but you wouldn't wish what happened at Rotherham on your worst enemy. If it had happened to Harlequins, I'd have been furious.

While the battle for survival at Harlequins was going on, the 2002 Six Nations Championship began with a match against Scotland. Two years before, they had won – in the final match of the championship to deny us the Grand Slam – so we were determined that, on our first trip back to Murrayfield since that defeat, we would beat them. We were much more pragmatic this time than we had been in 2000. We simply hadn't looked at the conditions or attempted to take them into account before. This time, we did. We trained in open places where we were battered by the wind, and in the cold and wet all the time. We understood what was in store for us and we were properly prepared to deal with it.

When it came to the match, we didn't play the game we wanted to, attacking the wide channels and going in close with our forwards. We'd hoped to play a mix-and-match game so the opposition didn't know what was going on – I'm not sure we quite achieved this, but at least we won (3–29)! I was on for the last five minutes because Julian

White broke his nose. I was amazed to get a huge cheer when I came on to the pitch in Edinburgh. I later discovered that it was because apparently I was one of the few Englishmen to stay on the pitch two years ago and clap the Scots as they received their medals. Most of the other England players had walked off the pitch because it was freezing cold. It was very rewarding to get such a good reception.

Our first home game of the championship was against Ireland, and we desperately wanted to win this time, having lost to them at Lansdowne Road. The way we played in the first 50 minutes was definitely better than against Scotland, with much more attacking width and an attacking edge to the game. I came on when Graham Rowntree came off injured. The players and coaches were disappointed that England didn't play as well as they could have for the last 20–30 minutes; Ireland tried to make a good game of it, and came back into the action in the last quarter. We took our foot off the pedal for the simple reason that everyone was absolutely knackered! The result was an easy win – 45–11 – but not the performance that we had hoped for. After the match we felt both a joy at winning and a disappointment at our performance. But we still felt, at this stage, that the Six Nations Grand Slam could be ours this year.

The game against France is always billed as the game of the Six Nations, and this year was no exception. Indeed, people were joking that it was France's turn to beat us since Wales, Scotland and Ireland had done it in turn. Britain seemed to be divided into England fans and France fans as the Scots, Irish and Welsh backed the French to knock us over! Much has been made of the fact that England had lost one game each year – to each of the home nations sides in turn. To me, it just shows that you can't take winning for granted any more – not against anyone There's so much competition that games are getting closer and closer.

We prepared well for the game against France – we had a very good week and felt confident going into the match so there was nothing wrong about our preparation that could account for what happened. The simple truth is that France played well – they outplayed England as England had hoped to outplay France. They played us at our own game and beat us 20–15.

There was real confidence in that France side. England didn't perform well – not nearly as well as we had the year before – but all credit is due to France. The worst thing for me was that as well as losing to France we'd also shown that we'd gone backwards as a squad. We weren't as good as we had been the previous year and, as a team of players, you always want to believe that you're going forwards. You may lose occasionally or have blips on the way but, basically, you want to know that you're heading in the right direction.

There were lots of reasons for our loss of form but the main one was sheer exhaustion. It was the end of an awfully long season – the British Lions tour had taken up the previous summer and we'd rolled straight into a tough autumn international season, the delayed Ireland match and then straight into this Six Nations. Certain players looked jaded and tired. I knew I was one of them.

I knew the season was taking its toll. We didn't have the zip and snap we had the year before. There was an irony in the fact that while we were all tired and needed a break, we also needed more sessions together as a team.

But, how could any of us work any harder when we were already knackered? We couldn't neglect our duties to our clubs when they pay our salaries and need our week-in, week out support, so we were stuck. I knew that I had to give my all in club games because Harlequins were struggling so much, but it all added up to making me – and the rest of the boys – feel exhausted.

There have been many efforts to reduce the number of club games and allow the England squad to spend more time together. These have helped, but we're still not there. If England are to be truly successful, the players and coaches need more training sessions together. Against France we played like a team that hadn't played together for a while – that's no good when you're facing a professional outfit like the French, who were prepared to outplay us at our own game. They chose options well. They put us under huge pressure in set pieces – so our entire game was under siege. We were getting caught in the tackle – and spilling, turning or kicking the ball badly. You can't do that to France because they're a great side – they'll pick you off with space, find a gap, attack the channel and then they've got you. France 20; England 15.

The good thing about this England team is that we don't worry about the 'one game in a Six Nations lost every time' thing that seems to absorb everyone else. We are aware of every game that we play but we don't worry, like the press seems to, about the defeats – we worry about learning from them and trying to put things right. I can honestly say that we did learn from that defeat against France, as we do from all our defeats Certainly, by the time the game against Wales came round, we were steaming and raring to go.

Against Wales we were very keen to get back to winning. We'd had a good run until the France game and we wanted to get back on the winning road. It meant that there was an extra bite to training that week – feisty to say the least. Preparation was spot on and England were very dominant by the end of the game. We won 50–10 – we had reasserted ourselves completely.

It was at this time that Graham Henry left his job as Wales coach and Steve Hansen, his assistant, took over. I had obviously got to know Graham quite well on the Lions tour over the summer and I knew how much he enjoyed his role with Wales. But he'd had a string of defeats, so his position was considerably weakened. The Lions tour itself was a difficult time for him – he came under considerable criticism, some of it justified, some of it unfair. Then, when Wales did not come up to the mark, he was asked to leave.

It is never an easy occasion when a coach goes. Graham Henry liked coaching Wales; he loved all the characters in the set-up and had even got used to the pressure of being the Wales coach. On tour over the summer he had talked about his role with the national side with great affection. Steve Hansen, the man who stepped up to take on the main job, is something of a mystery – no one seems to know that much about him. But he worked with Graham Henry for a long time and has the support of the players, so I'm sure he'll be fine. I might regret saying this, but I hope they sort everything out in Wales and manage to get a good, strong team again.

The final game of the Six Nations was against Italy in Rome. By this stage, of course, we had nothing to play for except pride, but that was enough. Italy had given us quite a fright when we first played them at the stadium in Rome, two years before, and we wanted to make sure that we didn't end up losing to them on our second visit there – that would have ended the season on a complete downer. The strange thing about this match, for me, was that I was sitting on the bench with three other guys who have captained England at some time – me, Matt, Lawrence and Johnno – all four of us with faces like thunder because we were desperate to come on the pitch.

When we did come on to the pitch, the Italians must have wondered what had hit them. We played some good stuff and beat them comfortably – 9–45. Matt said, as we left our seats on the bench, 'Let's go out there and do the basics properly. Not many England players are hitting the rucks and mauls with real gusto – let's take 'em on.' Lawrence, Johnno and I, being forwards, thought it was a marvellous idea to hit rucks and mauls, so on we ran ready to belt anything that moved. The second we got on the pitch, Johnno charged the ball down and I barged in there: Johnno and I were in the thick of the ruck – exactly as planned. Where was Lawrence? Filing his nails? Combing his hair? No – worse. He was pretending to be a back, standing outside Wilko. He'd been on the pitch for less than five minutes and he was scoring.

'We're supposed to be hitting rucks,' I said to Lawrence, as he celebrated his try. 'Na, you guys were doing that,' he said, waving to the crowd – we couldn't believe it. In his first game back, he scores five minutes after getting on the pitch – jammy git.

The Six Nations as a whole was a disappointment for England. We had started so well with the autumn internationals that we had hoped to capitalize and notch up some great victories in the tournament. Parts of it went well and parts were average – certainly it was not as good as the year before. The main reason, as I've said before, was that it had been a long, hard, non-stop season and we hadn't spent enough of it being together as a group. This meant that we hadn't been able to play the type of game that had been so successful the year before. In all the games, there'd not been the zip and snap that had been there in the previous season – the atmosphere wasn't crackling as it had been before. You didn't get the sense that everyone was confident and up for it.

That can all be rectified and the process began in summer 2002 with most of the guys in the England team taking the summer off instead of travelling to Argentina. It's always risky to take time off because great new players can emerge in your place. The guys who toured to Argentina over the summer did well and several big-name players faced a battle to get their places back but, having said that, it's important to take breaks when you can get them, especially when the following year – 2003 – involves a tour to New Zealand and Australia and the rugby World Cup in Australia.

There is no more exciting challenge in rugby than the World Cup, and no greater test than a tour to New Zealand. As the season ended, I found myself looking forward to the future more than ever and reflecting on the season just gone with a smile on my face – whatever else may have happened we'd had a lot of funny moments along the way. The funniest? Without doubt, watching Austin Healey getting so much grief from both players and supporters for his advertising campaign with a hair loss company. If you've seen it, you'll know why!

CHAPTER TWENTY

The World Cup

These World Cups seem to come around quicker all the time. Or perhaps I'm just getting old! The build-up to the 2003 tournament began with the autumn internationals in 2002. We had back-to-back matches against New Zealand, Australia and South Africa – the three teams to have previously won the World Cup. Win those three and we'd know we were in good shape. If we lost, we had a year to sort ourselves out before meeting them again in Sydney 2003.

The three-match series began with New Zealand We'd had a good week leading up to the match. Everyone had been writing off Jonah Lomu and saying that he wouldn't make it into our side. I was never very sure about that – I'm all in favour of 6'6" wings. In the end, as if to prove the guys wrong, he went and scored two tries – a class player. I was on the bench for this game and watched as England hung-on for a hard-fought victory. Ben Kay snatched a line-out five metres from our line on a New Zealand throw. The final whistle came seconds later and we'd beaten them 31–28. England had shown dogged determination in a huge triumph.

The victory felt like the first of many tiny steps that we would make towards the World Cup. Even though it was a narrow victory – it was a victory all the same. We'd been under pressure and we'd kept cool and won the day.

I came back in for the game against Australia because Trevor Woodman was injured. Lawrence was dropped to the bench for the Australia game, a decision that I thought was harsh because even though we didn't play well against New Zealand, we still beat one of the best sides in the world. Although Grewcock was also dropped, it felt a little bit as if Lawrence was getting all the blame. It wasn't all his fault

In the end, it was quite funny because we were doing well, then Lawrence came on as a blood replacement. While he was on, Australia made something of a comeback and scored about 15 points. Some bloke in the crowd shouted, 'Oy, Dallaglio – we were fucking winning before you got on.' In the end, we did win – by one point. We beat Australia 32–31 to make it two victories in a row.

The third game was against South Africa – a team that had been through a lot of changes and came to us on the back of defeats in France and Scotland. Rudi Straeuli, the coach, needed his side to put in a very feisty performance against England to prove they had what it takes. To be fair to them, they did! Although probably not in the way that Straeuli would have wanted. I'm not one to complain about matches being too physical but there were a lot of things going on in the game that really have no place on a rugby pitch. There were fists flying, boots flying and real violence going on. Any parents watching who were considering sending their kids to rugby training might have thought twice after what they witnessed. During the game, I wasn't aware of how bad it was. It was only when I saw the match played back to me on video that I realized how bad it had been. The management showed us the video as a debrief because Clive had decided to highlight his concerns to the press. I was genuinely shocked when I saw the video. As a spectacle, the match wasn't up to much because South Africa played with 14 men for much of it after the early sending-off of Jannes Labuschagne. We beat them 53–3 – the biggest Test defeat in South Africa's history. Another win. Three out of three.

Afterwards, there was a real sense of a job well done. We'd set out to beat the three most successful rugby nations in the world, one after the other, and that's exactly what we'd done. It gave us a confidence going into World Cup year and gave us a renewed sense of purpose as we prepared for the Six Nations championship.

The game against France, to open the 2003 Six Nations, was to be my 100th match for England. I'm really not one to sit and count the caps but plenty of people were on hand to tell me that I'd made it to my century. I was looking forward to the match – if we beat France, it would be another huge step forward to the World Cup after our successful run in the autumn internationals.

As we gathered at our training base to prepare for the game, I had no idea of the devastating news that would follow. A few days before we played France, Nick Duncombe, a friend and fellow player at Harlequins, died very suddenly. He was 21. He had won two caps for England in the 2002 Six Nations, but was struggling with a hamstring injury so had gone away to Lanzarote for a week of training and recuperating.

Mark Evans turned up at Pennyhill Park to tell us the news. He rang me and asked whether I could get the Quins lads together. I suggested we all meet in my room and I called Dan Luger and Will Greenwood. When Evs walked in we knew something was very seriously wrong. He was in an absolute state. He'd been crying and was jittery, nervy and shaky. We looked at him and couldn't work out what had happened, but I can honestly say that not in a million years would I have thought there could be anything wrong involving Nick. He was such a lively, cocky little thing – so full of life and with so much to live for.

When Evs told us, we were all in complete shock. It was like being hit by a sledgehammer. I'd sent a text to him earlier in the week asking how he was. I got a text back from him saying 'it's absolutely great. I'm sitting around the swimming pool. It's 60/70 degrees, I'm in my shorts getting a suntan and drinking a beer.' Marvellous, I thought. That little monkey's knocking back San Miguel in the sunshine and I'm at Pennyhill Park getting absolutely flogged. A few days after sending that text, Nick was dead.

Will and I were good friends with Nick, but Dan was a very very good friend – they were always out together socially. Dan was really heart-broken. I remember saying to Will – let's keep an eye on him because he's quite fragile at the moment. We made sure we popped into his room whenever we could and made sure he wasn't on his own too much. Once Evs had broken the news about Nick, he explained how it had happened. Nick had suffered from a particularly virulent form of blood poisoning. The first he knew about his illness was when he found himself in a great deal of pain. Nathan, his mate who was with him in Lanzarote, took Nick to hospital and they did some tests. He passed away in the night. When you lose a friend like Nick – a 21-year-old with everything to live for – it hurts. Thinking about it eats away at you. You have to try to think of the positive side and celebrate his life, instead of mourning his death. Nick was happy when he died – he was playing a sport he loved and he was very good at it. He was popular and enjoying life. You've just got to try to think about that.

Running out at Twickenham for my 100th cap was strange, in light of what had happened. I ran out on my own and had a fantastic reception. The noise hit me as I emerged from that tunnel – it was great, really superb and humbling as ever. Unfortunately, the happy feeling didn't last all the way through the game. I managed to get myself into a tackle with my head between my knees and a France player wrestling me on the floor. Not an unusual position for me to be in, but when another France player bundled in, I found myself effectively squashed down with my head somewhere between my knees and my ankles. Something had to give – in this case my hamstring, which was already as taut as it could be. I felt an almighty snap but managed to get up and run around for a couple of minutes before I realized that I had no change of pace (which people have probably been saying about me for years!). Something was definitely wrong and I knew I'd have to come off the pitch. I was gutted. The only time I've ever found a hamstring in my life, and I end up pulling it. My 100th Test for England and I was coming off injured. I later discovered that the point at which the hamstring goes up to your bum has three tendons attached onto it and I'd torn one off completely.

There was good news and bad news from the specialists.

The good news was that it had already started fusing back. The bad news was that they thought I was probably looking at about 12 weeks for the thing to fully repair itself. It signalled the end of my Six Nations. I had no choice but to work very hard on getting the injury better as soon as I could. I worked just below the level at which I'd have done further damage to the injury – out there every day. It worked, and I ended up coming back within five weeks, which was brilliant.

I missed the next game of the Six Nations against Wales in Cardiff, and it felt really odd to go there and watch the match as a spectator. I saw the game – we didn't play particularly well but we won 9–26 which meant we'd lined up quite a row of victories and there was a real sense of belief in the team. The nice thing for me was that Robbie Morris was getting his first cap, and Clive asked me to come in and present his first shirt to him. That made me feel involved with the team.

While the guys went on to beat Italy at Twickenham, I kept working on my hamstring – pushing it and pushing it. They won 40–5 and, by some sort of miracle, I was pronounced fit for the Scotland game. Before they decided that I was fit to play, Dave Reddin, the fitness trainer, put me through the most torturous, punishing routine he could devise. He was trying to see if he could get a reaction out of the hamstring. I trained every day of that week with him. At the end of it, he said, 'If you can go through that, you'll find 80 minutes an absolute doddle.'

By the time the Scotland game came along, we were getting better. England have always been slow starters in the Six Nations but now we were starting to play well. We won 40–9. Then, it was on to Ireland for the grand slam. We were so determined not to let another grand slam slip away that we went out there certain that nothing would get in our way. We were playing from right to left, we were told, so when we ran out, we went to the right-hand side and stayed there. That's what we would always do at Twickenham. We didn't know that the Irish always go to the right-hand side. We had no idea of the problems we were causing by standing there. Some poor bloke was sent to Johnno to ask him to move. We were all lined up waiting for the Irish President, Mary McAleese. It was just minutes before kick-off.

Johnno was not moving anywhere. He's not in the most sociable frame of mind when he's about to go out and play. He told the fella where to go – rightly so. But the guy was sent back to talk to him again. Johnno explained, more clearly this time, and so the guy was in absolutely no doubt at all, that he and his team were not moving anywhere. The poor fella had to trudge off and tell his bosses that it wasn't going to happen. While we stood there, the whole Ireland team ran round behind us and lined up on the other side – off the red carpet completely. It was ridiculous – the President had to walk through the mud to shake hands with the Ireland players. People suggested afterwards that we had been playing mind games. That's not true. We just lined up where we thought we should and once we were there we didn't want to be messed around.

The match itself was close for 60 minutes. There was wave after wave of Irish attack, but our defence was great. It was by far our best match of the entire Six Nations. It pleased us that we'd managed to save our best till last. Once again, it was a huge step forwards and another confirmation with the World Cup getting ever closer. We had a hefty old party that night. The victory was a weight off our shoulders and something of a relief because we'd let so many grand slams go. Those who said we couldn't win away from Twickenham and couldn't win high-pressure games had to think again.

The summer tour to Australia and New Zealand was the next stop for us. They were two huge matches. Facing New Zealand in their own backyard is never an easy thing, but facing them when they are dead set on avenging the defeat of Twickenham is even harder. The fact that we'd become Six Nations champions in the meantime just made us even more of a scalp for them. Much of the match was a blur for me because I tackled someone and their kneecap made contact with my head – right between the eyes. I was out on my feet in ga-ga land for the next 10 minutes. I managed to make it to half-time, and the England doctor asked me a series of questions to check how alert I was. 'What hotel are we staying in?' he said. I looked at him with a blank face then said, very slowly, 'The Intercontinental.'

'Where are we?' he asked. Wellington, I replied. Again, after about 30 seconds. 'What floor are we all staying on?' Third floor, I said. 'All great answers, Jason,' he said. 'But you're not answering very quickly, are you?' A lot of people might think I'm slow anyway but I'd really like to think that I'd remember the name of the hotel I'm staying in a bit quicker! I was replaced for the second half by Phil Vickery. We won the match, notching up our first victory in New Zealand (13–15) for 30 years, and setting ourselves up nicely for our encounter with Australia.

We flew to Melbourne full of confidence, only to be greeted by a very anti-English press who described the England forwards as 'Orcs on steroids' – now, we're no oil paintings but we're not Orcs! They also described us as grumpy old men and Johnno as the king of the grumpy men. I remember thinking – well, that's fair enough. Johnno is a grumpy old man. No one can complain about that. None of the criticism really bothered us at the time, but we were surprised by exactly how sharp it was. The Australian press said 'you're not going to win a World Cup playing like that' just after we beat Australia 14–25. It was the first time we'd beaten Australia in Australia. What point were they trying to make? As far as we were concerned, it was fantastic.

The training for the 2003 World Cup was harder than any other training I've ever done, but it was all specific to the game and quite varied – so you never got bored. Knackered – yes, but not bored! We worked so hard in that time – training in the scorching heat to prepare ourselves for Australia (and, in the event, it seemed to rain all the time we were in Australia for the World Cup so that was a waste of time). There were three warm-up games for the tournament – in which Clive worked with different players and different combinations before announcing his final squad. I was captain for the Wales game in Cardiff and was pleased that there were some new guys in the side – players who hadn't played in the grand slam match against Ireland – guys like Stuart Abbott, Alex King, Danny Grewcock and Simon Shaw. We beat them 9–43 – a record margin – as everyone in the side tried to lay down a marker for the World Cup.

Next match was France in Marseilles. This was our first match in the new skintight shirts. I'm not sure those shirts are the most flattering designs for front-row forwards. Dorian West spent the whole of the national anthems with his stomach held in! We had an experimental side out for this match as well – I was on the bench. France had their number one team out. Considering that, the fact that we were only narrowly beaten 17–16 wasn't bad at all. We were all fighting to give Clive and the selectors the biggest headache we could. When we got to Twickenham for the last of our warm-up games, and the last match before the World Cup, things were different. We beat France 45–14. The big margin gave us that sense of a job well done. It meant we were moving into the World Cup in good shape and full of confidence.

Our preparation immediately before the World Cup was quite different from the preparation we did in 1999 – there were no army assault courses or complicated team-building sessions. I think Woodward had learnt the lessons from 1999 and our training was quite specific to the task in hand and less harsh than it had been. We didn't feel we had the natural enthusiasm trained out of us – we went into the tournament feeling fresher and fitter. We have this saying, 'Don't train like Tarzan and play like Jane'. We were all conscious that while we were putting the work in on the training park, the real work would come in the tournament itself.

I was thrilled when I heard I was in the squad. When the letter came through the door it was a mixture of happiness and relief. What was a surprise was hearing that so many big-name players had missed out. Guys like Simon Shaw, Graham Rowntree and Austin Healey were all out of the squad. It was humbling to realize the standard of the squad I was involved in, when you think of the standard of players who hadn't made the final group.

Our first game was against Georgia – something of an unknown quantity. When we saw the forwards, many of whom looked like bit-part actors from James Bond films, we realized that we'd been right not to dismiss them. In the end we beat them 84–6. It was a good scoreline but, to be honest, we felt pretty disappointed with the way we played. Our performance was not as good as it should have been. We were all aware that we didn't want to have our best game of the tournament in the first match but, equally, we wanted to play a decent game of rugby.

Our big pool game was against South Africa. This was especially big given what had happened at Twickenham the last time we'd played against them. We knew just how important it was to win and go through to the quarter-final in pole position. We won 25–6 but there was a feeling that we could have done so much better. We'd played two very bruising games and faced Samoa next. They raised their game considerably against us. They overplayed their expectations. This was their World Cup final – their big match of the tournament. Against South Africa afterwards, they were nowhere near the team they'd been against England. They just couldn't raise their game twice. For a little while they looked like beating us but still there was no sense of panic from England. We all knew that if we kept our heads, we would win, and we did.

Before our final pool game against Uruguay, I had some fantastic news. My partner, Sandra, gave birth to Francesca Belle – our first daughter. Sandra and I had decided that I would not go back for the birth because the other two children had arrived so quickly. If this baby had come at the same speed, by the time I'd flown halfway round the world, she'd have had it. We were also a bit worried about me turning up for a couple of days then leaving again. The boys – Harry and Jack – would have found that very difficult to deal with. It may have ended up making things harder, not easier, for Sandra.

In the event, I received a call in the early hours of the

morning in the week leading up to the Uruguay match from Sandra saying she was going into labour. I kept the phone with me all day and got a call later in the day from a friend who was with Sandra in the delivery room. Her friend said that the baby was almost there. The next call was from Sandra, herself, to say that everything was brilliant and we had a daughter. I felt immensely proud of Sandra. That night was the only time we managed to pop out for a beer during the World Cup.

Our game against Uruguay was another physical one but an easy victory – we won 13–111 then watched Wales on the television as they played New Zealand. We were all madly cheering Wales on. It may sound surprising, but we were all very enthusiastic and wanted Wales to do well.

The quarter-final pitched us against Wales in Brisbane. It was the match in which I would equal Philippe Sella's 111 caps record and become the joint most capped player of all time. Wales played well but I think it was our fitness which told in the end. Johnno's presence was also key to our success. 'Is anyone here knackered?' he asked at half-time. 'No', we replied. Our fitness was good. The Welsh boys had nothing else to give in the second half but we were all still fine. Clive made substitutions which speeded the game up and we were suddenly in control. We won 17–28 and faced France in the semi-final – one of our greatest rivals, and a team prone to achieve surprise victories in World Cups.

The game against France was the first time in the tournament we'd seen the real England play. I was on the bench for this game. I could see French heads dropping as we went into their half. We played sensible rugby given the limitations of the rainy conditions. The France players looked like they didn't want to be there. When I came on in the second half, I became the most capped player. I got a fantastic reception from the crowd. I went straight to a line-out and stood in front of Johnno. 'Anyone would think you'd achieved something special,' he said with a wry smile, just to bring me down to earth. Victory by 24–7 meant we were in the final. Matt Dawson managed to get his hands on a match ball for me to celebrate becoming the world's most capped player, despite the officials trying to stop him taking it away. There was elation in the changing room – we'd got to the World Cup final without playing particularly well. We were exactly where we wanted to be.

The week-long build-up to the final was quite relaxed. We could feel the support growing and our hotel had fans stationed outside, watching us eat and move around inside the hotel. Every time we went out, we were cheered. The whole seafront was packed full of people just trying to get a glimpse of us. We felt like pop stars for the week. The hardest thing before that match was the announcement of the 22 in the squad. We all desperately wanted to be selected so it was extremely tough for the eight guys who didn't make it. They'd miss out on the game of their lives but every single one of them dealt with it brilliantly. Their attitude and their support lifted the squad and was crucial to us on match day.

I was on the bench at the start of the match and it was clear that there were real problems in the front row. There were loads of penalties against England and people have been very critical of Andre Watson, the referee, but – to be honest – I think Watson was right. They were all penalties. It's just that, in the nature of the game, he could have reset the scrum instead of penalising all the time. I think he wanted to make a point to the front rows and was penalising to show them that he would not tolerate ill-discipline. When

I went on, I said to Andre, 'I'll go forwards or backwards but I won't go up or down. You'll have no problems with me.' He said that's exactly what he wanted to hear. I think he'd become frustrated with what was going on and so had the players. It did seem to calm everything down once I'd spoken to him – it took the heat out of it and things got better.

By full time, we had drawn with Australia, 14–14. Johnno spoke to us and told us just to carry on playing as we had been, and we would win 'Everything's OK,' he told Clive when he ran onto the pitch. 'Everything is just fine.' Johnno was right. The moment when Jonny kicked the ball that would win us the World Cup, all I remember was the sound of leather on leather. I knew it was going over. It just sounded like a good connection. He belted it with his wrong foot, under all that pressure yet still, it seemed certain that it was going over the posts. I looked up and saw it sail over. The crowd roared and Catt drilled the ball off the pitch for the final whistle. We'd done it. We were the world champions.

It was chaos after the match – there was so much going on. Everyone was running around, trying to seek out family and friends. It was so emotional. The Australia players looked tired and dejected. Ben Darwin – the guy who'd been injured in the semi-final against New Zealand – was there, and I wanted to seek him out and see if he was OK. Johnno was calm, collected and gracious, as ever. Everything you want from a captain. He deserved every second of the joy he got from victory. What Johnno did for England that day can't be expressed in words. He was pivotal, immense. The heart and soul of the side. When he was handed the Cup, he handed it straight to the team. The Australian Prime

Minister practically threw our medals at us but I couldn't have cared less. Daws jumped on my shoulders and nearly throttled me in the process.

We ended up not going out that night until midnight – some boys were out until 3pm the next day. I simply can't condone that sort of behaviour. They became known as the Sydney Five and I can't possibly reveal to you whether I was one of them. I can't name names. The next night it was the IRB Awards dinner. We went out afterwards again until 4am then we got up at 8am to fly home. When we arrived at Heathrow, the reception was staggering. It had been a good flight – a few beers, a bit of sleeping and a few trips down the plane with the Cup. When we arrived at Heathrow, security officers told us that we would have to get off in twos and threes for safety – because of the number of people there. It was for their safety more than ours. There was a feeling that if we all got off together, there'd have been mayhem and people would have got hurt. To be honest, I thought this was a wind-up. I really didn't believe that, at that time in the morning, there would be so many people out.

When I stepped off that plane, the sound hit me before anything else. It was so noisy, it nearly knocked me off my feet. Unbelievable: cameras and TV crews were everywhere and there were thousands of people all screaming and cheering. I remember getting onto the bus and driving away, and as we left Heathrow, all we could see were thousands of cars, abandoned on the side of the road, up on grass verges, on double yellow lines and on the pavement. It was incredible. We got back to Pennyhill Park and I asked Clive whether I could slip away. I hadn't seen my new daughter and was desperate to get home. The World Cup was wonderful but the highlight of the whole thing for me was having the door opened by Sandra holding my beautiful baby daughter.

The biggest change that I noticed straight away back in England was not so much that more people recognised me than before – people have always noticed me, I must have one of those faces! It was more that guys who wouldn't have previously have known one rugby player from the next, suddenly had a real interest in the game. Guys who'd been football supporters all their lives started to take an interest in the sport. That, for me, was the biggest change. Suddenly rugby was a big deal for everyone.

We heard that a parade was to be organised through London, followed by a trip to Buckingham Palace and tea at 10 Downing Street, and my first thought was, 'Oh no.' We'd had these awful grey World Cup suits that we had to wear during the tournament for official engagements. They came with tan-coloured shoes. I had managed to leave my trousers behind in Australia and I'd given my shoes to the guy who was cleaning the room in Australia. What on earth was I going to wear to the Palace? In the end, they managed to find me some shoes and I had to borrow some trousers which were far too small – I think they must have been Jason Robinson's. I was scared to bend over at the Palace in case they ripped!

The parade was incredible – I was gob-smacked. No one could have prepared us for the number of people who were there. We stood there and looked around at the hundreds of thousands of faces – it was fantastic. There was champagne on the bus with beer and wine and it all got drunk during the day. We just loved every minute of it.

Going straight to the Palace from that was surreal. We were still in shock after the parade then suddenly there we were having afternoon tea at the Palace. After that, it was off to Downing Street to meet Tony Blair. All of us were feeling shell-shocked by this time. A few of the boys asked Gordon Brown if we could have our winnings tax-free. As I recall, he didn't seem to think he could arrange that. The final honour was discovering that we'd all been appointed MBE in the New Year Honours List and Clive had been knighted. I already had an MBE so I was appointed OBE. The feeling for me was exactly the same as when I got the first award. I thought it was lovely to be honoured but that there were far more deserving people out there. You think of the charity workers – people who devote their lives to looking after others. All I do is play rugby.

A lot of people were asking me, at the time, whether it was difficult to keep your feet on the ground. The answer is a definite 'no'. With a house full of young kids your feet are never far from the ground, and rugby-wise, we came back from the World Cup on Tuesday and I was on the bench for Harlequins on the Saturday. There was no time to sit back and think 'Gor Blimey, we won the World Cup.' It was back to the club to catch up with old mates. By the time we all met up again for the 2004 Six Nations, we hadn't seen each other for a while, so it was great to meet up again. It felt strange not having Johnno there but his decision to retire was something he had not taken lightly. He'd thought it all through, and decided the time was right. I respected that and I fully supported the appointment of Lawrence as captain – he's got very much the same qualities as Johnno and leads from the front.

It was at the beginning of the Six Nations that I started thinking about my own retirement. I know I'm fitter than I've ever been, and could probably go on for a while longer but you get to the stage when you can keep saying that and keep going, 'just another year'. For me, the real motivation was the family. With three children and a partner back home, I didn't want to be away as much. I'd got to the stage of dreading going to New Zealand and Australia and being away from the family for four weeks again. I just didn't want to do it.

The first two matches of the Six Nations Championship just confirmed my feelings – being away to Italy and Scotland meant being away, effectively, for two weeks and I didn't like it one bit. I kept thinking to myself that I didn't think I could do four weeks away – it would hurt too much. That's when I knew it was time to retire.

I didn't want to announce my retirement in an England week because I didn't want the guys to have any distractions, so I decided to wait until the Ireland game, then I phoned Clive and told him that I wouldn't be available for the tour in the summer and would be calling it a day after the Six Nations. Clive was great. He said he was disappointed but that he understood and respected my decision, and he would be very keen for me to get involved in coaching. At that point, I had no idea what I would do after retiring – I still had Harlequins to concentrate on, but I certainly hadn't ruled out coaching. It was nice that Clive genuinely thought I'd make a good coach.

My most abiding memory of the first two Six Nations games was seeing the Princess Royal's face when she spotted me in the line-up. She was amazed that I was still playing – we had quite a laugh about that. Her face was a picture when she saw me standing there – I've been meeting her at those matches for over a decade now!

Not being selected for the Ireland game and the Wales

game was obviously a huge disappointment, but I understand the management's decision to bring on Matt Stevens, a new young prop who is the future of the game. I remember when I was that new, young prop, many years ago. I remember all the support that everyone gave to me and how welcoming they were. That is a part of rugby that has not changed. Much in the sport has altered while I've been involved but that team spirit is as alive today as it ever was. I hope Matt, and every other new young player who comes into this England side, has the amount of fun and satisfaction that I have had from rugby. It's been the most astonishing journey – one with no regrets and full of fabulous people and astonishing experiences. I've loved every minute of it.

JASON LEONARD

Career Statistics

SEASON	CLUB	TOURNAMENT
1988/89	Saracens	Courage League Division 2
1989/90	Saracens	Courage League Division 1
	Total	
1990/91	Harlequins	Courage League Division 1
1991/92	Harlequins	Courage League Division 1
1992/93	Harlequins	Courage League Division 1
1993/94	Harlequins	Courage League Division 1
1994/95	Harlequins	Courage League Division 1
1995/96	Harlequins	Courage League Division 1
1996/97	Harlequins	Courage League Division 1
1997/98	Harlequins	Allied Dunbar Premiership 1
1998/99	Harlequins	Allied Dunbar Premiership 1
1999/00	Harlequins	Allied Dunbar Premiership 1
2000/01	Harlequins	Zurich Premiership
2001/02	Harlequins	Zurich Premiership
2002/03	Harlequins	Zurich Premiership/Wildcard
2003/04	Harlequins	Zurich Premiership
	Total	
	Grand Total	

JASON'S TRIES

13/01/90	Saracens	vs Bristol (Bramley Road)
27/10/90	Harlequins	vs Liverpool St Helens (Stoop)
18/09/93	Harlequins	vs Wasps (Sudbury)
14/12/96	ENGLAND	vs Argentina (Twickenham)
01/02/98	Harlequins	vs Gauteng Falcons (Stoop)
07/05/01	Harlequins	vs Cornwall (Launceston)
01/12/01	Harlequins	vs Sale Sharks (Stoop)

LEAGUE			EUROPE						ALL GAMES		
APP	T	PTS	APP	T	PTS	APP	T	PTS	APP	T	PTS
8	–	–									
11	1	4								1	4
19	1	4									
8	1	4	5	–	–				17	1	4
6	–	–	3	–	–				9	–	–
9	–	–	5	–	–				16	–	–
11	1	5	4	–	–				16+1	1	5
13	–	–	3	–	–				17	–	–
9	–	–	3	–	–				12	–	–
19+1	–	–	2+1	–	–	5	–	–	27+2	–	–
17	–	–				7	–	–	24	1	5
19+2	–	–	1	–	–				20+2	–	–
13+3	–	–	0+1	–	–	5+1	–	–	19+5	–	–
14+2	–	–	3	–	–	7	–	–	25+2	1	5
18	1	5	3	–	–	3+1	–	–	25+1	1	5
17	–	–	2	–	–	3	–	–	22	–	–
3+2	–	–				2+1	–	–	3+2	–	–
176+10	3	14								5	24
195+10	4	18	34+2	0	0	32+3	0	0	252+15	6	28

CAP	DATE	TEST NO	VENUE	OPPONENTS
ENGLAND TEST MATCHES				
1	28 Jul 90	421	Buenos Aires – Velez Sarsfield	Argentina
2	4 Aug 90	422	Buenos Aires – Velez Sarsfield	Argentina
3	3 Nov 90	423	Twickenham	Argentina
4	19 Jan 91	424	Cardiff – National Stadium	Wales
5	16 Feb 91	425	Twickenham	Scotland
6	2 Mar 91	426	Lansdowne Road	Ireland
7	16 Mar 91	427	Twickenham	France
8	20 Jul 91	428	Suva – National Stadium	Fiji
9	27 Jul 91	429	Sydney Football Stadium	Australia
10	3 Oct 91	430	Twickenham	New Zealand
11	8 Oct 91	431	Twickenham	Italy
12	11 Oct 91	432	Twickenham	United States
13	19 Oct 91	433	Paris – Parc des Princes	France
14	26 Oct 91	434	Murrayfield	Scotland
15	2 Nov 91	435	Twickenham	Australia
16	18 Jan 92	436	Murrayfield	Scotland
17	1 Feb 92	437	Twickenham	Ireland
18	15 Feb 92	438	Paris – Parc des Princes	France
19	7 Mar 92	439	Twickenham	Wales
20	17 Oct 92	440	Wembley Stadium	Canada
21	14 Nov 92	441	Twickenham	South Africa
22	16 Jan 93	442	Twickenham	France
23	6 Feb 93	443	Cardiff – National Stadium	Wales
24	6 Mar 93	444	Twickenham	Scotland
25	20 Mar 93	445	Lansdowne Road	Ireland
26	27 Nov 93	446	Twickenham	New Zealand
27	5 Feb 94	447	Murrayfield	Scotland
28	19 Feb 94	448	Twickenham	Ireland
29	5 Mar 94	449	Paris – Parc des Princes	France
30	19 Mar 94	450	Twickenham	Wales
31	4 Jun 94	451	Pretoria – Loftus Versfeld	South Africa
32	11 Jun 94	452	Cape Town – Newlands	South Africa

TOURNAMENT	RESULT	SHIRT NO	NOTES	GAP	MINS
	Won 25–12	1		–	80
	Lost 13–15	1		7	80
	won 51–0	1		91	80
5NC	Won 25–6	1		77	80
5NC	Won 21–12	1		28	80
5NC	Won 16–7	1		14	80
5NC	Won 21–19	1		14	80
	Won 28–12	1		126	80
	Lost 15–40	1		7	80
RWC	Lost 12–18	1		68	80
RWC	Won 36–6	1		5	80
RWC	Won 37–9	1		3	80
RWC–QF	Won 19–10	1		8	80
RWC–SF	Won 9–6	1		7	80
RWC–Final	Lost 6–12	1		7	80
5NC	Won 25–7	1		77	80
5NC	Won 38–9	1		14	80
5NC	Won 31–13	1		14	80
5NC	Won 24–0	1		21	80
	Won 26–13	1		224	80
	Won 33–16	1		28	80
5NC	Won 16–15	1		63	80
5NC	Lost 9–10	1		21	80
5NC	Won 26–12	1		28	80
5NC	Lost 3–17	1		14	80
	Won 15–9	1		147	80
5NC	Won 15–14	1		70	80
5NC	Lost 12–13	1		14	80
5NC	Won 18–14	1		14	80
5NC	Won 15–8	1		14	80
	Won 32–15	1		77	80
	Lost 9–27	1		7	80

CAP	DATE	TEST NO	VENUE	OPPONENTS
33	12 Nov 94	453	Twickenham	Romania
34	10 Dec 94	454	Twickenham	Canada
35	21 Jan 95	455	Lansdowne Road	Ireland
36	4 Feb 95	456	Twickenham	France
37	18 Feb 95	457	Cardiff – National Stadium	Wales
38	18 Mar 95	458	Twickenham	Scotland
39	27 May 95	459	Durban – King's Park	Argentina
40	31 May 95	460	Durban – King's Park	Italy
41	11 Jun 95	462	Cape Town – Newlands	Australia
42	18 Jun 95	463	Cape Town – Newlands	New Zealand
43	22 Jun 95	464	Pretoria – Loftus Versfeld	France
44	18 Nov 95	465	Twickenham	South Africa
45	16 Dec 95	466	Twickenham	Samoa
46	20 Jan 96	467	Paris – Parc des Princes	France
47	3 Feb 96	468	Twickenham	Wales
48	2 Mar 96	469	Murrayfield	Scotland
49	16 Mar 96	470	Twickenham	Ireland
50	23 Nov 96	471	Twickenham	Italy
51	14 Dec 96	472	Twickenham	Argentina
52	1 Feb 97	473	Twickenham	Scotland
53	15 Feb 97	474	Lansdowne Road	Ireland
54	1 Mar 97	475	Twickenham	France
55	15 Mar 97	476	Cardiff – National Stadium	Wales
56	15 Nov 97	480	Twickenham	Australia
57	22 Nov 97	481	Old Trafford	New Zealand
58	29 Nov 97	482	Twickenham	South Africa

TOURNAMENT	RESULT	SHIRT NO	NOTES	GAP	MINS
	Won 54–3	1		154	80
	Won 60–19	1		28	80
5NC	Won 20–8	1		42	80
5NC	Won 31–10	1		14	80
5NC	Won 23–9	1		14	80
5NC	Won 24–12	1	Temp rep by Rowntree	28	67
RWC	Won 24–18	1		70	80
RWC	Won 27–20	3	After 40 successive caps he missed his first Test when he is "rested" for the Samoa match in Durban	4	80
RWC–QF	Won 25–22	1		11	80
RWC–SF	Lost 29–45	1		7	80
RWC–3rd/4th	Lost 9–19	1		4	80
	Lost 14–24	1		149	80
	Won 27–9	3		28	80
5NC	Lost 12–15	3		35	80
5NC	Won 21–15	3		14	80
5NC	Won 18–9	3		28	80
5NC	Won 28–15	3		14	80
	Won 54–21	3	Rep by Hardwick	252	70
	Won 20–18	3	Captain/Try	21	80
5NC	Won 41–13	3		49	80
5NC	Won 46–6	3		14	80
5NC	Lost 20–23	3		14	80
5NC	Won 34–13	3	Misses two England Tests in Argentina because he is on tour with the British Lions in South Africa, also missed the two match tour of Australia after	14	80
	Drew 15–15	1		245	80
	Lost 8–25	1		7	80
	Lost 11–29	1		7	80

CAP	DATE	TEST NO	VENUE	OPPONENTS
59	6 Dec 97	483	Twickenham	New Zealand
60	7 Feb 98	484	Paris – Stade de France	France
61	21 Feb 98	485	Twickenham	Wales
62	22 Mar 98	486	Murrayfield	Scotland
63	4 Apr 98	487	Twickenham	Ireland
64	14 Nov 98	492	Huddersfield – McAlpine Stadium	Netherlands
65	22 Nov 98	493	Huddersfield – McAlpine Stadium	Italy
66	28 Nov 98	494	Twickenham	Australia
67	5 Dec 98	495	Twickenham	South Africa
68	20 Feb 99	496	Twickenham	Scotland
69	6 Mar 99	497	Lansdowne Road	Ireland
70	20 Mar 99	498	Twickenham	France
71	11 Apr 99	499	Wembley Stadium	Wales
72	26 Jun 99	500	Sydney – Stadium Australia	Australia
73	28 Aug 99	502	Twickenham	Canada
74	2 Oct 99	503	Twickenham	Italy
75	9 Oct 99	504	Twickenham	New Zealand
	15 Oct 99	505	Twickenham	Tonga
76	20 Oct 99	506	Twickenham	Fiji
77	24 Oct 99	507	Paris – Stade de France	South Africa
78	5 Feb 00	508	Twickenham	Ireland
79	19 Feb 00	509	Paris – Stade de France	France
80	4 Mar 00	510	Twickenham	Wales
81	18 Mar 00	511	Rome – Stadio Flaminio	Italy
82	2 Apr 00	512	Murrayfield	Scotland
83	17 Jun 00	513	Pretoria – Loftus Versfeld	South Africa
84	24 Jun 00	514	Bloemfontein – Free State Std	South Africa
85	18 Nov 00	515	Twickenham	Australia
86	25 Nov 00	516	Twickenham	Argentina

CAREER STATISTICS

TOURNAMENT	RESULT	SHIRT NO	NOTES	GAP	MINS
	Drew 26–26	1		7	80
5NC	Lost 17–24	1		63	80
5NC	Won 60–26	1		14	80
5NC	Won 34–20	1		29	80
5NC	Won 35–17	1	Opted not go on the England "nightmare" tour to the southern hemisphere	13	80
WCQ	Won 110–0	1		224	80
WCQ	Won 23–15	1		8	80
	Lost 11–12	1		6	80
	Won 13–7	1		7	80
5NC	Won 24–21	1		77	80
5NC	Won 27–15	1		14	80
5NC	Won 21–10	1		14	80
5NC	Lost 31–32	1		22	80
	Lost 15–22	1	Not selected for the RWC warm–up match against the US Eagles at Twickenham	76	80
	Won 36–11	18	Repl Rowntree	63	30
RWC	Won 67–7	1	Rep by Rowntree	35	65
RWC	Lost 16–30	1		7	80
RWC	Won 101–10	21	Bench	–	
RWC–Playoff	Won 45–24	1	Rep by Rowntree	11	27
RWC–QF	Lost 21–44	1		4	80
6NC	Won 50–18	1	Rep by Woodman	104	70
6NC	Won 15–9	1		14	80
6NC	Won 46–12	1		14	80
6NC	Won 59–12	1	Rep by Woodman	14	71
6NC	Lost 13–19	1		15	80
	Lost 13–18	1		76	80
	Won 27–22	1	Sin binned	7	70
	Won 22–19	1		147	80
	Won 19–0	1	Rep by Flatman	7	70

CAP	DATE	TEST NO	VENUE	OPPONENTS
87	2 Dec 00	517	Twickenham	South Africa
88	3 Feb 01	518	Cardiff – Millennium Stadium	Wales
89	17 Feb 01	519	Twickenham	Italy
90	3 Mar 01	520	Twickenham	Scotland
91	7 Apr 01	521	Twickenham	France
92	20 Oct 01	525	Lansdowne Road	Ireland
	10 Nov 01	526	Twickenham	Australia
93	17 Nov 01	527	Twickenham	Romania
	24 Nov 01	528	Twickenham	South Africa
94	2 Feb 02	529	Murrayfield	Scotland
95	16 Feb 02	530	Twickenham	Ireland
96	2 Mar 02	531	Paris – Stade de France	France
	23 Mar 02	532	Twickenham	Wales
97	7 Apr 02	533	Rome – Stadio Flaminio	Italy
	9 Nov 02	535	Twickenham	New Zealand
98	16 Nov 02	536	Twickenham	Australia
99	23 Nov 02	537	Twickenham	South Africa
100	15 Feb 03	538	Twickenham	France
101	22 Mar 03	541	Twickenham	Scotland
102	30 Mar 03	542	Lansdowne Road	Ireland
103	14 Jun 03	543	Wellington – Westpac Trust Stad.	New Zealand
	21 Jun 03	544	Melbourne – Colonial Stadium	Australia
104	23 Aug 03	545	Cardiff – Millennium Stadium	Wales
105	30 Aug 03	546	Marseilles – Stade Velodrome	France
106	6 Sep 03	547	Twickenham	France
107	12 Oct 03	548	Perth	Georgia
108	18 Oct 03	549	Perth	South Africa
109	26 Oct 03	550	Melbourne – Colonial Stadium	Samoa
110	2 Nov 03	551	Brisbane – Suncorp Stadium	Uruguay
111	9 Nov 03	552	Brisbane – Suncorp Stadium	Wales

TOURNAMENT	RESULT	SHIRT NO	NOTES	GAP	MINS
	Won 25–17	1		7	80
6NC	Won 4–15	1	Rep by Woodman	63	61
6NC	Won 80–23	1	Rep by Woodman	14	68
6NC	Won 43–3	1		14	80
6NC	Won 48–19	1	Temp rep by Flatman	35	79
6NC	Lost 14–20	1	Misses three England tests in North America because he is on tour with the British Lions in Australia	196	80
	Won 21–15	17	Bench	–	
	Won 134–0	3		28	80
	Won 29–9	17	Bench	–	
6NC	Won 29–3	17	Repl White	77	5
6NC	Won 45–11	17	Repl Rowntree	14	64
6NC	Lost 15–20	17	Repl Rowntree	14	7
6NC	Won 50–10	17	Bench	–	
6NC	Won 45–9	17	Repl Rowntree	36	24
	Won 31–28	17	Bench	–	
	Won 32–31	1		223	80
	Won 53–3	1		7	80
6NC	Won 25–17	1	Rep by Rowntree	84	33
6NC	Won 40–9	3	Missed two tests	35	80
6NC	Won 42–6	3		8	80
	Won 15–13	3	Rep by Vickery	76	40
	Won 25–14	17	Bench	–	
	Won 43–9	1	Captain	70	80
	Lost 16–17	17	Rep White (temp) & Rowntree	7	21
	Won 45–14	17	Rep White	7	17
RWC	Won 84–6	17	Rep Woodman (temp) & Vickery	36	31
RWC	Won 25–6	17	Rep Woodman	6	7
RWC	Won 35–22	1		8	80
RWC	Won 111–13	1		7	80
RWC–QF	Won 28–17	1	Rep by Woodman	7	44

CAP	DATE	TEST NO	VENUE	OPPONENTS
112	16 Nov 03	553	Sydney – Stadium Australia	France
113	22 Nov 03	554	Sydney – Stadium Australia	Australia
114	15 Feb 04	555	Rome – Stadio Flaminio	Italy
	21 Feb 04	556	Murrayfield	Scotland

BRITISH & IRISH LIONS TEST MATCHES

1	26 Jun 93	55	Wellington – Athletic Park	New Zealand
2	3 Jul 93	56	Auckland – Eden Pk	New Zealand
3	21 Jun 97	57	Cape Town – Newlands	South Africa
	28 Jun 97	58	Durban – King's Pk	South Africa
4	30 Jun 01	60	Brisbane – Wooloongabba	Australia
5	7 Jul 01	61	Melbourne – Colonial Stadium	Australia

*TESTNO – is England's match number since they began in 1871. GAP – is days since last cap. MINS – Total minutes on the field of play.

CAREER STATISTICS

TOURNAMENT	RESULT	SHIRT NO	NOTES	GAP	MINS
RWC–SF	Won 24–7	17	Rep Vickery (temp) & Woodman	7	3
RWC–Final	Won 20–17	17	Rep Vickery	6	19
6NC	Won 50–9	17	Rep Vickery	85	11
6NC	Won 35–13	17	Bench Missed next test	–	
				TOTAL	**7328**

	Won 20–7	3	Not selected for the first Test of the series in Christchurch	–	80
	Lost 13–30	3		7	80
	Won 25–16	16	Repl Smith	1449	1
	Won 18–15	21	Bench. Not selected for third Test in Johannesburg	–	
	Won 29–13	16	Repl Smith	1470	1
	Lost 14–35	16	Repl Vickery. Not selected for the third Test in Sydney	7	15
				TOTAL	**177**

CAP	DATE	TEST NO	VENUE	OPPONENTS
ENGLAND B				
1	31 Oct 89		Headingley RFC	Fiji
2	3 Feb 90		Paris – Stade Jean Bouin	France B

CAP	DATE	TEST NO	VENUE	OPPONENTS
ENGLAND XV				
1	18 Jul 90		Tucumán	Tucumán
2	21 Jul 90		Buenos Aires	Buenos Aires XV
3	29 Sep 90		Twickenham	Barbarians
4	7 Jul 91		Sydney – Waratah Park	New South Wales
5	14 Jul 91		Brisbane – Ballymore	Queensland
6	7 Sep 91		Twickenham	Soviet Union
7	14 Sep 91		Gloucester – Kingsholm	Gloucester
8	21 Sep 91		Cambridge – Grange Road	England Students
9	21 May 94		Durban – King's Park	Natal
10	28 May 94		Johannesburg – Ellis Park	Transvaal
11	30 Nov 96		Twickenham	NZ Barbarians
12	19 Jun 99		Brisbane – Ballymore	Queensland

TOURNAMENT	RESULT	SHIRT NO	NOTES	GAP
	Lost 12–20	1		
	Drew 15–15	1		

TOURNAMENT	RESULT	SHIRT NO	NOTES	GAP
	Won 19–14	1		
	Lost 23–26	1		
	Won 18–16	1		
	Lost 19–21	1		
	Lost 14–20	1		
	Won 53–0	1		
	Won 34–4	16	Repl Rendall	
	Won 35–0	1		
	Lost 6–21	1		
	Lost 21–24	1		
	Lost 19–34	1		
	Won 39–14	1		

JASON LEONARD

CAP	DATE	TEST NO	VENUE	OPPONENTS

BRITISH & IRISH LIONS TOUR MATCHES

CAP	DATE	VENUE	OPPONENTS
1	22 May 93	Whangarei – Okara Park	North Auckland
2	29 May 93	Wellington – Athletic Park	NZ Maori
3	2 Jun 93	Christchurch – Lancaster Park	Canterbury
4	8 Jun 93	Invercargill – Homestead	Southland
5	16 Jun 93	New Plymouth – Rugby Park	Taranaki
6	22 Jun 93	Napier – McLean Park	Hawke's Bay
7	24 May 97	Port Elizabeth – Boet Erasmus	E.Province Inv. XV
8	31 May 97	Cape Town – Newlands	Western Province
9	7 Jun 97	Pretoria – Loftus Versfeld	Northern Transvaal
10	14 Jun 97	Durban – Kings Park	Natal
11	17 Jun 97	Wellington – Boland Stadium	Emerging Springboks
12	24 Jun 97	Bloemfontein – Free State Std	Free State Cheetahs
13	1 Jul 97	Welkom – NW Stadium	Northern Free State
14	8 Jun 01	Perth – WACA	Western Australia
15	12 Jun 01	Townsville – Dairy Farmers Std	Queensland President's XV
16	19 Jun 01	Gosford – NorthPower Stadium	Australia A
17	26 Jun 01	Coffs Harbour	NSW Country Cockatoos
18	3 Jul 01	Canberra – Bruce Stadium	ACT Brumbies

TOURNAMENT	RESULT	SHIRT NO	NOTES	GAP
	Won 30–17	1		
	Won 24–20	16	Repl Popplewell	
	Won 28–10	1		
	Won 34–16	1		
	Won 49–25	3		
	Lost 17–29	3		
	Won 39–11	3	Captain	
	Won 38–21	3		
	Lost 30–35	3	Rep by Young	
	Won 42–12	18	Repl Smith	
	Won 51–22	3	Captain	
	Won 52–30	21	Repl Rowntree	
	Won 67–39	1	Captain. rep by Rowntree	
	Won 116–10	21	Repl Vickery	
	Won 83–6	21	Repl Smith	
	Lost 25–28	1		
	Won 46–3	1	Rep by Morris	
	Won 30–28	16	Repl Young	

CAP	DATE	TEST NO	VENUE	OPPONENTS

LONDON DIVISION

1	9 Dec 89		Imber Court	South West
2	1 Dec 90		Otley – Cross Green	North
3	8 Dec 90		London – The Stoop	Midlands
4	15 Dec 90		Gloucester – Kingsholm	South West
5	5 Dec 92		Sudbury – Wasps RFC	Midlands
6	12 Dec 92		Gloucester – Kingsholm	South West
7	19 Dec 92		London – The Stoop	North
8	16 Oct 93		Newcastle – Kingston Park	North
9	23 Oct 93		Twickenham	New Zealand XV
10	30 Oct 93		Leicester – Welford Rd	Midlands
11	29 Nov 95		Twickenham	Samoa

BARBARIANS

1	2 Jun 96		Kyoto	Kansai RFU
	28 May 00			Ireland XV
2	31 May 00		Murrayfield	Scotland XV
3	4 Jun 00		Twickenham	Leicester Tigers

CUP FINALS

	4 May 91		Twickenham	Northampton
	1 May 93		Twickenham	Leicester Tigers
	24 Feb 01		Twickenham	Newcastle Falcons
	20 May 01		Headingley	Narbonne

TOURNAMENT	RESULT	SHIRT NO	NOTES	GAP
	Won 28–12	1		
	Won 18–12	1		
	Won 25–24	1		
	Drew 12–12	1		
	Won 26–16	1		
	Lost 24–26	1		
	Lost 20–24	1		
	Won 22–21	1		
	Lost 12–39	1		
	Won 23–14	1		
	Lost 32–40	1		
	Lost 66–76	3		
	Won 31–30		Bench	
	Won 45–42	1		
	Won 85–10	20	Repl Du Randt	
Pilkington Cup	Won 25–13	1		
Pilkington Cup	Lost 16–23	1		
Tetley's Bitter Cup	Lost 27–30	1		
European Shield	Won 42–33	1		

Index